My
iPad®
for Kids

Sam Costello

que®

800 East 96th Street,
Indianapolis, Indiana 46240 USA

My iPad® for Kids, Second Edition

Copyright © 2013 by Pearson Education, Inc.

ISBN-13: 978-0-7897-4864-5

ISBN-10: 0-7897-4864-9

The Library of Congress cataloging-in-publication data is on file.

Printed in the United States of America

First Printing: November 2012

Trademarks

All terms mentioned in this book that are known to be trademarks or service marks have been appropriately capitalized. Que Publishing cannot attest to the accuracy of this information. Use of a term in this book should not be regarded as affecting the validity of any trademark or service mark.

Warning and Disclaimer

Bulk Sales

Que Publishing offers excellent discounts on this book when ordered in quantity for bulk purchases or special sales. For more information, please contact

U.S. Corporate and Government Sales
1-800-382-3419
corpsales@pearsontechgroup.com

For sales outside of the U.S., please contact

International Sales
international@pearsoned.com

Editor-in-Chief
Greg Wiegand

Acquisitions Editor
Laura Norman

Development Editor
Charlotte Kughen

Managing Editor
Kristy Hart

Project Editor
Anne Goebel

Copy Editor
Charlotte Kughen

Indexer
Lisa Stumpf

Proofreader
Water Crest Publishing

Technical Editor
Jennifer Ackerman-Kettell

Publishing Coordinator
Cindy Teeters

Cover Designer
Anne Jones

Compositor
Mary Sudul

Contents at a Glance

Table of Contents

11   Using Your iPad in Fifth Grade   223

12   Using Your iPad in Sixth Grade   247

13 Using Your iPad in Seventh Grade 269

14   Rock Out: Music on the iPad   **291**

Online Extras

Visit www.informit.com/title/9780789748645 where you'll find all sorts of additional content we weren't able to squeeze into this book, including content on everything from building slideshows in the Photos app to a slew of other handy educational apps you can download to help you with coursework!

About the Author

Sam Costello is a writer and web marketer living in Providence, Rhode Island. He has written about technology, movies, books, comics, food, and more for magazines and websites large and small, including *PC World*, CNN.com, *Rue Morgue*, *Cape Cod Magazine*, and *InfoWorld*. His writing has been published on five continents.

Sam has been the About.com Guide to iPhone and iPod since 2007. At that site—http://ipod.about.com—he writes reviews, how-to's, and tech support articles about the iPhone, iPod, iTunes, and other Apple technologies.

In addition to nonfiction writing, he also writes comics and short stories.

By day, Sam is a technology manager at the Boston office of Digitas, a leading digital marketing agency.

Sam lives with his girlfriend Jenn and their two cats, Oni and Clarence. He holds a Media Studies degree from Ithaca College.

Website: http://www.samcostello.net

Twitter: @samcostello

Dedication

To my parents, David and Stephanie. Thank you for supporting my love of reading and books, and for encouraging me to write. I wouldn't be here without you—literally.

Acknowledgments

Thanks to Jenn, my parents, and my brother Jeff for your support. Thanks to my friends for being understanding of my disappearance from our social calendars for the months I've been working on this book. I'll see you all soon.

Thanks to the people who generously loaned me iPads and accessories that helped with the completion of this book: J.D. Harper and Laura Mullen.

Thanks, too, to everyone at Pearson who helped bring this book to life: Laura Norman, Charlotte Kughen, Cindy Teeters, Anne Goebel, Jennifer Kettell, and anyone I may be forgetting.

We Want to Hear from You!

As the reader of this book, *you* are our most important critic and commentator. We value your opinion and want to know what we're doing right, what we could do better, what areas you'd like to see us publish in, and any other words of wisdom you're willing to pass our way.

We welcome your comments. You can email or write to let us know what you did or didn't like about this book—as well as what we can do to make our books better.

Please note that we cannot help you with technical problems related to the topic of this book.

When you write, please be sure to include this book's title and author as well as your name and email address. We will carefully review your comments and share them with the author and editors who worked on the book.

Email: feedback@quepublishing.com

Mail: Que Publishing
           ATTN: Reader Feedback
           800 East 96th Street
           Indianapolis, IN 46240 USA

Reader Services

Visit our website and register this book at quepublishing.com/register for convenient access to any updates, downloads, or errata that might be available for this book.

Learn More with Online Extras!

If you want to learn even more about how to use your iPad for fun and school and get recommendations on tons more cool apps, check out the many online extras for this book at www.informit.com/title/9780789748645.

You'll learn advanced tips on how to get the most out of ringtones, email, and Pages. Discover where to get free e-books, suggestions for more learning apps for school, and how to play games from your iPad on an HDTV.

Discover the iPad's
ports and buttons.

Learn to control
the iPad by touch.

Get to know the
iPad's home screen.

Congratulations! You have an iPad. It's an exciting, fun, helpful gadget. You're going to love it. To get the most you can out of it, you need to learn how to use it. Let's start with the basics:

- → How the iPad works
- → Knowing which iPad you have
- → Understanding the buttons and ports
- → Controlling by touch
- → Using the home screen
- → Knowing your OS

Please Touch: How the iPad Works

If you put an iPad next to a computer, you might think they don't have much in common. One has a big screen, a DVD drive, a keyboard, and mouse; the other is just a flat slab of plastic and metal and glass. But appearances can be deceiving. It might not look like it, but the iPad is just a computer in a different package.

Just like a desktop or laptop computer, with the iPad you can run software, get on the Internet, play games, watch videos, listen to music, and communicate with your family, teachers, and friends. Unlike your desktop computer, you can chuck your iPad in your backpack so you have it with you wherever you go.

The On/Off/Sleep/Wake Button

Unlike a traditional computer, the iPad doesn't have a button labeled "On" or even one that's obviously designed to turn it on. But that doesn't mean it doesn't have one. In fact, the iPad's On button does much more than a normal On button.

If you hold your iPad so that the screen is taller than it is wide (called portrait mode) and the Home button is at the bottom, you see a small flat button on the iPad's top-right corner. This button does a lot of things: It turns the iPad on and off, puts it to sleep and wakes it up, and restarts the iPad.

Turning an iPad On and Off

To turn your iPad on or off, you just hold down this button. If you want to turn on the iPad, hold down the button until the white Apple logo appears. This means the iPad is starting up, and you can let go of the button.

To turn off the iPad, hold down the button until a red slider appears at the top of the screen. Slide it to the right, and the iPad shuts down.

Naptime for the iPad: Putting It to Sleep

Sometimes you don't want to turn the iPad off, but you do want to save battery life and prevent other people from seeing what you're doing. In that case, you can put the iPad to sleep.

To do this, press the On/Off button once. The iPad's screen goes dark, indicating it is now in sleep mode.

To wake up the iPad, press the button again or press the Home button—but not for as long as you did when you turned the iPad on, or you might accidentally turn it off!—and the screen lights up. Move the slider at the bottom of the screen to the right and your iPad is ready for use again.

Smart Covers

Another cool way to put the iPad to sleep and wake it up is with Smart Covers. These are the colorful covers you've probably seen on some iPads. They attach by magnets, and your iPad is smart enough to know when the Smart Cover is on. When it's over the screen, the iPad goes to sleep. Open the Smart Cover and the iPad wakes up. If you don't have one already, you can buy one at the Apple Store.

Nice to Meet You: How to Know Which iPad You Have

As you probably know, there's more than one kind of iPad. In fact, Apple releases a new version of the iPad every year. Each new version of the iPad is called a generation, as in the first-ever iPad was the first-generation model. Each generation of the iPad has hundreds of changes and improvements from the last model. Some of those changes—usually software changes— work on all iPads, but changes that depend on the iPad's hardware—the electronics that make it work—usually only work on the latest model. Because of that, it's important to know which iPad you have.

The two most recent models of the iPad are the iPad 2 (the second-generation model) and what's called "the new iPad" (the third-generation model). The iPad 2 came out in 2011, and the new iPad was released in 2012.

Almost everything you read in this book applies to both the iPad 2 and the new iPad. There are two things that work only on the new iPad: 4G wireless networking (learn more in the "The Two Kinds of iPads" section of Chapter 4, "Surf's Up: Using the Internet") and Siri, the digital assistant (read more in "Meet Your Digital Sidekick: Siri" in Chapter 2, "Getting Started: Set Up and Sync Your iPad").

Discovering What iPad Model You Have

Each generation of iPad has a different model number given to it by Apple. The best way to figure out what iPad you have is by looking at the model number. To do this, flip your iPad over so you're looking at its back. At the bottom of the iPad's back, under the word "iPad," you'll see a lot of small writing. On the first line, you'll see "Model."

Model A1416, A1430, A1403—new (third generation) iPad

Model A1395, A1396, A1397—iPad 2

Model A1219, A1337—original iPad

Understanding the Buttons and Ports

Compared to a traditional computer, with all its ports and buttons, the iPad is very simple. To use the iPad, you just need to be familiar with these buttons, ports, and features:

- **Front camera**—The tiny lens on the front above the screen is one of the iPad's cameras. This one is lower resolution than the rear camera, meaning it takes less-detailed pictures. It's mostly used for video chats via FaceTime, which I cover in Chapter 6, "Get Ready for Your Close Up! It's FaceTime!"

- **Home button**—The Home button is very important. You see it coming up over and over in this book. You use it when you're restarting the iPad, rearranging your app icons, and much more.

- **Headphone jack**—This hole is where you plug in headphones and certain other accessories.

- **On/Off/Sleep/Wake button**—Earlier in the chapter, you read about this flat button that you use to turn on and off the iPad as well as to put it to sleep and wake it up.

- **Switch**—The little switch on the side of the iPad (it's on your right when you look at the screen, and on the left when you look at the back) has two purposes: It can lock the iPad's screen so that it doesn't rotate when you turn the iPad (more in the "Side Switch for Screen Lock or Mute" section later in this chapter), and it can also mute the speakers.

- **Volume button**—This button lets you raise or lower the iPad's volume without touching the screen.

- **Speaker**—The little group of holes at the bottom of the back of the iPad is its speaker. Obviously, you get better-quality sound from a good pair of headphones, but the speaker does the job when you don't have any better options.

- **Dock connector**—This rectangular port is used for two things. First, it's where you plug the iPad's included USB cable in when you want to sync it to your computer (more on syncing in "Setting Up and Syncing Your iPad," in the next chapter). It's also the place where you connect a lot of accessories, especially speaker docks.

- **Back camera**—The small circle on the back of the iPad is the other of its two cameras. This camera takes still photos and videos and has a higher resolution—meaning the images look better—than the front camera.

Front camera ——

Home button ——

On/off button   Back camera

Headphone jack ——

Switch ——

Volume button ——

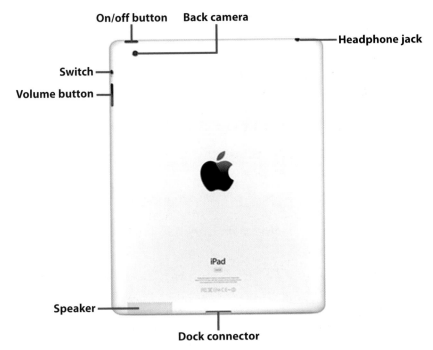

Speaker ——

Dock connector

MicroSIM Card Port

Not all iPads have a MicroSIM card port, just ones that have 4G Internet access from AT&T (more on what this is and how to know if you have it in Chapter 4). This slot on the right side of the iPad holds the card that allows the AT&T-compatible iPad to access cell phone networks to get on the Internet.

Side Switch for Screen Lock or Mute

You can use the iPad's switch to do a couple different things: lock the screen and mute the volume.

The iPad automatically changes the orientation of its screen depending on how you hold it. If you hold it up and down (portrait mode), the screen is oriented that way. But turn iPad to the side (landscape mode) and the screen turns to match it. The switch locks the screen so that when you turn the iPad, the screen doesn't move.

You can also use the switch to turn off sound on the iPad.

Changing How the Side Switch Works

To choose which action the iPad's side switch performs, tap the Settings app on the Home screen and follow these steps:

1. Tap General.

2. In the box called Use Side Switch To, choose Lock Rotation if you don't want the screen to move when you move the iPad. Choose Mute to shut off the sound. You can change this setting whenever you want by repeating these steps.

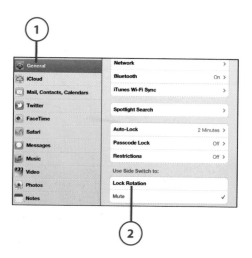

Controlling by Touch

Just because the iPad is really a computer doesn't mean it works just like any other computer. It doesn't—and that's because the iPad doesn't work only with a keyboard or mouse. Instead, you control it by touching the screen or tilting the iPad side to side.

Tap, swipe, and pinch might sound like things you want to do to your brother or sister, but they are actually movements you use to control the iPad:

- **Tap**—When you want to select something on the iPad's screen, tap it with your finger. You don't have to tap hard; just touching works. Use taps to launch apps, play songs, and use other onscreen controls.

- **Double-tap**—This is similar to a tap, but instead of just one, it's two taps in a row done quickly. Double-taps don't come up too often, but they're useful for zooming in and out of things, especially magazine or comic book pages and websites (more on this in "Zooming In and Out" in Chapter 4).

hold

- **Tap and hold**—This is just like a tap, except you keep your finger pressed down on the screen. Tapping and holding is used for moving apps, deleting things, and getting some menus to pop up.

- **Tap and drag**—Like tap and hold, except you move your finger across the screen. Moving your finger also moves the thing you just tapped (if it can be moved). To drop the item in a new place, just take your finger off the screen. You usually have to put an app into Edit mode in order to tap and drag things.

- **Swipe**—This is when you drag your finger lightly across the screen. Sometimes you use it for a slider bar that you're moving. Other times, you're swiping the entire screen to move to a new set of options or apps. You can swipe from almost anywhere. From the home screen, swiping to the right reveals the search tool, and swiping to the left reveals other screens of apps.

- **Four- or five-finger swipe**—If you have multitasking gestures turned on (see the "Using Multitasking Gestures" margin note at the end of this section), you can use this really handy gesture. Take four or five fingers, put them on the screen all at the same time, and swipe left or right to move between apps you've used recently.

- **Pinch**—To pinch something on your iPad's screen, spread your thumb and index finger apart. Then put them on the iPad's screen and bring them together so that they stay on the screen and meet in the middle. This is a pinch. You can also pinch out by starting with your fingers together and then spreading them apart. You most often use pinching in documents and websites where you want to control zooming in and out.

- **Four- or five-finger pinch**—When multitasking gestures are turned on, this neat shortcut takes you back to the home screen without tapping the Home button. Spread four or five fingers apart and place them on the iPad's screen. Then, while keeping your fingers on the screen, pinch them all together and you jump back to the Home screen.

- **Rotate**—If you haven't locked your screen rotation (learn more about this in the "Side Switch for Screen Lock or Mute" section earlier in this chapter), your iPad's screen automatically rotates to match how you're holding it.

- **Shake and tilt**—Besides touching the iPad's screen, you can also control some apps based on how you move the iPad. Some apps respond when you tilt the iPad from side to side or shake it back and forth.

Using Multitasking Gestures

Want to use the four- or five-finger gestures just mentioned? Then you need to turn on multitasking gestures. To do this, go to the General page in the Settings app, scroll down to Multitasking Gestures, and move the slider to On.

Using the Home Screen

The most common screen you see when using your iPad is the home screen. You use it practically every time you use your iPad. And if that's case, you better learn what all those icons, apps, and other things on the screen do, right?

Wi-Fi indicator   Clock   Lock indicator   Battery level

Wallpaper   Page indicator   Apps   Dock area

- **Wi-Fi/4G Signal Strength**—This icon tells you whether you're connected to the Internet and how strong that connection is. If you're connected using Wi-Fi, you see this icon. If you're using 4G, you'll see the word "4G," the company you're using for access (usually AT&T or Verizon) and cell phone-like bars. Whether you're on Wi-Fi or 4G, the more bars you have, the faster your connection will be.

- **Clock**—A handy clock that lets you know what time it is.

- **Lock or Mute**—Depending on how you set your side switch option earlier in the chapter, this icon either shows that, when used, your screen is unlocked, or that your volume is muted.

- **Battery Meter**—See how much battery life you have left with this percentage and graphic—100% is a fully charged battery. The closer you get to 0%, the sooner you need to plug your iPad in for a recharge.

- **Wallpaper**—The image behind your apps is called the wallpaper. You find out all about wallpaper, and how to change it, in Chapter 3, "It's All Yours! Customizing Your iPad."

- **Apps**—Each one of these icons is an app that lets you do different things (like access the Web, play games, or listen to music). To launch one, just tap the icon. You can add new apps to your iPad using the App Store. You see how to do this in Chapter 2.

- **Screens**—These dots let you know how many screens of apps your iPad has. Swipe left to see the other screens. Swipe right to go to Spotlight, the iPad's search tool. Learn how to use Spotlight in Chapter 2.

- **Dock**—These four apps across the bottom of the screen are in the Dock. The Dock is where you can store your favorite and most-used apps for easy access. Learn how to move things in and out of the Dock in Chapter 3.

Know Your OS

Throughout this book there are references to iOS 5 and iOS 6, and the different features and options your iPad offers depending on which one you have. Because some things in this book work on one version of the iOS but not the other, it's important to know which you have. But first, you need to know what iOS is.

iOS is the name of the software, or operating system, which runs on the iPad, iPhone, and iPod touch. Other operating systems you might know are Windows or Mac OS X. The operating system is the basic software that lets your iPad work. All of the apps that you get run on it.

Just like with Windows, there are different versions of the iOS. Each version adds features, fixes bugs, and changes how things look. All versions of the iOS are free (to find out how to get new versions—when they're available—check out www.informit.com/title/9780789749512). Apple releases a major new version with a full number like iOS 6 every year. Smaller updates, with point numbers like iOS 5.1.1, come out a few times a year.

Finding Out What Version of iOS You're Running

Because the version of the iOS running on your iPad can help determine what features and options you can use, it's important to know what version you have.

1. Tap Settings on your home screen.

2. Tap General.

3. Tap About (not pictured).

4. Look for the Version line. It says something like 5.1.1 or 6.0. That's the version of the iOS you're running. Now, as you read this book, pay attention to which features of the iPad require one version of the iOS or another.

Get new music, movies, and
apps using built-in apps.

Set up Find My iPad to
track lost or stolen iPads.

Search your iPad
using Spotlight.

Before you can put your iPad to work, there are a few steps you need to follow to set it up and ensure that it works the way you want it to. In this chapter, you learn all about those steps, including:

→ Setting up and syncing your iPad

→ Getting an Apple ID

→ Getting music, apps, and more at the iTunes Store

→ Setting up Find My iPad

→ Using Spotlight search

→ Meeting your digital sidekick: Siri

Getting Started: Set Up and Sync Your iPad

The basics of how you control the iPad are pretty simple, as you learned in Chapter 1, "Please Touch: How the iPad Works." The techniques you learned—tapping, dragging, pinching—work in practically everything on your iPad. But how do you get the apps, music, videos, and other things that make the iPad so much fun onto it in the first place? And where do those things come from?

The answers to these questions depend on a number of the things you learn in this chapter. Sometimes music or books come from your desktop or laptop computer. Other times you download videos from the Web. And in other situations, you buy apps and games from online stores.

Before you do any of those things, though, you need to set up your iPad. The setup process helps you decide how your iPad will work and what content it will have on it. It also helps you set up the accounts you need to buy new things.

The steps that are part of setting it up can be a little tricky and some of them require your parents' help. So, before you start on this chapter, ask your parents to help you with these tasks to make sure that everything goes smoothly.

Setting Up and Syncing Your iPad

To start using your iPad, you need to choose some basic settings and decide what content—such as music and movies—you want to sync from your computer to your iPad so you can begin using it.

Setting up your iPad is a two-step process. First, you choose some settings on the iPad itself. Then you connect it to your computer (if you have one; you can still use the iPad even if you don't have a computer) to transfer music, movies, and other content to it.

One of the most important parts of the setup process is creating your Apple ID. As you see throughout this book, an Apple ID is an account that you use with your iPad for a wide range of things. It's important for using FaceTime and finding lost iPads, for buying music or downloading new apps and games. Your Apple ID is also the way you pay for things on your iPad. Getting an Apple ID is free and crucial to getting the most out of your iPad.

>>>Go Further

THE MANY USES OF APPLE IDS

You'll probably need help from your parents when it comes to your Apple ID. That's because it can be complicated. You and your parents need to decide whether you should have your own Apple ID or use theirs. If you have your own, you can buy from iTunes or the App Store using an iTunes Allowance (learn what this is in "iTunes Allowance: What It Is and Why Your Parents Should Give You One" later in this chapter) and do some other things, such as use FaceTime, separately from them. In that case, make sure your parents know your Apple ID username and password so they can help you if problems crop up. Alternatively, you can use your parents' Apple ID, which enables you to all share music, apps, and other iTunes purchases. I recommend that everyone have their own Apple IDs because it's easier in the long run—if you don't get one now, you'll need to later, but all of your music, apps, and other purchases will be stuck with your parents' Apple ID—but this is a decision you and your parents should make together.

Setting Up the iPad

Begin by pressing the iPad's power
button to turn it on. Then follow
these steps:

1. Drag the slider to the right to
    begin the setup process.

2. Choose the language you want
    the iPad to use (I'd strongly rec-
    ommend it be a language you
    speak!) and then tap the arrow in
    the top-right corner to continue
    (not shown here).

3. Choose the country where you'll
    be using the iPad and tap the
    Next button in the top-right
    corner.

4. Any nearby Wi-Fi networks that
    you can use to connect to the
    Internet appear. Tap the one you
    want to connect to.

5. If the network you selected is
    password-protected, you need
    to know and enter its password
    to access to it. If you're setting
    up your iPad at home, ask your
    parents for the name of your
    Wi-Fi network and its password. If
    you're trying to connect at school,
    ask one of your teachers if there's
    a Wi-Fi network you can use and
    what the password is. After you've
    entered the information, tap
    Join in the onscreen keyboard to
    access it.

No Wi-Fi

If there isn't a nearby Wi-Fi network, tap Connect to iTunes and use the included cable to plug your iPad into a USB port on your computer. At that point, skip the rest of these steps and move on to the "Syncing with iTunes" section.

6. Decide whether you want to enable Location Services. When you're connected to the Internet, Location Services lets your iPad know where you are and gives you information and search results based on that. If you're in a certain neighborhood and want to know where to get a burrito or what time a movie is playing at the local theater, you need Location Services. I recommend using it. Make your choice and tap Next.

7. Choose whether this is a new iPad or if you have data already backed up somewhere else that you want to download to it. For most of you, this is probably your first iPad. If you've already had one or had an iPod or iPhone whose data you want to use, choose Restore from iCloud Backup or Restore from iTunes Backup (for instructions on how to put backed-up data on your iPad, check out "Restoring Your Data from Backup" in Chapter 17, "Fixing Problems Yourself"). When you've made your choice, tap Next.

8. Log in with your Apple ID or create a new one. Although having an Apple ID isn't required, you need one to get apps, download music, and use FaceTime, so I strongly recommend you get one.

No ID?

If you don't have one, you can set up one in this step. Skip to the next section, "Creating an Apple ID on the iPad," to learn how.

9. Choose whether you want to receive product and promotional emails from Apple. Make your choice and tap Next.

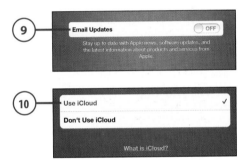

10. Agree to the terms of using the iPad and iTunes by tapping Agree. Then you need to decide whether to use iCloud. iCloud is a free service from Apple that enables you to back up data to the Internet and share it, too. I recommend using it, but it's not required. Make your choice and tap Next.

Learn About iCloud

You can learn more about iCloud by tapping the What Is iCloud? link beneath the selection shown here.

11. Your iPad can automatically back up its data, so if something goes wrong, you won't lose it. Choose whether you want to back up to iCloud automatically each day (for this to work, you need to have turned on iCloud in the last step and be connected to the Internet) or to your computer. If you choose your computer, the back-ups happen only when you sync. Make your choice and tap Next.

12. If you ever lose your iPad, you can try to get it back using the Find My iPad feature. This feature uses Location Services (which you turned on in step 6, right?) to find your iPad on a map and help you get it back. You don't have to use this feature (and you can always turn it on later), but using it is pretty smart. Make your choice and tap Next.

13. Siri, Apple's voice-activated digital assistant, can do all kinds of things. With it turned on, you can speak to your iPad and have it turn what you say into text. You can also ask Siri to search the Web for you or give you information about restaurants, movies, and sports. (To learn more about Siri, check out "Meet Your Digital Sidekick: Siri," later in this chapter.) For all of these cool features to work, though, you have to turn Siri on. Tap Use Siri and then tap Next.

No Siri?

Siri is only available on iOS 6 and higher. If you're running iOS 5, you can use Dictation instead.

14. Apple asks you if it can use information about how your iPad works (or doesn't!) to improve its software. If you choose this option, Apple doesn't get any personal information about you or watch what you're doing, so you don't have to worry. Make your choice and tap Next.

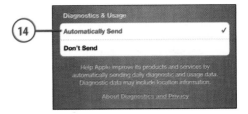

15. Tap Start Using iPad to get on your way! If you've already set up an Apple ID, skip to "Syncing with iTunes." If not, go to the next section.

Creating an Apple ID on the iPad

You need an Apple ID (aka an iTunes account) for many features of your iPad and to buy things at the iTunes or App Store. You can create a free Apple ID directly on your iPad. This is definitely a place where you should have your parents' help because they may be paying for the music and apps you buy or so they can help you use your account. When you get to the Apple ID screen of the iPad setup process, as shown in step 8 in the previous section, if you don't have an Apple ID, tap Create a Free Apple ID and follow these steps:

1. Enter your birthday using the spinners.

2. Agree to Apple's terms for having an Apple ID by tapping the Agree button at the bottom right and then the Agree button in the pop-up window.

3. Enter your first name and last name.

4. Choose what email address you want to use for your Apple ID (use an address you'll have access to for a long time). If you don't have an email address, or want to get a new one, tap Get a Free iCloud Email Address. If you do have one you want to use, tap Use Your Current Email Address. Then tap Next.

5. If you chose to use your current email address, enter it and tap Next.

6. Choose a password that's at least eight letters long, with at least one capital letter, one lowercase letter, and one number. Enter it a second time to make sure you know it and then tap Next.

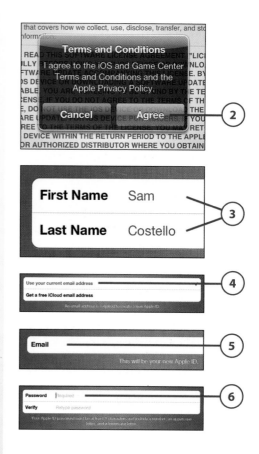

Getting an iCloud Email

If you don't have an email address, or don't want to use your main one for your Apple ID, you can choose to get a free iCloud email address. To do that, just tap that option and tap Next. The next screen lets you create your new icloud.com email address and continue.

7. Enter a reminder in case you forget your password. Choose a question from the spinner or add one of your own in the Question field. Choose something you'll remember but that even some-one who knows you won't be able to guess.

8. Enter the answer into the Answer field.

9. If you want Apple to send you emails announcing new prod-ucts or sharing other news, leave the Email Updates slider On. Otherwise, move the slider to Off and tap Next. You see a screen with Apple's terms for having an Apple ID. You must agree to these terms to use your Apple ID at the iTunes or App stores. When you do this, your Apple ID is created and you're ready to go.

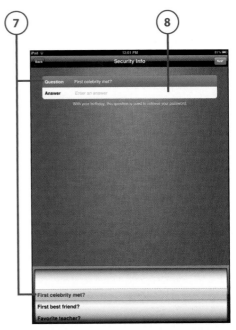

GOOD PASSWORDS

>>>Go Further

Make sure to use a good, secure password and don't share it with anyone except your parents or immediate family (don't even share it with your best friends). A good password is something that you'll remember but that someone else isn't likely to guess. "Password" or "1234" aren't good. The name of your favorite stuffed animal when you were little or a nickname that no one calls you anymore is a good choice. You should keep your pass-word secret because if someone knows it, they can buy things you don't want (and charge you for them!) or make it look like you're doing things that you're not and maybe get you in trouble.

Syncing with iTunes

You can use an iPad if you don't have a computer; but if you do have one, there's a good chance it's full of music, photos, and other things you'd like to put on your iPad. To do that, you have to sync (syncing also backs up the data on your iPad to your computer for safe keeping).

Syncing is an easy and useful way to get content from your computer to your iPad. What it's not, though, is a way to get new music or movies that you don't already have. For that, you need to use the iTunes Store app or iTunes on your computer (or App Store for new apps). Check out "Getting Music, Apps, and More at the iTunes Store" later in this chapter for tips on that.

It's also important to keep in mind that your iPad doesn't have unlimited storage space, so you might have to choose what you want on it. Learn more about that in "Go Further: Your iPad's Storage Space" later in this section.

There are two ways to sync, but the easiest is to plug your iPad into your computer using the cable that came with it. Begin by plugging one end of the iPad cable into the dock connector. Plug the other end into a USB port on your computer. If you're not sure how to do this, an adult should have no trouble helping you.

If it's not already running, iTunes launches and the screen that lets you manage all the content on your iPad appears.

Each tab on this screen lets you control different kinds of content on your iPad. Click a tab (each one is discussed in one of the next several sections) to access that content. When you've made all your changes and want to save them and sync again, click the Apply button. You can do this after changing the settings on each tab or after you've completed all of them.

The Summary Tab

The Summary tab is the overview screen where you perform basic activities:

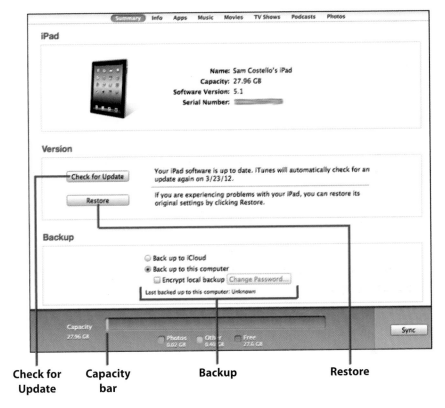

Check for   **Capacity**   **Backup**   **Restore**
Update   **bar**

- **Check for Update**—Click this to check for, and install, an updated version of the iOS, the software that makes the iPad work (you can find instructions on this in the online extras at www.informit.com/title/9780789740512.

- **Restore**—If your iPad is having major problems, sometimes you need to erase it and start from scratch. That's what this option does. (Learn more about this in Chapter 17's "Restoring Your Data from Backup.")

- **Backup**—This option lets you decide whether the data on your iPad is saved for safekeeping. The default setting is based on what you chose in step 10 of "Setting Up the iPad," earlier in this chapter.

- **Capacity bar**—This color-coded bar at the bottom of iTunes shows how much of your iPad's storage space you're currently using and how much is still available. The default information shows you how much space is being taken up by each type of data—music, apps, books, and so on. If you click a category at the bottom (for example, Audio), you see other information, such as how many songs or apps are on your iPad.

>>>Go Further

YOUR IPAD'S STORAGE SPACE

There are three different models of iPad, and each offers a different amount of storage space. The smallest is 16GB, the largest 64GB, with a 32GB model in between. The more storage you have, the more music, movies, apps, and other content you can put on your iPad. If you want to put something on your iPad but don't have enough space, you have to remove something else to make room. To remove things, sync your iPad, uncheck items, and then click Apply and you free up space. When you make these choices, keep in mind that not all items are created equal. A two-hour movie takes up more space than a five-minute song. A game with lots of nice graphics and voiced characters takes up more space than a book.

The Info Tab

The Info tab is where you sync calendars, addresses, and email accounts. Here are the main options on this tab:

- **Sync Contacts**—If you have your friends' and family's names, addresses, phone numbers, and emails stored on your computer, you can sync them to your iPad by checking this box. If you have this information stored in different programs, you need to merge it all into one because the iPad can only sync with one address book program. On a Mac, your iPad syncs with the built-in Address Book program. On a PC, you can choose to sync with Outlook, Outlook Express, Windows Address Book, or Windows Contacts.

- **Sync Calendars**—You can also sync your calendar or a family calendar to the iPad, which is good for keeping track of your days off from school, big homework assignments, and people's birthdays (learn more in Chapter 8, "Get Organized with Calendar and Reminders"). If you want to sync calendars, check this box, click Selected Calendars, and choose the calendars you want. You can also sync all the calendars on your computer by checking the All Calendars box.

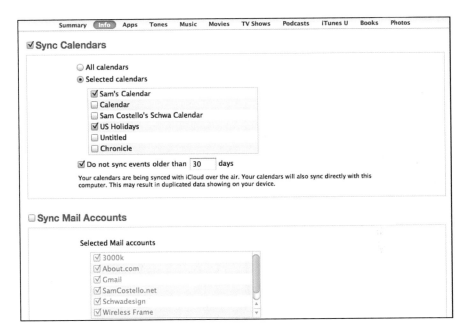

- **Sync Mail Accounts**—If you have an email address set up on your computer, you can add it to your iPad by checking this box and then clicking the account you want to add. If you don't have an email address, that's okay. You can set one up in Chapter 5, "Talk to Me: Texting, Chatting, and Email."

- **Sync Bookmarks**—If you have your favorite websites saved as bookmarks in the web browser on your computer, you can sync all of those bookmarks to your iPad, too. Just check the box next to Sync Bookmarks. If you use a Mac, you're done. On a PC, click the menu to choose what browser's bookmarks you want to sync. Select the browser you use most often.

The Apps Tab

Here's where things start to get really fun: adding apps to your iPad. When you use iTunes to download apps and games, they show up in this area. Here's how you install them on your iPad:

Choose which apps you want to sync.

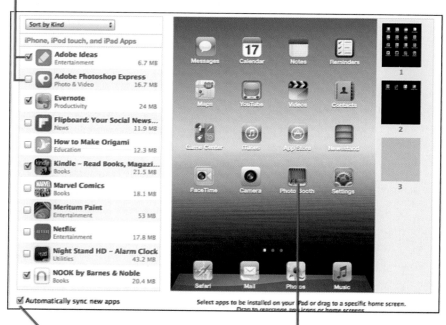

Check this box to ensure any apps purchased on your computer are synced to your iPad.

Drag and drop app icons to rearrange them on the screen.

- **Sync apps**—Check this box to turn on the ability to sync apps. When you do this, the apps in the column below it light up.

- **Select apps**—To choose apps to sync to your iPad, check the box next to each app.

- **Arrange apps**—On the right is a picture of your iPad's home screen. Next to that picture are other boxes with apps on them. These are other screens. Click the #2 screen to see the apps that will be installed there. If you want to put those apps somewhere else, you can drag and drop them onto another screen or to another place on the same screen. Check out "Arranging Apps" and "Making Folders" in Chapter 3, "It's All Yours! Customizing Your iPad," for more information.

- **New screens**—To create a third screen for your apps, click an app with your mouse and drag it over to the gray box labeled "3" next to the picture of your iPad screen. Let go of the mouse button to drop the app there; you've just added another screen of apps. Repeat to create more screens.

- **Automatically sync new apps**—If you get apps using iTunes on your computer instead of using the App Store on your iPad, use this option. Check it if you want new apps that you download on your computer to be added to your iPad every time it syncs.

The Tones Tab

Tones are the sounds made by the iPad to let you know you have a FaceTime call, new email, text message, or reminder. The iPad comes with dozens of sounds, but you can also add your own to make your iPad more personal.

To sync tones to your iPad, click the Sync Tones button. You can sync all the tones on your computer by clicking All Tones. Alternatively, you can choose just some of them by clicking Selected Tones.

Read more about sounds and tones, and where to get them, in the "Choosing Your Sounds" section of Chapter 3.

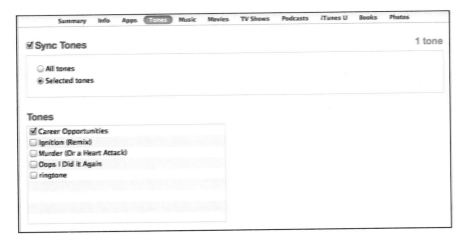

The Music Tab

Here's another fun tab. You can add music to your iPad so that you have your favorite songs with you wherever you go.

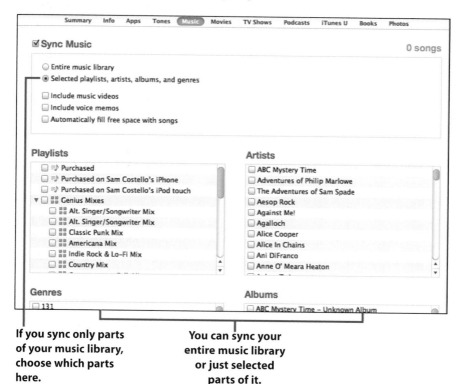

If you sync only parts of your music library, choose which parts here.

You can sync your entire music library or just selected parts of it.

- Click the Sync Music box so a checkmark appears in it (if the box is already checked, you don't need to click) to turn on the ability to add music to your iPad.

- Chances are your iPad won't have enough space to hold all your music, apps, games, books, and everything else, so your best bet is to click Selected Playlists, Artists, Albums, and Genres so that a black dot appears. Then you can choose what music you want to have on your iPad.

- If you have music videos you want to watch on your iPad, click that box so a check mark appears in it. You can ignore the other two for now.

- If you decide to sync only selected songs, you have to choose which songs you want. There are four ways to do that: by playlist, artist, genre, and album:

    - If you have created any playlists in iTunes and want to sync them, check the box next to the name of each playlist you want to add.

    - If you want to add all the songs and albums by your favorite bands to your iPad with just one click, check the box next to their names.

    - To sync all albums and songs in a certain genre, click the box next to the genre you want.

    - To sync just one album at a time and have more control over what ends up on your iPad, click the individual album names.

The Movies Tab

If you rent or buy movies from iTunes, or download video files from the Web, you can watch them on your iPad. This is especially fun if you're taking a long trip and want some entertainment.

- **Sync Movies**—Check this box to turn on the ability to sync movies to your iPad.

- You have two choices for syncing movies: automatically and one at a time:

    - To choose automatically, check that box and then select the number of movies you want to sync in the drop-down menu.

    - If you want to choose your movies, check the box next to each movie you want to sync. Taking a movie off your iPad, but leaving it on your computer, works the same way: Uncheck the box next to that movie.

You can sync your entire movie library or just selected parts of it.

Choose only certain movies by checking the boxes.

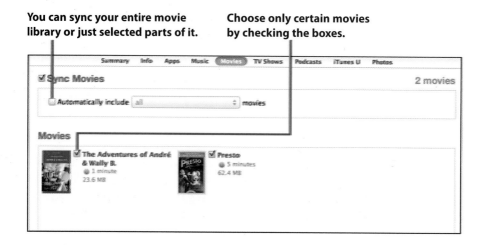

The TV Shows Tab

Just like with movies, you can also watch your favorite TV shows on your iPad. Here, however, you have a bit more flexibility because you can choose the specific episodes you want to sync.

Check the box to put TV shows on your iPad.

Use the Automatically Include options to have iTunes sync your TV shows automatically.

Use the Shows and Episodes sections to pick which episodes of which shows to sync.

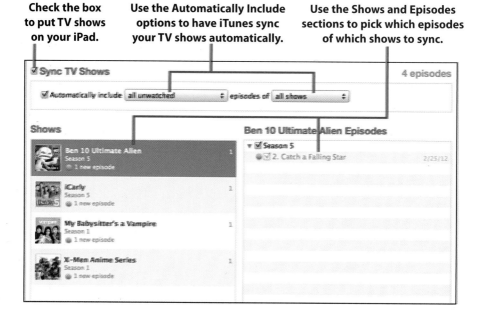

- Begin by checking the Sync TV Shows box. Just like with movies, you can either automatically sync shows or choose which ones you sync on a show-by-show basis.

- If you choose to automatically sync, you then decide what you want to sync. In the first drop-down box, your choices are all unwatched episodes, the newest shows, the newest shows you haven't watched, and the oldest shows. Pick the one you want from the drop-down.

- Use the second drop-down box to choose whether you want this choice to apply to all shows or just the ones you selected. I recommend using just the ones you select, because you might want to keep shows you've seen on your computer, but don't want to add them to your iPad.

- If you want to choose specific shows to sync, don't check the box next to Automatically Include. Instead, check the boxes next to the show you want to add to your iPad and then click the box next to each episode you want to sync. You can do this for as many shows and episodes as will fit on your iPad.

The Podcasts Tab

Podcasts are like radio shows that you can download and listen to any time. Most of them are free, and there are thousands to choose from on all kinds of topics at the iTunes Store. In fact, you can even subscribe to your favorites so that when a new episode comes out, it's automatically downloaded to your computer.

Check this
box to put
podcasts on
your iPad.

Use the Automatically
Include options to
have iTunes sync your
podcasts automatically.

Use the Podcasts and
Episodes sections to
pick which episodes of
which podcasts to sync.

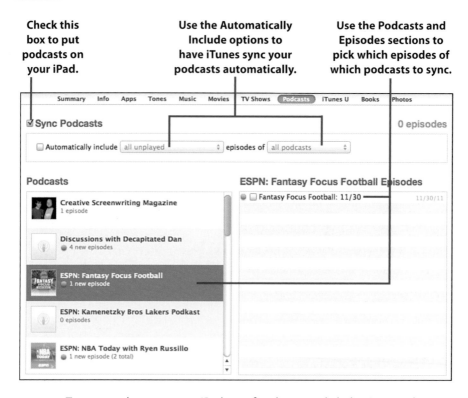

- To sync podcasts to your iPad, you first have to click the Sync Podcasts check box so that a check mark appears in it.

- Choosing what podcast to sync is a lot like choosing what TV shows to sync. You have to decide if you want to sync podcasts automatically or one at a time.

- If you choose automatically, then choose how many podcasts and whether you want to only sync ones you haven't heard or all of them.

- If you want to sync only some podcasts, don't check the box next to Automatically Include. Instead, check the box next to the podcast you want to sync. Then check the box next to each episode of that podcast that you want to sync.

The iTunes U Tab

iTunes U is one of the best ways to use your iPad for learning. At the iTunes Store, you can download audio and video recordings of all kinds of classes on topics such as history, math, art, and English. Most of the stuff at iTunes U is for college students, but some of it is aimed at grade school audiences, so you might find something you like.

Syncing iTunes U classes works the same way as TV shows and podcasts.

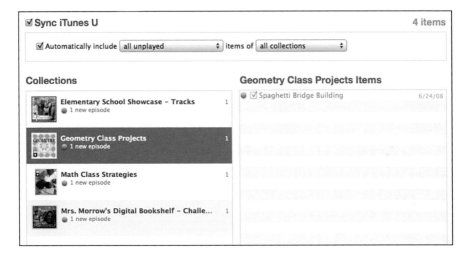

The Books Tab

You can get e-books and audiobooks from iTunes and other sources. The iPad is a great place to read or listen to books because it can hold hundreds of them and the books can have pictures, sound, and animations:

- To sync books to your iPad, first click the check box next to Sync Books so a check mark appears there. If you enable this option, use the buttons below to choose whether to sync all the books on your computer or just some of them.

- If you choose selected books, click the box next to the books you want.

- Adding audiobooks to your iPad works the same way. Scroll down the page to see and configure the Audiobooks options.

**Check the box to put
books on your iPad.**

**Choose which books you
want to sync to your iPad.**

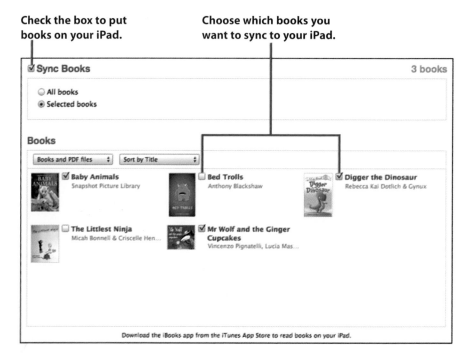

The Photos Tab

With its big screen, the iPad is awesome for looking at pictures—and having
the built-in digital cameras makes it even better. If you store photos on your
computer, you might want to sync your favorites to your iPad so you can
have them with you wherever you go:

- Begin by clicking the Sync Photos check box and then choosing where to
  sync photos from the list. If your computer is a Mac, choose iPhoto. If you
  use Windows, choose the program you use (there can be a lot of options,
  depending on what you have installed on your computer, but Windows
  Live Photo Gallery is the most common).

- Just like with other things, you first have to decide whether you want to
  sync all your photos or just some. You might have more photos on your
  computer than you can store on your iPad. Because of that, it's usually
  best to sync only your favorite photos.

- If you choose to sync only selected photos, you then have to choose
  what albums, events, or people (this option only works if you use iPhoto)
  to sync. Click the boxes in those sections.

Check this box
to put pictures
on your iPad.

iTunes lets you pick whether to
sync all your photos in a location
or just some of them.

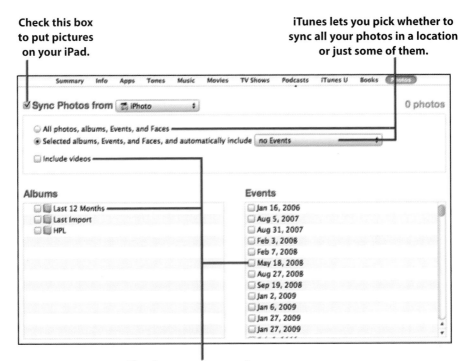

Use these sections to choose
which specific photos you
want to sync to your iPad.

SAVING YOUR CHANGES

>>>Go Further

Don't forget that after you've changed all these settings, they're not per-
manent until you click Apply in the bottom-right corner of iTunes. When
you do that, the settings are saved and the music, movies, and apps you've
chosen are added to your iPad. Now, whenever you sync your iPad, these
settings will be used (until you change them).

After you've synced your iPad, you should eject it before you can unplug
it from your computer. To do that, click the Eject button next to the iPad
icon in iTunes.

Sync Via Wi-Fi

You can always sync using the cable that comes with your iPad, but if you want to be really high tech, you should sync over Wi-Fi. To do this, you have to change a setting on the Summary page in iTunes when your iPad is synced.

On that page, click the box that says Sync with This iPad over Wi-Fi and then click Apply. After you do that, any time your iPad and computer are on the same Wi-Fi network, your iPad pops up in iTunes and syncs. Super easy!

Getting Music, Apps, and More at the iTunes Store

One of the best things about the iPad is that there's a nearly unlimited supply of new music, apps, and games you can get at the iTunes Store. This isn't a store where you can walk in and look at products, though. It's an online store run by Apple that lets you buy things that work on your iPad (and iPhone, iPod, and computer). Instead of going to the store in person, you go to it in an app—the iTunes app that comes with your iPad.

The iTunes app is where you go to buy music, movies, TV shows, and audio-books; it's also one place you can download podcasts and iTunes U classes. Some things in iTunes are free, like free songs and iTunes U, but you have to pay for most things. That's why you either need an iTunes Allowance or your parents' permission to buy things using their credit cards.

These general instructions apply to getting basically any kind of content at iTunes. For specific steps for getting books, check out "Buying E-Books at the iBookstore" in Chapter 9, "E-books and iBooks." To learn how to get movies and TV shows, read "Watching Videos from YouTube or iTunes" in Chapter 15, "Lights, Camera, Action: Videos and Photos."

Downloading Using the iTunes App

To use the iTunes Store and find out what music, movies, and other content is available for you to add to your iPad, make sure you're connected to the Internet and then tap the iTunes app to launch it. I'll take you on a tour!

Tap a feature item to learn more about it or buy it.

Browse by category.

Search for music and movies.

Choose the kind of content you want to view.

The first thing you see is the main screen for Music on the iTunes Store. You know you're in the Music section because the Music button at the bottom of the screen is highlighted. You can tap any of the other buttons to move the sections for Movies, TV Shows, and so on. Tap the button for the kind of content you're interested in.

When you're in the section you want, there are three ways to find content. You can tap the More button to see a list of all content in that section by type (for instance, in music you see Country or Rock; in TV shows you see Animation or Sports). You can also tap the Search box and type in the thing you're looking for. Or you can tap one of the featured items. To see more featured items, swipe the rows left and right, and swipe the screen up and down.

You can also jump to different ways of sorting items by tapping the buttons at the top of the screen. Tap All to return to the front page of each section.

Tap these buttons to learn more about an album, movie, or TV show.

Buy an album or a song with just two taps.

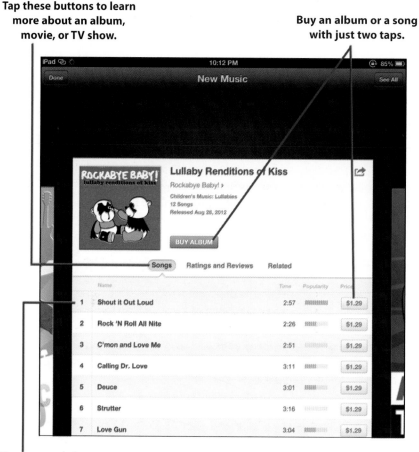

Hear a sample by tapping the number next to a song title.

When you've found something you're interested in, tap it. A window pops up with more information about it. You see the item's price and buttons across the middle of the window (what those buttons are depends on what kind of content you're looking at). When you're looking at an album, the Songs button shows you all the songs on the album. Tap Ratings and Reviews to see what other iTunes users say about the item. Tap Related to see other, similar items you might enjoy.

If you want to hear a clip from a song to see if you like it, tap the number next to the song's name and it starts playing.

To buy a single song, tap the price next to it and then tap Buy Song. To buy the entire album, tap the price at the top of the list and then tap Buy Album.

Logging In to Your Apple ID

If you're not already logged in, you need to log in with your Apple ID. If you haven't bought from iTunes before, you have to agree to terms and conditions and try your purchase again.

The new music, movie, or TV episode automatically downloads to your iPad. When the download is complete, the new item is ready for you to use. Music downloads to the Music app, and movies and TV shows download to the Videos app.

Downloading Using the App Store App

The App Store is like the iTunes Store—it's an online store run by Apple where you can download apps and games for your iPad (programs from the App Store don't work on desktops or laptops). Just like iTunes, you need to have an Apple ID to use it. Many apps and games are free, but some you have to pay for, so in that case you either need an iTunes Allowance or your parents' permission to buy things.

Tap the App Store app to launch it. Just like in iTunes, there are three ways to find content. You can tap the Search box and type in the name or kind of app you're looking for. You can also swipe the rows left and right to see more apps and tap one of the featured items. Lastly, you can tap the More button at the top of the app and browse through categories like Education, Games, and Photo & Video.

When you've found something you're interested in, tap it. You see a screen with more information about the app. On that screen, you can find the app's price and three buttons across the center. Tap the Details button to see screenshots from the app (swipe left and right to see them), a description of the app, and some other basic information. Tap Ratings and Reviews to see what other users think of the app. Tap Related to see other, similar apps that you might enjoy.

Tap a featured item to learn more about it or buy it.

Browse apps by category.

Search for apps.

Swipe left or right to see more apps.

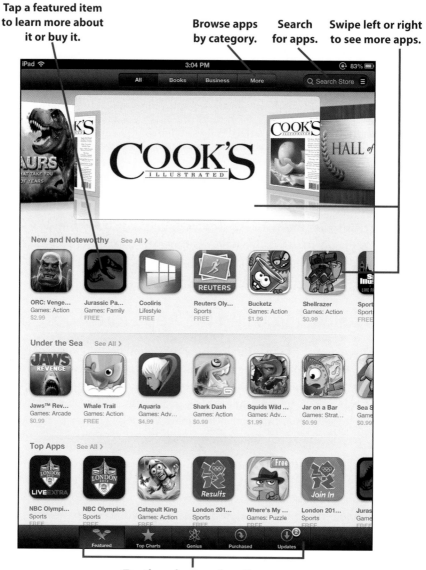

Tap these buttons for other ways to browse the App Store.

To download a free app, tap Free and then tap Install App. If the app costs money, you see its price instead. To buy a paid app, tap the price and then tap Buy App.

Just like with iTunes, if you're not logged into your Apple ID, you're asked to do that. After you do, the app or game starts downloading to your iPad. When it's done, it will be on your home screen. Tap it to start using it.

>>>Go Further

BUYING AT ITUNES ON YOUR COMPUTER

Although buying things at iTunes via your iPad is very easy, you can also get music, apps, movies, and other things from the iTunes Store via the iTunes program on your computer. Doing this is very similar to using the iTunes Store app, except there's no separate App Store app; you get everything in iTunes. When you download items to your computer, just sync your iPad and they'll be added.

Remember that when you buy at the iTunes or App Stores, you need to have a credit card or PayPal account on file in your iTunes account to make the purchase. If you don't want to or can't make purchases using a credit card with your account, you can buy using an iTunes Allowance.

Learn all about apps by tapping these buttons.

Tap the app's price to buy it. This will say free if there's no charge.

An app that's downloading or installing has a small progress bar on it.

Loading...

iTunes Allowance: What It Is and Why Your Parents Should Give You One

Do you or someone you know get an allowance? Allowances—money that your parents give you to spend on just about anything you want—are pretty great. There's a virtual version of an allowance, called an iTunes Allowance, that lets your parents give you money just to spend at iTunes or the App Store.

With an iTunes Allowance, your parents can put $10–$50 in your iTunes account every month. That way, you always have money to buy songs, apps, movies, and books at the iTunes or App Stores, and you don't have to ask your parents to buy something for you. Yeah, it's pretty great.

If your parents set one up for you, whatever amount of money they give you gets put into your iTunes account each month. You keep any money that's left over at the end of the month (so, if you have $2 at the end of the month plus you get a $10 allowance each month, you have $12 at the start of the next month—the leftover $2 + the normal $10). An iTunes Allowance can come in pretty handy if your parents are okay with setting one up.

Of course, if your parents don't want to give you an allowance every month, they can always give you the occasional iTunes Gift Card so that you have some money to spend at the iTunes or App Stores.

Setting Up an iTunes Allowance

If your parents want to give you an iTunes Allowance (there are some tips on how to convince them in a minute), you need to have an iTunes account (like the one you set up earlier this chapter) and your parents need their own separate account. Then have one of your parents launch the iTunes program on a computer, log in with their account, and then follow these steps:

1. At the iTunes Store, click Buy iTunes Gifts.

2. Scroll to the Allowances section near the bottom of the screen.

3. Click the link Set Up an Allowance Now.

4. On the iTunes Allowance screen, fill out all the information.

5. Click Continue to create the allowance. Now, you'll be able to get new music and apps and other iTunes goodies every month! The money from your iTunes Allowance is available in iTunes on your computer or the iTunes or App Store apps on your iPad. Just sign in to your account, and it will be there next to your username in the right corner of the screen.

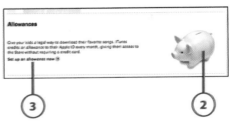

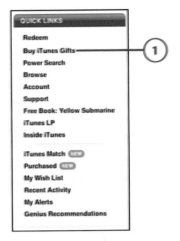

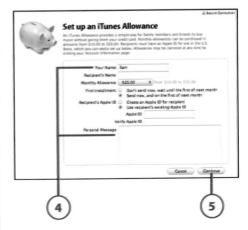

HOW TO CONVINCE YOUR PARENTS TO GIVE YOU AN ITUNES ALLOWANCE

After hearing about it, you probably want an iTunes Allowance. But you might have to convince your parents first. Here are a few reasons they might want to give you one:

- It helps them budget and know for sure how much you'll spend at iTunes each month.

- It prevents large, unexpected charges to their iTunes accounts that you could ring up by mistake.

- It helps you learn the value of items and how to manage money.

- It helps you to be independent and learn how to set priorities.

- It keeps you from bugging them every time you want to buy something new at iTunes!

Lost and Found: Find My iPad

With anything as expensive as an iPad, you really need to take care with where you put it; something this portable can be easily lost or stolen. If you ever lose your iPad, it doesn't have to be the end of the world. In fact, it doesn't even mean that you necessarily have to buy a new one. Thanks to a cool technology from Apple called Find My iPad, you can use the Internet to figure out where your iPad is (all the details on how to do that are in Chapter 17).

To use Find My iPad, you have to turn it on *before* you need to use it. That's why Apple makes turning on this feature part of the iPad setup process. If you chose not to turn it on then, though, the good news is you can still turn it on later.

Setting Up Find My iPad

To turn on Find My iPad, start by opening the Settings app and then follow these steps:

1. Tap iCloud and log in using your Apple ID.

2. Move the Find My iPad slider to On.

3. A window pops up asking you to allow iCloud to use your iPad's location, which also enables Find My iPad. Tap Allow.

4. With that done, Find My iPad is enabled.

Now that Find My iPad is turned on, you'll be able to track your iPad if it gets lost or stolen. To learn how to use Find My iPad, check out Chapter 17's "Finding a Lost iPad."

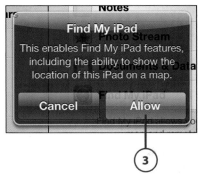

Spotlight Search

Ever known there was something on your computer but you just couldn't find it? You probably used your computer's search tool to find it. Your iPad works the same way.

The iPad's search tool, Spotlight, is very powerful. Search on some computers only looks at the names of files, not what's in them. That's like trying to find an important fact in a library full of thousands of books just by looking at their covers, not reading them. Not very accurate! Spotlight does a better job, though, because it can search what's in the built-in apps that came with your iPad. This means that Spotlight almost always finds what you're looking for—on your iPad, that is. To search the Web, use the iPad's built-in Safari web browser.

Using Spotlight

If you want to find something on your iPad using Spotlight:

1. From your iPad's home screen, swipe to the right until all the apps disappear and you see a search bar at the top of the screen and a keyboard at the bottom.

2. Type what you want to find. This could be a person's name (which gets you their address book entry and any emails or texts they've sent you), the name of a book or a song (one tap on the search results opens or plays it) or a piece of information (if that information is in a document or email, it appears). Tap Search and you see a list of results.

3. Tap the search result that you want to view.

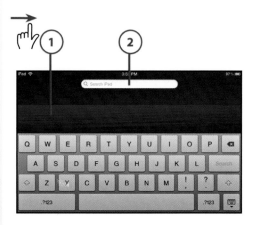

Meet Your Digital Sidekick: Siri

You might not realize it, but if you have iOS 6 (released in fall 2012) on your iPad, you have a digital sidekick that can help you do all kinds of things. (Learn more about how to upgrade your iOS online at www.informit.com/title/9780789749512.) Your sidekick is named Siri.

Siri is unlike other features of your iPad in an important, and very cool, way: Instead of tapping on Siri, you speak to it. And Siri talks back!

Siri is a voice-activated tool only available on the third-generation iPad (not iPad 2 or the original iPad) that can help you do all sorts of things. To use it, make sure you're connected to the Internet and then just hold down the Home button to activate Siri (a window pops up at the bottom of the screen) and speak to your iPad.

When this window appears, speak to your iPad to tell it what tasks to perform and what information you need.

>>>Go Further

WHAT SIRI CAN DO

Siri isn't exactly its own app. Instead, it's part of a lot of the iPad's built-in apps, and it has a few features that stand on their own. I cover how to use Siri for these apps in upcoming chapters, but here are a few cool things Siri can do that you won't find in those chapters:

- Launch apps just by saying the app's name. For example, you can say, "Launch Temple Run," to launch that app.

- Tell you the day's, or upcoming days', weather forecast. Try saying, "What will the weather be like tomorrow?" or "Is it going to rain today?"

- Show you sports scores and player statistics. For example, try asking, "What was the score of the Lakers game?"

- Find out what movies are playing near you and what time they're showing. For example, ask Siri, "When is *The Dark Knight Rises* playing today?"

- Suggest restaurants based on your location or what kind of food you want to eat. For example, "Where can I get a good burrito?"

Learn to Use Siri

Not sure how to start using Siri? Then you're in luck, because Siri comes with a built-in tutorial that gives you some suggestions.

1. Hold down the Home button until Siri's What can I help you with? menu pops up.

2. Tap the I icon.

3. A list of the kinds of commands Siri responds to pops up. This is a good place to see what apps you can use Siri with, as well as suggestions for how to speak to Siri.

4. The phrases you see in this menu aren't the only way to talk to Siri. For example, to see other ways to use the Music app, tap Play the Light of the Sun. To get tips on creating reminders, tap Remind me to call mom.

5. To use what you've learned, tap the Siri icon and speak something you want Siri to do.

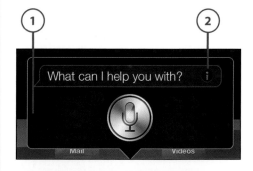

Turning Siri Off

Have you tried Siri and decided it's not for you? You can turn it off. To do that, tap the Settings app on your home screen. Then tap General. Tap Siri and move the slider to Off. You can always move it back to On if you want to use Siri again later.

Getting Answers with Siri

Besides doing things for you, Siri can also help you answer questions. Want to know the population of the United States? Ask Siri. How about the number of ounces in a pound? Siri knows.

Siri can do this because it gets information from a website called Wolfram Alpha, which is designed to help people answer questions.

If you want Siri to tell you the distance from the sun to the Earth, hold down the Home button and when Siri pops up, ask, "How far is the sun from the Earth?" You should get the answer in no time.

Having Fun with Siri

Siri is a powerful and useful tool to help you get information and use your iPad. But Siri isn't completely serious; it also has a silly side. Try asking Siri questions like "What's the meaning of life?" or "Will you marry me?" and see what answers you get. Siri can be pretty sassy if you ask the right questions.

It's Not All Good

WHAT SIRI CAN'T DO

Siri is pretty powerful, but it's not omnipotent. (Not sure what that means? Ask Siri for the definition of *omnipotent* to find out.) It can help you do things on your iPad, but it can't do things your iPad can't do to begin with. Siri can't stream movies that aren't on your iPad or in an app because your iPad can't do that anyway. Siri and Wolfram Alpha can also only answer questions of fact. So, you can find out when the Declaration of Independence was written, but not whether LeBron James is a better basketball player than Kobe Bryant. That's an opinion, and Siri doesn't have opinions.

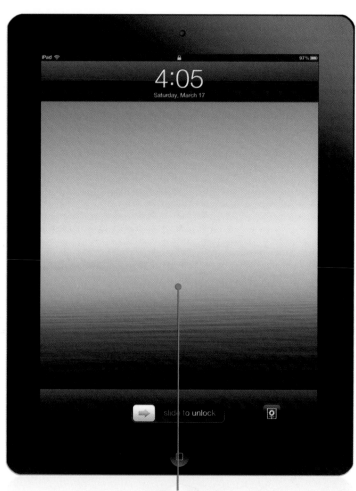

Learn how to
customize your
iPad, starting with
the wallpaper.

There are many ways to change how your iPad looks to make it more your own. From how you arrange your apps to the pictures you use for your wallpaper to the sounds your iPad makes, you have lots of options for customization. In this chapter, you learn about:

→ Changing the wallpaper and lock screen
→ Arranging apps and making folders
→ Customizing your iPad's sounds
→ Getting new tones
→ Changing screen brightness

It's All Yours! Customizing Your iPad

If you have your own room, what's one of the first things you did when you got it? You decided where your bed and dresser would go, where you'd store your toys or dolls or books, and what you'd put on the walls. Your choices make you feel at home in your room. You made it yours. By customizing its look and sounds, you can do the same thing for your iPad.

Changing the Wallpaper and Lock Screen

Just like on a desktop or laptop computer, you use a picture as the background on your iPad's screen. Think of that background as being like the paint or wallpaper in your room. Everything else—pictures, posters, shelves—sits in front of it. On your iPad, the background picture is the wallpaper and your apps are like posters floating on top of it. When you press the power button to wake your iPad up, you'll see the same picture used as your background. Even though they're the same picture, they're not actually the same thing. The image in the background is the wallpaper. The image shown when the iPad wakes up is the lock screen. They're often the same picture, but they don't have to be. You can choose different pictures for each one.

Setting Your Wallpaper and Lock Screen

Your iPad comes preloaded with pictures for you to choose from for your wallpaper and lock screen. To change the wallpaper, lock screen, or both, start on the home screen by tapping Settings and then follow these steps:

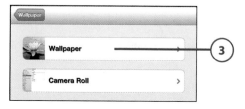

1. Tap Brightness & Wallpaper to access these options.

2. Tap Wallpaper.

3. Choose the collection of images you want to pick the wallpaper from. Unless you add your own images to your iPad (or use Photo Stream; more on that in a minute), your only choice is Wallpaper. Tap that.

4. Tap the image you want to see in full size.

5. At the top of the screen, you see options for how you want to use the image. To use it for both the wallpaper and lock screen, tap Set Both. You can also choose either Set Lock Screen or Set Home Screen to use it in just one of those locations. Tap Cancel if you've changed your mind and want to use something else entirely. After you've chosen an image, press the Home button to go back to your home screen and, if you picked an image for the wallpaper, you see it underneath your apps.

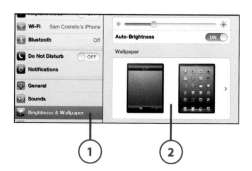

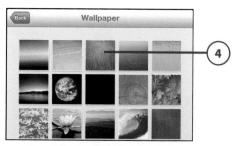

Adjusting Brightness

When you're on the main wallpaper screen, you see one other option: Brightness. That's another setting that controls how your iPad looks when you use it. Check out "Changing Screen Brightness" at the end of this chapter to learn more about it.

Putting Pictures on Your iPad

Even though your iPad comes with pictures to use as wallpaper or on the lock screen, you may want to add your own. There are a few places you can get them.

- **The iPad cameras**—You can take pictures with the iPad's cameras and use one as your wallpaper (read more about taking pictures with the iPad in Chapter 15, "Lights, Camera, Action: Videos and Photos"). When you've taken a picture that you want to use, follow the steps in the "Setting Your Wallpaper and Lock Screen" section, up to step 4.

- When you're looking at the Wallpaper option, choose Camera Roll. This is where your pictures are saved. Choose the picture you want and set it as your wallpaper or lock screen using the earlier instructions.

- **Photo Stream**—One neat feature of iCloud that puts pictures on your iPad is called Photo Stream. With it, your friends and family can share photos with you that automatically appear in your Photos app. You and your friends need iCloud accounts to use Photo Stream.

- **The Internet**—You can use the iPad's Safari web browser to save pictures you find on the Internet and use them as your wallpaper or lock screen.

- **Apps**—There are both free and paid apps in the App Store that offer collections of pictures. If you get one of these apps, you often just choose the picture from within the app, rather than following the other steps, to use it as your wallpaper.

- **Your Computer**—You can also use the pictures synced from your computer to your iPad as wallpapers. For tips on how to sync photos from your computer, check out Chapter 2, "Getting Started: Set Up and Sync Your iPad."

Saving Pictures from the Internet

If you want, you can use the Safari browser to get pictures from the Internet and use them as your wallpaper (learn more about getting online in Chapter 4, "Surf's Up! Using the Internet"). To do that, tap the Safari icon to launch it and follow these steps:

1. Go to a web page that has the picture you want to use.

2. Tap and hold on the picture until a menu pops up. From the pop-up menu, tap Save Image.

3. The picture is saved to your Camera Roll. Follow the steps from "Setting Your Wallpaper and Lock Screen," but choose Camera Roll instead of Wallpaper in step 2, to use the picture for either or both of those screens. Pick a picture close to the same size as the iPad's screen; otherwise, it looks blurry when it gets enlarged to fit the iPad screen.

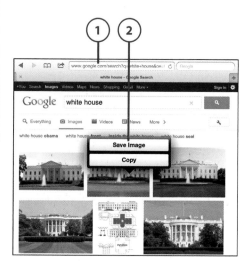

Arranging Your Apps and Making Folders

Even though your apps come arranged one way, they don't have to stay that way. You can move them around however you want or even put similar apps together into folders to keep things neat and tidy.

Although you can arrange your apps however you want, there is one set of them that has to stay sort of the same: the Dock. The Dock, the bar across the bottom of the iPad's home screen, starts with four apps in it, but you can change them up so that it features the apps you use the most. About the only thing you can't do with it is get rid of it. Your iPad's home screen always has the Dock.

Arranging Apps

Almost everyone rearranges their apps, but different people do it different ways. Some people put the apps they use the most near each other. Other people like to put similar apps together. Some order them alphabetically. You can pick whichever method you like the best and then arrange them using these steps:

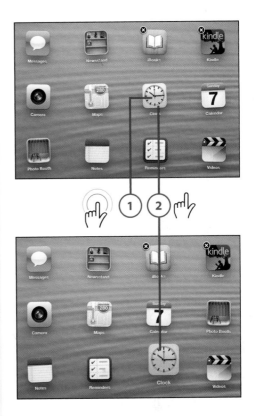

1. Tap the app you want to move and hold it until all your apps start jiggling. When this happens, you can move any of the apps—not just the one you started with.

2. Drag the app to the new location where you want it. The other apps move to make room for it. Take your finger off the screen and let the app drop into the new place.

3. Press the Home button to save the new arrangement.

It's Not All Good

ACCIDENTALLY DELETING APPS

The steps that help you move apps are very similar to the ones you use to delete apps, so be careful. When your apps start jiggling, an X appears on apps you've installed (but not on apps that came with your iPad, such as Music or Photos). Tapping the X deletes the app. You might want to do that sometimes, but if you mean to move the app instead, make sure to just tap the app itself, not the X. If you do accidentally delete an app, it's okay. The next time you sync your iPad, just add the app again (the same way you learned in Chapter 2), or if you don't sync with a computer, check out "How to Redownload Purchases" in Chapter 17, "Fixing Problems Yourself," to learn how to get it back.

Moving Apps to New Screens

Your iPad comes with all your apps on a single screen, but if you install more apps on your iPad than the 20 apps each screen can hold, they automatically start bumping over to another screen. You can also move apps to new screens yourself to either make room or to group similar apps together.

1. Tap and hold an app until they all start jiggling, just like you're going to move the app.

2. Drag the app you want to put on a new screen to the far-right edge of the screen, so that about half of the app is hidden. When you do this, the screen should move to the left and show you a new, blank screen. Let go of the app to drop it into place.

3. Press the Home button to save the arrangement. Now you have two screens for apps. Just swipe left and right to go from one screen to the other. You can create up to 11 screens on your iPad.

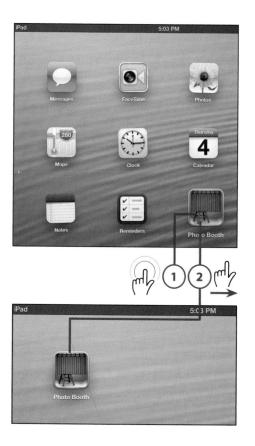

Making Folders

Besides moving your apps around, another great way to customize your iPad and keep everything organized is to create folders to put your apps in. All your music apps could go in one folder and all your school apps in another, for example. Folders have to have at least two apps in them and can have up to 20.

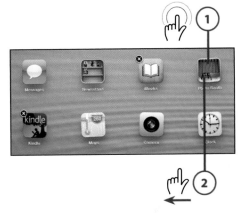

1. Tap and hold the app you want to put into a folder until it's jiggling.

2. Drag the app toward a second app you want to be in the same folder.

3. Drop the first app onto the second app. It kind of sinks into the second app and a folder is created.

4. Your iPad automatically gives the folder a name. If you want to change the folder's name, tap the X at the end of the bar and type in a new one. When you're done and want to save the folder, press the Home button.

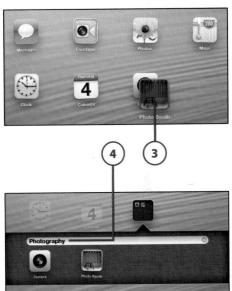

Editing and Deleting Folders

After you've created a folder, you're not necessarily done. There are a lot of other things you can do with folders:

- To add more apps to them, just drag and drop other apps onto them in the same way that you created the folder in the first place.

- To change the name of a folder, tap and hold the folder until it starts jiggling. Then tap the folder again. Tap the X in the name bar and then type in a new name. Press the Home button to save it.

- To move a folder, do it the same way you move an app: Tap it and drag it to a new place, and then press the Home button.

- To delete a folder, tap and hold it until it jiggles. Then drag the apps out of it. When there's just one app left, the folder disappears.

Adding Extra Apps to Your Dock

Even though the iPad comes with four apps in the Dock, you're not limited to four—and those don't have to be the four you have in there. You can have up to six apps, whichever ones you want, in your Dock.

1. Tap and hold the app you want to add to the Dock until it starts jiggling.

2. Drag the app to the Dock and drop it there.

Arranging the Dock

You can move the apps around the Dock so that they're in the order you want, and you can drag apps off the Dock to remove them from it. You can even add folders to your Dock to store even more apps there.

3. Press the Home button to save your changes.

Arranging Apps in iTunes

You can also arrange apps, make folders, and add new screens to your iPad using iTunes. To do this, your iPad needs to be synced to your computer. For more tips on doing this, check out "Syncing with iTunes" in Chapter 2.

Customizing Your iPad's Sounds

Your iPad makes a lot of noises. Some of the sounds are fun, like the sound that comes from playing music or games or videos. Some of the sounds are helpful, like the ones that let you know when you send or receive email, get tweets, and remind you of things on your calendar. Others are just part of the iPad experience, such as the typewriter sounds when you type on the onscreen keyboard. You can even turn them all off and use your iPad in silence. Controlling all its sounds is an important part of how you customize your iPad.

Choosing Your Sounds

To control what causes a sound and what sounds you hear, tap Settings and then Sounds.

On this screen are all the different kinds of sounds you can control. For each one, tap the menu to see a list of options. Tap a sound to hear it play.

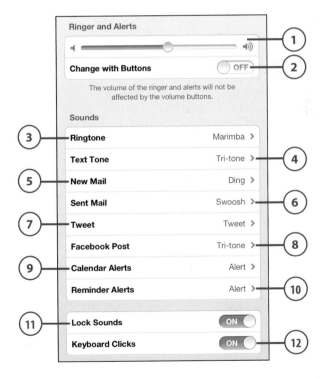

1. **Ringer and Alerts**—This slider controls the overall volume of the sounds played on your iPad. You can also raise or lower the volume at any time by clicking the volume buttons on the side of the iPad.

2. **Change with Buttons**—When this is Off, the volume buttons on the side of the iPad can't control the volume of ringers and alerts. I recommend keeping it turned On so they keep working.

3. **Ringtone**—This is the sound that lets you know when you're getting a FaceTime video call (you can learn more about this in Chapter 6, "Get Ready for Your Close Up! It's FaceTime!").

4. **Text Tone**—The sound that plays when someone sends you a text using Messages.

5. **New Mail**—The sound that plays when new email shows up on your iPad.

6. **Sent Mail**—The sound that plays when you send an email from your iPad.

7. **Tweet**—This sound plays when you receive a new tweet that mentions you.

8. **Facebook Post**—If you use the Facebook app and sign in, you hear this sound whenever things happen in your Facebook account, such as a friend posting on your wall.

9. **Calendar Alerts**—If you've created an alert to remind you of an appointment in your calendar, this sound plays when the reminder comes up.

10. **Reminder Alerts**—This sound works the same as the Calendar Alerts, but it's for the Reminders app.

11. **Lock Sounds**—Don't want your iPad to make that locking sound when you put it to sleep? Slide this to Off.

12. **Keyboard Clicks**—Sick of hearing your iPad make noise whenever you type? Slide this to Off.

Silence

Even though all of these items can have sounds, they don't have to. You can decide not to have any sound play for everything except Ringtone. If that's what you want, tap the item you want to be silent and choose None.

This is also important because it's the only way to be completely sure your iPad will be silent. Turning down the volume using the buttons on the side or using the Mute switch doesn't keep all the different sounds from making noise. Only setting each one to None can do that.

Screen Brightness

Have you ever tried to read a book or magazine in a dark room? You need a light to brighten things up and make it easier to read. But sometimes too much light doesn't help either—think about what it's like to go outdoors on a really sunny day. It can be hard to see then, too. You can change the brightness of your iPad's screen to fit the situation you're in and make it comfortable on your eyes.

Changing Screen Brightness

To change how bright your iPad's screen is, start by tapping Settings and then follow these steps:

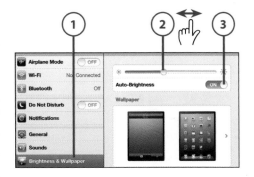

1. Tap Brightness & Wallpaper.

2. Move the slider to the left to make the screen dimmer and to the right to make it brighter. Move the slider around until you're happy with how your iPad looks.

3. You can also have your iPad automatically adjust for whatever amount of light is around you. Just slide the Auto-Brightness slider to On.

Auto-Brightness

Your iPad has a sensor in it that can detect how much light there is in the room. Using that sensor, the iPad can adjust the brightness of its screen automatically. Thanks to that sensor, Auto-Brightness makes the screen brighter or dimmer to adjust for the ideal condition for your eyes. As an added bonus, using Auto-Brightness also helps make your battery last longer!

Bookmark your favorite sites so they're easy to go back to.

Browse more than one site at a time using tabs.

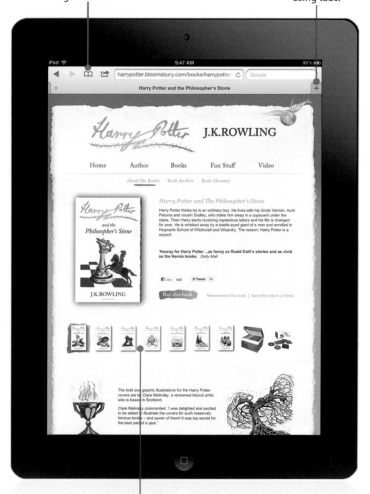

Surf the web using the iPad's built-in web browser, Safari.

You're going to be spending a lot of time online with your iPad. With it, browsing the Web is easy, fast, and fun—and touching websites to control them is way better than using a mouse. Here's what you learn in this chapter:

→ The two kinds of iPads
→ Using the iPad web browser
→ Why some sites and videos don't work
→ Being safe on the Internet
→ Awesome apps

Surf's Up! Using the Internet

One of the best things about the iPad is getting to use the Internet in all sorts of places—in bed, on the couch, in school, and out and about. But you can do that on a laptop with Wi-Fi, too, so what's so special about the iPad? Three things: its shape, how you get online, and the way you control the iPad. Because it's smaller than a laptop and much lighter, the iPad is easier to carry and use with just one hand. Some iPad models can get online almost anywhere, even if there's no Wi-Fi network nearby. And finally, because of its touch-screen and lack of a keyboard, you can surf the Web on it by touch.

The Two Kinds of iPads

All iPads may look basically the same on the outside, but on the inside they can be different in two ways. The first way is the amount of storage they have (check out "Go Further: Your iPad's Storage Space" in Chapter 2, "Getting Started: Set Up and Sync Your iPad," for more on this). The second is how they connect to the Internet. When it comes to Internet connection, there are two kinds of iPads: Wi-Fi only or Wi-Fi + 4G. Where and how you can surf the Web depends on what kind of iPad you have.

These black strips are found only on iPads with 3G and 4G.

- **Wi-Fi** is the wireless Internet that you might have at home, school, or even your local McDonald's or Barnes & Noble. It's how you connect a computer and some video game systems to the Internet without any wires. Every iPad can get on the Internet this way.

- **Wi-Fi + 4G** iPads are kind of like cell phones. They can get online using Wi-Fi, but they also have 4G, the same technology that lets cell phones make calls or browse the Web. Only some iPads have 4G. They have a black strip of plastic on the top of their back sides. If you have a Wi-Fi + 4G iPad, you can get online almost anywhere.

3G Versus 4G

The iPad that came out in 2012 was the first one to use 4G networking. The previous models used 3G. There are two important differences between 4G LTE (the full name of 4G) and 3G. First, 4G is faster than 3G. Second, 4G is a newer technology, so it's not available everywhere. When you're in a place where 4G is available and you have cellular data turned on (more on that later in this chapter), your iPad automatically uses it. If there's no 4G near you, but 3G is available, your iPad automatically connects to the 3G network. You don't need to worry about choosing between 3G and 4G networks. Your iPad chooses the fastest one for you.

Wi-Fi iPads

If you're like most people, you have a Wi-Fi iPad. This means that you can get online anytime there's a Wi-Fi network near you—sort of.

Some people put passwords on their Wi-Fi networks to keep other people from using them. If you want to use one of those, you have to know the password. (If you have Wi-Fi at home and you don't have a password, you should tell your parents to use one. It makes your network much safer.) If you don't, though, there are lots of networks open.

Finding and Using Wi-Fi Networks

To see if there are any Wi-Fi networks near you, start by tapping the Settings app on the home screen and then follow these steps:

1. Tap Wi-Fi to access the Wi-Fi options.

2. In the Wi-Fi box, make sure the slider is On.

3. If there are any Wi-Fi networks nearby, they're listed under Choose a Network. Networks with a lock next to them have passwords. If you know the password, tap that network's name.

4. Type the password and tap Join. If you have the right password, you'll be online in no time.

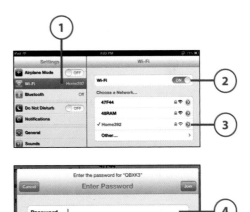

Unlocked Networks

Networks that don't have the lock icon are open to everyone. Tap one of those and your iPad connects. There are also some unlocked networks (often at places like restaurants and coffee shops) that you have to register to use. To use them, just tap them and, when the window pops up, agree to the network's terms of use (with your parents' permission). After you've done this, you'll be free to use it.

5. When you've successfully connected to a Wi-Fi network, the Wi-Fi signal strength icon appears in the top-left corner of your screen. The number of bars tells you how strong and how fast your connection is. Now you're on the Internet—happy surfing!

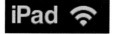

>>>Go Further
FINDING WI-FI NETWORKS

Some of the most common places to find Wi-Fi networks are at home, at school, at the library, and in public places such as restaurants. Not every school has Wi-Fi that you can use, but if yours does, ask one of your teachers if you're allowed to use it and how to access it. More and more stores offer Wi-Fi. When you're in one of those places with your iPad, you can use the Internet, often for free. Places such as McDonald's and Starbucks have Wi-Fi, and a lot of other stores and restaurants do, too. Some have passwords on their Wi-Fi, others don't. If you're in a store or restaurant that has a password, you can often ask someone who works there for it.

Wi-Fi + 4G iPads

If your iPad has both Wi-Fi and 4G, everything about using Wi-Fi to get on the Internet applies to you, but you've got something else too: You can get online with 4G.

To use 4G, you need to be in range of a 4G signal, which is kind of like a radio station signal. Just like with radio stations, sometimes it's hard to get good reception. However, instead of static, your Internet connection gets slow. Unlike using Wi-Fi, you don't have to connect to 4G; if you're in range, you use it automatically. Look for the little 4G (or sometimes 3G) icon in the top-left corner of your screen. That means you're connected.

It's Not All Good

WATCH OUT FOR 4G CHARGES

Just like with cell phones, when you have a Wi-Fi + 4G iPad, your parents (or maybe you!) pay for a monthly plan that lets you access the Internet to download a set amount of web pages, apps, songs, and other things. Be careful not to go over your monthly limit—extra charges can add up quickly!

If you see this 3G or 4G indicator, you have cellular Internet access.

If you can't get good 4G reception, you can always try Wi-Fi, but you should be able to get online from more places using 4G.

Let's Go on Safari: Using the iPad Web Browser

The iPad comes with a web browser called Safari. It isn't the only web browser you can use on your iPad (check out "Awesome Apps" later in this chapter for some suggestions), but it's a really good one.

Safari is a lot like other web browsers you've probably used (in fact, if you've used a Mac, you've probably used Safari). Here's what the buttons in Safari's top bar do:

- **Back/forward arrows**—Tap the left arrow to go back to the last web page you were on. If you've already tapped that at least once, the right arrow goes to the next page.

- **Bookmarks**—This menu stores your bookmarks (more on them in "Making Bookmarks," later in this chapter). You can store bookmarks in folders, change their names, and delete them by tapping this button and then tapping Edit. If you're using Reading List (read more about this feature later in this chapter), this icon turns into a pair of eyeglasses. If you sync bookmarks from your computer, they appear here.

- **Action box**—This box contains all kinds of neat options—for making a bookmark, emailing or printing a page, adding it to your Reading List, and adding a shortcut to a page to your home screen (this is like a bookmark, except it lives on your home screen, not in Safari).

- **Address bar**—Shows the address of the page you're on. Tap the address, tap the X at the end of the bar to delete the text all at once, and then type in the address of a new site you want to visit.

- **Search box**—If you want to search for something using Google or another search engine, tap this box, type in what you're looking for, and then tap the Search button on the keyboard.

- **New tab**—If you want to go to a new website but still keep the one you're looking at open, you need to open a new tab. Safari lets you open many websites at once, but because you can't browse four or five at the same time, it hides the ones you're not looking at. It lets you keep those hidden sites, and switch to them, by using tabs—little rectangles with the name of the hidden site on them. To open a new tab, tap the + sign. You can have up to nine tabs. Switch tabs by tapping the one you want to look at.

- **Close tab**—To close a tab and the site in it, tap the X on the one you want to close.

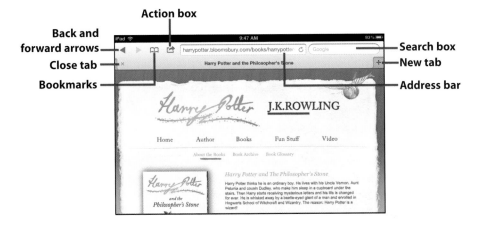

Action box

Back and forward arrows

Close tab

Bookmarks

Search box

New tab

Address bar

Those are far from the only things you can do with Safari, though. Read on for some tips on how to control Safari by touch and how to use some of its other features to get the most out of it.

USING SIRI TO SEARCH THE WEB

Searching for information on the Web is another way that Siri, the iPad's voice-activated digital assistant, can help you. When you hold down the Home button and Siri pops up, just say what topic you're looking for and Siri opens a web search on that topic. For example, say, "Web search Marie Curie," and you see a list of sites about the French scientist in no time. You can also specify where to search by saying, "Google Marie Curie," "Search Wikipedia for Marie Curie," or "Search Bing for Marie Curie."

Zooming In and Out

One of the really fun things about controlling the iPad by touch is that you can zoom in and out of websites using your fingers. There are two ways to do this:

- If you want to zoom in on a part of a web page, just double tap that section. That section of the page zooms to fill up more of the screen. To zoom out, just double tap it again.

- You can also pinch your iPad's screen for greater control. To do this, put your thumb and index finger (the one you point with) together and then place them on your iPad's screen. Without taking them off the screen, slide your fingers apart toward opposite sides of the screen. The page zooms in. To zoom out, put your thumb and index finger at opposite sides of the screen and then pinch together until they meet in the center.

Zooming Everywhere

Zooming in and out works in many iPad apps, not just Safari. Any time you want to zoom in or out in an app, try it. It usually works!

Opening a Link in a New Tab

By opening a web page in a new tab, you can see the new page without losing the one you're already on. To do this, open a web page in Safari and follow these steps:

1. Find a link you want to open and then tap and hold it until a menu appears.

2. When the menu pops up, tap Open in New Tab. When you do that, the new tab opens, but you stay on the page you were on.

3. To see the page that you opened in the new tab, tap the new tab.

4. To close either tab, tap the X.

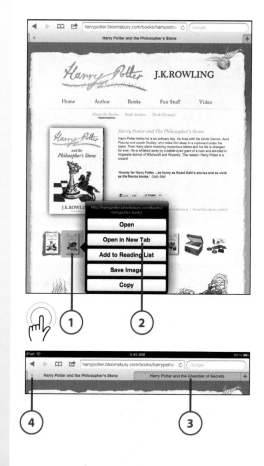

Emailing a Web Page

If there's a web page you want to
share with a friend, teacher, or family
member, you can email them a link
to it. A link is a shortcut that they
can click to take them to their web
browser and right to the page you're
sharing. To do that, go to the web
page you want to send and then follow these steps:

1. Tap the Action box.

2. Tap Mail.

3. This opens the email app. Enter
   the email address of the person
   you want to send the link to.

4. The email subject is automatically filled in with the name of
   the page, but you can change it
   to whatever you want. Just tap
   the subject line and make your
   changes.

5. If you want to write a message
   to send with the link, tap the
   body of the email and write your
   message.

6. Tap the Send button. This doesn't
   email the entire website, but it
   sends a link to the page so the
   person can easily check it out.

Emailing on Your iPad

Following these steps, of course,
means you have to have email set
up on your iPad. If you don't, you
can learn how to set up and use
email in Chapter 5, "Talk to Me:
Texting, Chatting, and Email."

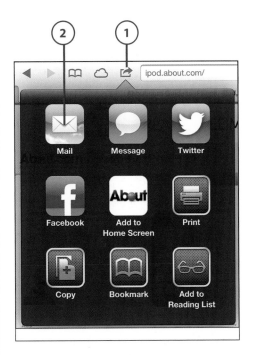

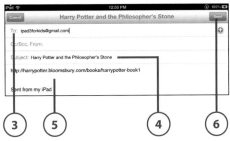

Printing a Web Page

Printing a page isn't that different from sending someone a link. You have to have an iPad-compatible printer (more about this in "Writing and Printing on the iPad" in Chapter 7, "Using Your iPad for School"). If you do, go to the web page you want to print and follow these steps:

1. Tap the Action box so that a menu appears.

2. Tap Print to access the print options.

3. Tap Select Printer in the Printer menu to choose an available printer (if your printer isn't already selected).

4. Tap the + and – buttons to change the number of copies of the page you're printing.

5. Tap Print.

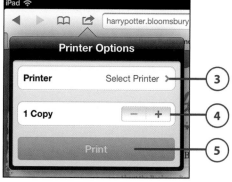

>>>Go Further

PRINTING FROM EMAIL

Not all printers are iPad-compatible, but even if you don't have one, you can still print the web page you're interested in. Follow the steps in "Emailing a Web Page" and send the link to the page you want to print to someone with a computer that's hooked up to a printer (maybe your parents). Then go to that computer, click the link you emailed to go to the web page, and print it there.

Making Bookmarks

Bookmarks are shortcuts that make it easy for you to visit your favorite websites without typing the address each time. With a bookmark, you go right to your favorite site with just a couple taps. To create a new bookmark, begin by going to the website you want to bookmark and then follow these steps:

1. Tap the Action box to open it.

2. Tap Bookmark.

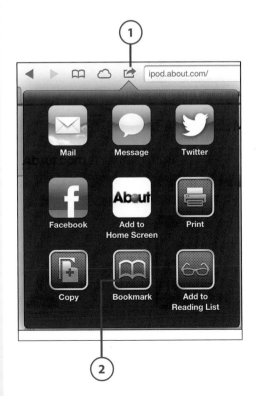

3. Each bookmark is named after the page you're bookmarking, but you can change that (which is a good idea because sometimes page names are long). To do that, tap the X in the top section and enter something shorter.

4. If you want to put the book-mark in a different folder, tap Bookmarks and select one.

5. Tap Save.

Why Some Sites and Videos Don't Work

Most websites look great on the iPad, but some sites look weird or don't work at all. A lot of the ones that don't work state that they need something called Flash. They might even say that you should download the Flash Player. Don't listen to them: Flash doesn't work on the iPad.

Flash is a technology that a lot of websites use for animations, audio and video, and sometimes games. YouTube uses Flash. So does the online video game site Kongregate.

But Flash doesn't work on the iPad because Apple controls what software works on the iPad, and Apple doesn't like Flash. Apple says, correctly, that Flash makes browsers crash too often and that it drains batteries too quick-ly—and nobody wants that. Because of that, Apple doesn't let Flash work on the iPad; you can't install it even if you want to. Kind of lame, right?

But is that a big problem? Maybe, maybe not. Lots of websites that use Flash also have special versions that work on the iPad, too.

For instance, there are two ways to use YouTube on the iPad. There's the YouTube app that comes with some versions of the iPad (check out "Watching Videos from YouTube or iTunes" in Chapter 15, "Lights, Camera, Action: Videos and Photos," for more on that) or you can go right to YouTube.com. Both of those options play movies using technology that works on the iPad, so you can still have fun with YouTube without Flash.

Some sites, such as Kongregate, don't have other versions; they require Flash and you can't use them on the iPad. This is definitely a pain, but there are fewer and fewer sites that have Flash without also having an iPad version. Plus, the App Store has so many great games, you might not miss sites such as Kongregate.

Save Your Favorite Pages with Reading List

Ever come across an article or a page on the Web that you're really interested in, and want to read, but don't have time for right now? Then you'll love Reading List. It's a part of Safari that lets you save articles and pages to read later. It's especially useful if you're using your iPad to do research for school and want to collect articles on the topic you're studying without having to read them all right away.

One especially cool feature of Reading List lets you read web pages even when your iPad isn't connected to the Internet. This only works in iOS 6 and above, but if you're running that version of the iPad's operating system, whenever you add something to your Reading List, it's saved to your iPad so you can read regardless of whether you have an Internet connection.

Adding Pages to Your Reading List

Adding pages or articles to your Reading List is simple; just follow these steps:

1. Use Safari to browse to a page you're interested in.

2. When you find an article you want to save for later, tap the Action box.

3. Tap Add to Reading List. The page is added to your list for you to read later.

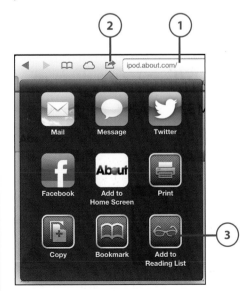

Reading Your Saved Articles

After you've saved some articles to your Reading List, you can go back to them later to check them out.

1. Open Safari.

2. Tap the Bookmark icon. (This icon changes to Reading List's eyeglasses icon when your Reading List is being synced to your other iOS devices or to the desktop version of Safari on your Mac.) This is where your Reading List is stored.

3. Tap on the eyeglass icon at the bottom to access your Reading List. You can also add articles to Reading List on a Mac and sync them to your iPad using iCloud.

4. To see all the pages in your list, tap All. To just see the articles you haven't read yet, tap Unread.

5. When you find the one you want to read, tap it and it loads in Safari.

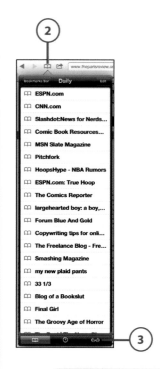

CLEAR UP THE CLUTTER WITH READER

Reader, another cool feature of Safari, lets you focus just on reading a page, rather than looking all the ads and other distractions that normally come with it. Look for the Reader icon in the address bar. You won't see it on every page, but when you do, tap it. You see a new version of the page in an easy-to-read format. Reader is especially good for reading longer articles.

Reader

There are a number of apps, such as Instapaper and Pocket, which combine the features of Reading List and Reader. If you like this kind of thing, you might want to check them out at the App Store.

Be Safe: On the Internet

The playground is a fun place, but it can also be dangerous: You can fall off the jungle gym or get bullied. The Internet is the same way. It's a pretty cool place, and it's full of interesting, exciting, and fun websites. However, you have to make sure you're safe when you use it. Follow these rules when you use the Internet to stay safe:

- Before you start using the Internet at all, talk to your parents. They'll want to help you use it and might have rules or suggestions that will keep you safe.

- The most important rule is to always talk to your parents or teachers. If someone or something makes you feel weird or uncomfortable, tell your parents or teachers. Tell them if you feel scared or unsure about anything that happens online. They're there to protect you, and they'll be able to help you figure out what to do.

- Never give your personal information—such as your name, phone number, or where you live—to someone online. They might tell you that they know you or someone you know, or they might be a total stranger. Either way, don't give them your information.

- Never give out passwords to your or your family's computer or other accounts, no matter who's asking for them.

- Don't send pictures of yourself to strangers or people who say they know people you know, no matter who's asking.

- If you only know someone online but not in real life, don't ever make plans to meet them in person. If someone asks to meet you, tell your parents right away.

- Don't sign up for things that ask for your personal information—such as a name or address—without getting your parents' permission first.

Awesome Apps

Here are some great web browsing apps that you might want to use. Search for them at the App Store:

- **Dolphin Browser HD**—This browser is a little faster than Safari and lets you sign into social media without using other apps. The coolest thing about it, though, is the little designs you draw on the screen that make things happen (such as drawing an up arrow to jump to the top of the screen). **Free**

- **Mercury Web Browser Pro**—This is another alternative browser app that has features Safari doesn't—such as different color themes and onscreen gestures to control the app. It also has an ad-blocking feature that lets you not have to see the ads on many websites. Mercury also usually loads web pages faster than Safari. **$0.99**

- **Mobicip Safe Browser**—Parents, you might find this app particularly interesting, since it filters websites for mature content and prevents your kids from visiting them. It offers multiple levels of filtering for kids of different ages and can be used together with a $10/year paid account to control what content your kids can browse with a high level of detail and specificity. **$4.99**

- **Wi-Fi Finder**—There's nothing worse than wanting—or needing!—to get on the Internet, but not being able to find a nearby Wi-Fi hotspot (not a problem for you lucky iPad Wi-Fi + 4G owners, of course). You won't have that problem again if you have this app, which features a directory of more than 650,000 Wi-Fi hotspots around the world. Just search based on your location, and it shows you where you can find nearby hotspots. **Free**

Text and chat with
your friends for free
using Messages.

Keep track of
everyone in your
life with Contacts.

Send and save emails
with Mail.

From email to chat to text messaging, the iPad makes it easy for you to stay in touch with almost anyone. In this chapter, you find out about:

→ Using Contacts
→ Using Messages
→ Texting
→ Chatting and instant messaging
→ Talking to friends with social media
→ Emailing
→ Staying safe while texting, chatting, and emailing

Talk to Me: Texting, Chatting, and Email

No matter how you want to stay in touch with your friends, family, or teachers, the iPad can help. You can use Apple's Messages app to send text messages to other iPhone and iPad users. Other apps let you send texts to friends' phones, chat on AOL or other instant messaging services, and send email. (If you're interested in video chat using FaceTime or Skype, check out the next chapter.) There are even apps for popular social media services such as Twitter and Facebook. With the right apps on your iPad, you can communicate with practically anyone, anytime.

Using Contacts

The Contacts app lets you store all the ways to contact your friends, family, teachers, and other people: email, phone, chat, and FaceTime. It also lets you keep handy their address, birthday, and other information and share that information with similar programs on your desktop or laptop computer, or with online address books from Yahoo! and Google. Many of the apps on your iPad that let you communicate with other people use Contacts, so it makes sense to put the people in your life into it.

Adding People to Your Contacts

To add people to Contacts, open the Contacts app on your iPad's home screen and follow these steps:

1. Tap the + button to add a new contact.

2. Type the person's first and last name.

3. Type the person's phone number. It is automatically added to the Mobile field. When you enter one phone number, the Contacts app automatically adds a line for a second in case you want to add another.

4. Choose the email address you want to add and enter it. Just like with phone numbers, you can choose the kind of email address you're adding by tapping the Home box and choosing from the pop-up list. After you add one email, a second email line is added.

5. Tap Ringtone to choose what sound plays when this person calls you. You can hear each tone by tapping on it. When you've made your choices, tap Save.

6. Tap Text Tone to choose what sound plays when this person texts you. You can hear each tone by tapping it. When you've made your choices, tap Save.

7. If the person has a website or blog, enter it on the Home Page line. If she has more than one, enter those on the lines that appear below the first one.

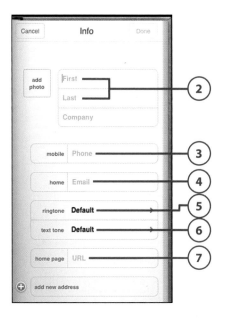

Changing the Type of Phone

If you want to enter a phone number other than a mobile phone, tap the word "mobile" to get a list of the other kinds of phone numbers. You can change the type of label on many lines by tapping it and selecting from the pop-up menu.

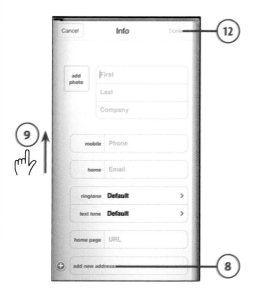

8. Tap Add New Address to enter the person's address. If you want to put in more than one address (work and home addresses, for instance), tap Add New Address again below the first one. Tap "home" next to the address to choose what kind of address it is.

9. Swipe up the screen to see more options.

10. Tap Add Field to add all kinds of other information about the person. You can choose fields like Nickname, Twitter account, Instant Messenger name, Birthday, and so on. You need to swipe through the menu because not everything fits on the screen.

11. From the list of options that appears, tap the field you want to add to the contact. To add another item, tap Add Field again.

12. Tap Done to save when you're done entering information.

Add Photos to Contacts

One of the fun things to add to your Contacts is pictures of people. When you do, their pictures show up in their emails, their chats, and when they contact you on FaceTime. To add photos to Contacts, open the Contacts app and follow these steps:

1. Tap the letter that begins the person's last name on the left or search for the person in the search bar.

2. Tap the person's name when you find it.

3. Tap the Edit button so that you can change the contact information to include a photo.

4. Tap Add Photo.

5. Tap Choose Photo to use a photo that's already on your iPad. From here you can select any of the locations on your iPad where you keep photos: Camera Roll, any folders you've added, and so on. To learn more about using photos on your iPad, check out Chapter 15, "Lights, Camera, Action: Videos and Photos."

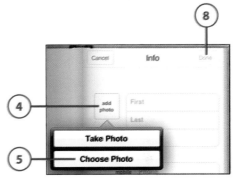

Taking a Quick Snapshot

If your contact is in the room with you, you can use your iPad to take a quick picture of them and immediately plug it into their contact page. Just tap the Take Photo button instead and use the Camera app to snap the photo.

6. After you've selected a photo, you can zoom in on the picture by pinching it or you can move it around by tapping and dragging.

7. Tap Use to select the photo.

8. When you have the picture you want added to Contacts, tap Done to save it.

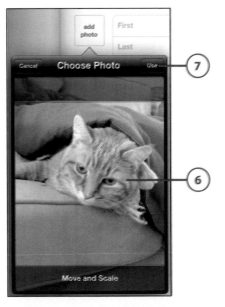

Editing Contacts

When someone moves or gets a new email address, you'll want to update the information you have about that person in Contacts. To do that, open the Contacts app and follow these steps:

1. Tap the letter that begins the person's last name on the left or search for her in the search bar.

2. When you find the person's name, tap it and then tap Edit.

3. Make the changes you want to make by tapping in any field and updating its contents.

4. Tap Done to save the changes.

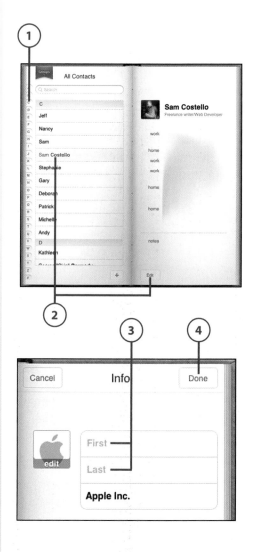

Deleting a Contact

If you want to delete someone from Contacts, open the Contacts app and follow these steps:

1. Tap the letter that begins the person's last name on the left or search for them in the search bar.

2. Tap the person's name when you find it.

3. Tap Edit.

4. Scroll down to the bottom and tap Delete Contact.

5. Tap Delete in the warning that pops up.

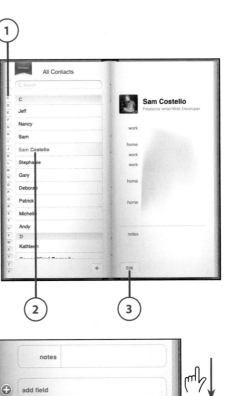

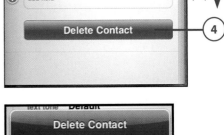

>>>Go Further

MAKING CONTACTS GROUPS

Even though you can see all the people in Contacts in one long list, you might want to put them into groups. For instance, you might want to put all your family members in one group and all your teachers in another.

Doing this can be very helpful, but you can't do it on the iPad. Instead, create the groups and put people in them on your computer (using the Address Book program on a Mac and a contacts program such as Microsoft Outlook on Windows). Then, when you sync your contacts to your iPad, they're automatically sorted into groups. Access them in the Contacts app by tapping the Groups ribbon in the top-left corner.

Awesome Apps

Contacts offers most of the features you need for your address book, with a few exceptions. One of the major exceptions is being able to send emails or texts to groups of people rather than just one person. Check out these suggestions for apps that can do just that as well as other neat things:

- **Remove Duplicate Contact**—Do you find yourself with a lot of duplicates cluttering up your Contacts? This app helps you easily find and delete all your duplicates. **$0.99**

- **Smart Group**—Want to contact a group of your friends all at once? SmartGroup allows you to send emails and text messages to groups of friends. You can use it to make groups on your own, or you can have it create "smart groups" of people that fit certain criteria. **$5.99**

Using Messages

Your friends like to text message, right? (And if they don't text, they probably want to.) With your iPad, texting and chatting comes free thanks to an app called Messages. Messages is a lot like other chat or texting apps you might have used on phones or computers. It lets you trade messages with your friends or send them photos or videos. In order to use it, though, your friends need to also have iPads, iPhones, iPod touches, or Macs that use Messages.

If your friends have cell phones, you can't text them using Messages unless they have iPhones—but don't worry, there's a way around that limitation that you find out about in the next section.

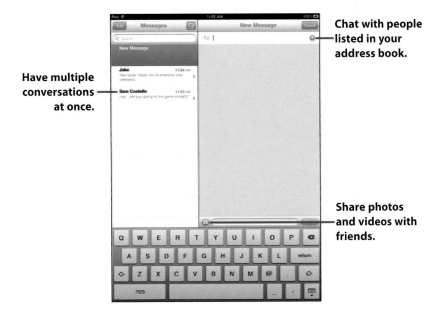

Have multiple conversations at once.

Chat with people listed in your address book.

Share photos and videos with friends.

Messages Account = Apple ID

Remember how your Apple ID is used for a lot of things? Here's more proof: Your Messages account, by default, is your Apple ID. The first time you open Messages, you're asked to sign in with your Apple ID to activate Messages.

Sending Messages Using Messages

Messages only works when you're connected to the Internet using Wi-Fi or 3G/4G. When you're online and want to message your friends, you just need to open the Messages app and follow these steps:

1. Tap the new message icon.

2. Messages lets you contact your friends using their phone numbers (if they have iPhones) or their email addresses (if they have iPod touches or iPads). Type in the name, email address, or phone number of the person you want to send a message to (it automatically goes into the To: line) or tap the + button to select the person from your Contacts.

3. Tap the text area at the bottom and type your message.

4. If you turned on Siri back in Chapter 2, "Getting Started: Set Up and Sync Your iPad," when you set up your iPad, you can speak your messages instead of typing them. To do that, tap the microphone and begin speaking. When you're done, tap it again. Siri converts your words into text (though you might have to edit them if it gets any words wrong).

5. You can also send photos or videos by tapping the camera icon. To send one that you already have, tap Choose Existing. To take a new one, tap Take Photo or Video.

6. When you're ready to send the message, tap Send. You know that your message has reached the person you sent it to when the word "Delivered" shows up under it.

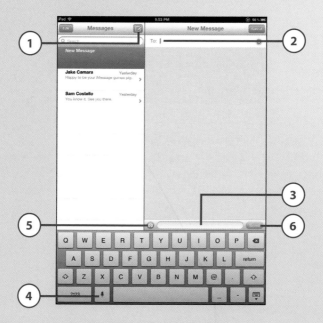

Names: Red Versus Blue and What That Means

If the person you're trying to contact isn't a Messages user, her name turns red. The app tells you that she isn't a Messages user and that it can't send your message. If the person is a Messages user, her name appears in blue.

It's Not All Good

WHO YOU CAN MESSAGE WITH MESSAGES

Remember, you can only use Messages to text other people with an iPad, iPhone, iPod touch, or Mac who also use Messages. If you want to text someone who doesn't use Messages, you need to use a texting app (more on those in a few pages).

Sending Messages with Siri

As mentioned earlier, you can use Siri to speak the messages you want to send to your friends from within the Messages app. But did you know you can use Siri to send a message from anywhere on your iPad? Here's how:

1. Press and hold the Home button until the Siri menu pops up.

2. Speak the message you want to send. Some examples of ways to speak your messages include

   • "Send a message mom to say practice is cancelled."

   • "Message 1-800-555-5555."

   • "Tell Bobby that the movie was great."

3. Depending on the message you want to send, Siri might ask some extra questions (such as "Which Bobby?" if you have more than one in your Contacts, or what message you want to send to 1-800-555-555). If it asks, answer the questions.

4. Siri might then ask if you want to send the message. Tap or say Send (or Cancel, if you change your mind) and the recipient will be reading your note in no time.

Undelivered Messages

Sometimes, a problem with either
your (or your friend's) Internet connection or software stops your message
from being delivered. You know the
message didn't go through because
a red exclamation point and a "Not
Delivered" message appears next to it.
To try again, follow these steps:

1. To resend the message, tap the
   red exclamation point.

2. Tap Try Again. In a lot of situations, this solves the problem
   and the message goes through.
   If it doesn't, you can always try
   again later.

Managing Multiple Messages Conversations

All Messages conversations have two parts: the message and the conversation. The message is the individual thing you send. The conversation is the collection of all the messages you've sent to and gotten from the person you're
talking to. You can delete either a single message or an entire conversation.

Deleting Messages

To delete just one or a few messages,
but keep the rest of the conversation,
follow these steps:

1. In Messages, tap the Action box.

2. Tap the circle next to the message you want to delete. A red check mark appears when you've selected it. To delete more than one message at a time, tap the circle next to all the messages you want to get rid of.

3. Tap Delete to complete the deletion process.

Forwarding Messages

You can also forward a message to someone else so you can share what that person has sent you. To forward the message, follow the first two steps to delete a message; instead of tapping Delete, tap Forward and then select a new recipient in the To: line.

Deleting a Conversation

To delete the entire conversation, not just a message or two, follow these steps:

1. Find the conversation you want to delete in the Messages column.

2. To delete the conversation, swipe across the name of the conversation in the Messages column.

3. Tap Delete to complete the deletion. If you decide not to delete the conversation, just tap the Messages column again and the deletion is canceled.

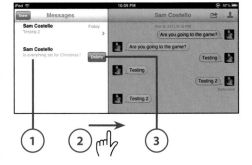

Finding Great Texting Apps

Messages is great, right? But not all of your friends have iPads, iPhones, or iPod touches, so what if you want to text them? In that case, you need regular texting. But if Messages only works with other iOS devices, what do you do?

Easy: You get some apps.

A bunch of texting apps at the App Store work on Wi-Fi (or 3G/4G) and allow you to send free or cheap texts to any user with a phone that can receive them, not just other Messages users. They also let your friends text you on your iPad. These apps are your best bet if you want to text friends who don't have iPads or iPhones:

- **HeyWire**—This free texting app is great if you text with people in other countries. It offers free text and picture messaging to phones in 45 countries, including the U.S., Canada, Mexico, China, and many more. **Free (turn off ads or add new features with paid upgrades)**

- **Textfree**—You get a free phone number from this app so that people with any kind of phone can send you texts as well as get them from you. You can also send picture messages. Textfree only works with some phone companies, but it's compatible with all the major ones. **Free (turn off ads for $5.99/year)**

- **TextNow**—Like the other apps on this list, TextNow gives you a free phone number that lets you send and receive text and picture messages. The basic app is free, and there are lots of add-on features you can buy. **Free (turn off ads and add new features with paid upgrades)**

It's Not All Good

PHONE NUMBERS YOU CAN'T CALL

The phone number you get with a lot of the free texting apps can generally be used for both texting and making phone calls over the Internet. It's important to realize, though, that those phone numbers only work on your iPad when it's connected to the Internet and you're running the app that gave you the phone number. Your friends can't call that number and have it ring your house phone or cell phone (unless you enable the call-forwarding features some of the apps offer).

Awesome Chat and Instant Messaging Apps

Another great way to talk to your friends is chat or instant messaging (IM) software. Chat/IM is similar to texting, but it's not quite the same thing. Chat/IM happens when you and your friend are using the app at the same time and talking live, whereas texting can happen at the same time, but doesn't have to. Think of chat as being more like talking on the phone, whereas texting is like sending email.

There are a ton of IM apps for the iPad—everything from AOL to Google Talk to Yahoo! Messenger and beyond. A lot of these apps let you talk with friends on all kinds of different chat systems from a single screen, which is much better than having to use a different app for each different chat system.

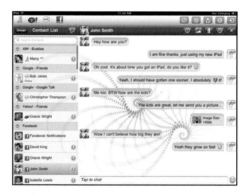

- **Agile Messenger HD Pro**—Agile lets you chat with friends on Facebook, Yahoo!, MSN, Google, AIM, and Skype. Beyond that, though, it also lets you use Facebook to check out friends' pages and post statuses as well as send voice and picture messages. **$7.99**

- **AIM for iPad**—This is the iPad version of the classic AOL Instant Messenger, or AIM, program. Along with AIM users, you can use it to chat with Facebook and Google users, too. **Free**

- **imo**—This free app lets you chat in Facebook, Google, Skype, MSN, AOL, Yahoo!, Jabber, and more, all from one screen. imo supports group chats, too. It also has a web-based version that lets you chat with your friends even when you're not in front of your iPad. **Free**

- **Yahoo! Messenger**—This is the iPad version of Yahoo!'s classic instant messaging app. It lets you chat with Yahoo! and MSN Messenger users and place phone and video calls to other users on your buddy list. You can even text users in the U.S. and Asia from this app. **Free**

Talk to Friends with Social Media

Texting, instant messaging, and chatting aren't the only ways to stay in touch with friends and family on the Internet. Some of the newest tools go beyond that to let you get information and updates directly from actors, athletes, writers, and other celebrities. The tools that let you do this fall into a broad category: social media.

You've probably heard of two of the most popular social media sites—Facebook and Twitter. They're both for social media, but that doesn't mean they're the same.

- **Facebook**—Facebook is designed to help you stay in touch with people you already know. When you have a Facebook account, you can "friend" people and add them to your network. When you do that, you can see the information and photos they post about themselves, and they can see the same about you. It's a great place to play games, share photos, listen to music, and plan events such as parties. Like most social media sites, Facebook is free.

- **Twitter**—Twitter is similar to Facebook in some ways, but different in some other important ones. On Twitter, you post short messages about what you're doing or thinking. These messages are posted to your public Twitter page and are automatically delivered to anyone who "follows" your tweets (being a follower on Twitter is like being a friend on Facebook). You can follow people and send private messages to other users.

Both Facebook and Twitter are interesting, and sharing to both of them is part of the iOS (just Twitter in iOS 5; both in iOS 6), but if you're a reader of this book, there's something very important about them that you need to know.

It's Not All Good

AGE LIMITS

Social media might sound like fun, but it's fun for slightly older kids and adults. In order to legally use Facebook, you have to be at least 13. There's no official age to use Twitter, but 13 is a good rule of thumb. So, until you turn at least 13, you shouldn't use Facebook or Twitter.

Facebook and Twitter put these limits on who can use their sites because there's stuff that happens on them that's too mature or upsetting or weird for kids. When you turn 13, if you want to get a Facebook or Twitter account, talk to your parents. They might let you, but they might also set rules for using your account, or they might want you to wait until you're a little older. Listen to what they have to say. Sometimes it can be frustrating to hear them say no, but they're trying to do what's best for you.

Email

Whether you use it to communicate with friends, to stay in touch with your relatives who live far away, or to send homework to your teachers, email is a big part of using an iPad.

Your iPad's email program, called Mail, has all the features you're probably used to from other email programs. The basic inbox screen in Mail lets you read email, reply to it, and store it in folders or delete it. You can also write a new message or search your emails from the main screen.

Before you can read or send emails, though, you need to learn how to set up email accounts on your iPad.

Setting Up Your First Email Account on Your iPad

You can add one (or more) email accounts directly on your iPad. To do this, start by tapping the Mail app and then follow these steps:

1. Tap the kind of email account you have.

2. If you have an iCloud, Exchange, Gmail, Yahoo!, AOL, or Hotmail email address, enter the information about your email account that the iPad asks for.

3. Tap Next.

Using Other for Email

If you don't have any of the kinds of email accounts listed here, you can tap Other to configure the account manually. That gets kind of complicated, so you should ask a parent or teacher to help you set one of these up.

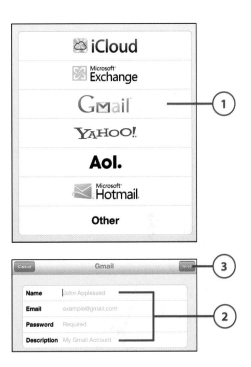

4. Some kinds of email accounts can also sync notes and calendars between your online accounts and iPad so that you can access them from multiple places. If these options appear, make your choices by leaving the default settings or moving the sliders to Off.

5. Tap Save. You go right to your new inbox and your email begins downloading. Tap the Inbox button to see the list of all your messages.

Add More Accounts

To add more accounts, go to the Settings page and, under Mail, Contacts and Calendars, tap Add Account.

It's Not All Good

EMAIL ERRORS

Sometimes when you're setting up email on your iPad, you don't get as far as your email downloading. Instead, you get an error. The most common time to get errors is when you're setting up an account. Your iPad confirms that all the information you enter about your account is right before letting you proceed. If it finds that something, like your password, is wrong, it lets you know and asks you to fix it. If you get errors when setting up or using your email double-check that all your settings, especially your username and password, are correct. If they are and you're still having problems, ask your parents or teachers for help.

>>>Go Further

WHAT TO DO IF YOU DON'T HAVE AN EMAIL ADDRESS

Don't worry if you don't have an email address; it's easy to get one—for free. Before you get one, though, you need to ask your parents' permission. Most free email services require you to be at least 13, so you need your parents' to help you sign up.

If you want an email address that works smoothly with your iPad, you can sign up for a free one at Google (gmail.com), Yahoo! (mail.yahoo.com), or Hotmail (hotmail.com). If you want one of those, go to the website and follow the instructions.

You can also get a free iCloud account from Apple. To get one of these, read "Creating an Apple ID on the iPad" in Chapter 2.

Losing Email

When you delete an email account on your iPad, you're also deleting all the email in that account from your iPad. It doesn't delete the email account itself or the emails in it. You can still get them on your computer or via the Web, depending on the type of email account. The messages just aren't accessible from your iPad's Mail app anymore.

Writing and Sending Email

Now that you've set up an email account on your iPad, it's time to start using it! To send an email, you need to be in the Mail app.

1. Tap the new email button to create an email.

2. Address an email. You have two ways to do this: Either type in the address of the person you want to send the email to in the To: field or, if you put the person in Contacts, tap the + and select them.

3. The CC: line lets you send the same email to another person at the same time. Enter the person's address or tap the + button.

4. BCC: lets you send a copy of the email to someone else without the people in the To: and CC: lines line knowing about it. Tap the CC/BCC: line to expand this option.

5. Tap the Subject line and type the subject of the email.

6. Tap Enter or tap the blank body of the message and start typing your email.

7. If you want to speak your messages instead of typing them, just make sure Siri is turned on. (You had the option when you set your iPad up in Chapter 2. If you didn't take it, tap Settings, then tap General, and then tap Siri and turn it on.) To learn how to use Siri to write email, check out the next section, "Using Siri to Send Email."

8. When you're done with the email and you're ready to send it, tap Send.

Choose Your Account

If you have more than one email account on your iPad, make sure to check the From: line to see which you're sending from. If you want to choose a different one, tap From: and then tap the account you want to use.

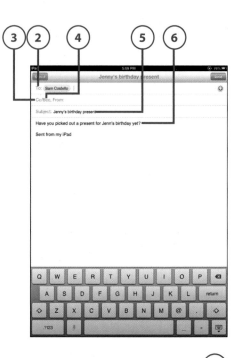

Using Siri to Send Email

If you're already in the Mail app with a blank email open in front of you, you can use Siri to dictate the email and send it. But did you know you can use Siri to send an email from basically anywhere on your iPad? Just like with Messages, you can tell Siri who to email and what to tell them, and then you can send the message without ever opening the Mail app.

1. Press and hold the Home button until the Siri menu pops up.

2. Tell Siri what email you want to send and who you want to send it to. Here are some examples of what you can say to send email with Siri:
    - "Send an email to John Smith saying, 'Do you want to come to my party on Saturday?'"
    - "New email to Ms. Jones."
    - "Email mom and tell her that she needs to sign my field trip permission slip."

3. Depending on what you say, Siri might ask you some follow-up questions. These questions can include things like clarifying which person you want to email (if you have more than one person in your Contacts with the same name) or exactly what you want to say (if you just said something like "New email to Ms. Jones"). Answer them.

4. When Siri has all the information it needs, it asks if you want to send the email. Tap Send and the email is sent. If you change your mind about sending the email, tap Cancel.

Replying to an Email

When you get an email that you want to reply to, just tap the Reply button and you get a new email with the old one copied in it, already addressed to the person you're replying to.

Sending Photos or Videos in Mail

In its first few versions, the only way to email photos or videos on the iPad was from the built-in Photos app or from photo and video apps from the App Store. But if you're running iOS 6, that's changed. Now, you can attach a photo or video to any email without ever leaving Mail. To do that, tap the Mail app to open it and follow these steps:

1. Tap the new email button to create a new blank email.

2. Address the email in the To: line and give the email a Subject: line like you normally would with any email.

3. Type the message you want to send.

4. When you're ready to include a photo or video, tap and hold on a blank area of the email until the magnifying glass appears. When it does, let go and a pop-up menu appears. Tap Insert Photo or Video.

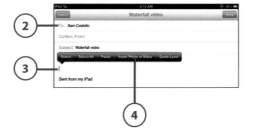

5. Tap the collection of photos that contains the photo or video you want to send. Unless you've added new Photo Albums (check out "Working with Photo Albums" in Chapter 15 to learn how to do that), tap Camera Roll.

6. Scroll through your Camera Roll until you find the item you want to send. Tap it.

7. If the item is a photo, you see a small version of it. If it's a video, you can tap the play button to watch it. If you decide you do want to use it, tap Use.

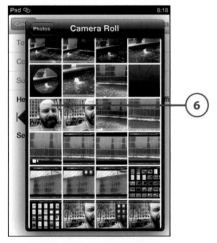

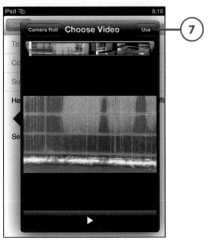

8. If the item is a photo, it is attached to your email. If it's a video, it is first compressed to be small enough to email and then attached. When you're done writing your email, tap Send to send it and the photo or video.

Don't Send Too Many

Photos and videos take up a lot of space, so most email accounts don't let you send more than a couple at a time to prevent email computers and accounts from filling up. A good rule of thumb is to just send three or four photos in one email, and only send one or two videos in an email.

Reading, Saving, and Deleting Email

Reading email on the iPad is simple: When an email shows up in your inbox, tap it. That's it! Well, OK, there's a little more to it. Here's what you need to know:

- If your iPad is in Portrait mode (taller than it is wide), tap the Inbox button to see a list of your messages for that email account. If your iPad is in Landscape mode (wider than tall), the inbox automatically appears on the side.

- The blue dot next to an email means you haven't read it yet.

- You can read your email one inbox at a time, or you can combine them all into one so that you don't have to go to each separate inbox to read your messages. To do that, keep tapping the Mailboxes button until you get to the Mailboxes screen and then tap All Inboxes.

In Landscape mode, you can tap here to back up and see your list of mailboxes for each email account you've set up.

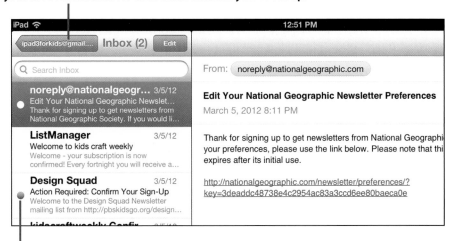

The blue dot means you have not yet read the email message.

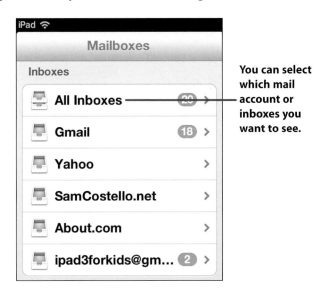

You can select which mail account or inboxes you want to see.

Deleting Email

Follow these steps to delete an email:

1. Swipe from left to right on the message you want to delete.

2. Tap Delete (or Archive, depending on which button appears. Different email accounts use different buttons).

Use the Trash

You can also delete an email by tapping it and then tapping the trash can icon above the message.

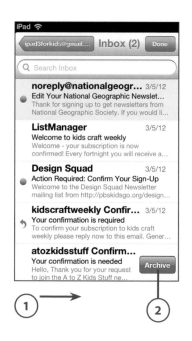

Moving Email

A lot of people like to just keep the emails they need to respond to or act on in their inboxes because it's easier to keep organized. If you're like that, you might want to move messages to another folder for storage. Start by selecting the message you want to move and then follow these steps:

1. Tap the Move to Folder button.

2. Tap the folder you want to move the email to.

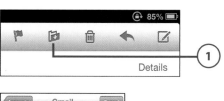

Be Safe: Texting, Chatting, and Emailing

It pays to be safe when you're texting, chatting, or emailing. Because you can't see who's messaging you, you can't be 100% sure they are who they say they are. Lots of people online are nice and are just there to have fun or learn, but some aren't so nice. Follow these rules to stay safe:

- If someone sends you something that makes you uncomfortable, tell a parent, teacher, or other adult you trust right away.

- If someone is being mean to you or one of your friends online, tell an adult.

- If someone asks you to be mean to someone else, or to gang up to tease or be mean to someone else, don't do it. Remember, you should always treat other people the way you want to be treated.

- If someone you don't know tries to chat with you, don't talk to them. If they keep trying to chat with you, block them.

- Never give your full name, address, phone number, or where you go to school to a stranger or anyone you don't know in real life.

- Never send a picture of yourself, your family, or your friends to a stranger or anyone you don't know in real life.

- If you get a file, picture, program, or other document emailed to you that you're not expecting, don't click it. Lots of emailed files have viruses in them.

- If you get an email with something in it that seems too good to be true (a free PlayStation or TV, for instance), it's probably a scam. Delete it and don't click any links or respond.

Take talking into the twenty-first century
with video chat using FaceTime.

Your iPad gives you a lot of ways to communicate with your friends and family, such as email, instant messaging, and texting. In this chapter, you learn all about another very cool way to stay in touch: FaceTime and other kinds of video conferencing.

→ What is FaceTime?

→ Making FaceTime calls

→ Skype: FaceTime for people without FaceTime

→ Being Safe on FaceTime and Skype

Get Ready for Your Close-Up! It's FaceTime!

FaceTime is one of the coolest features of the iPad. We've all seen science fiction movies in which people don't just have phone calls with each other, but have video calls where they can see each other while they talk. That's what FaceTime provides.

You can't have a FaceTime video chat with just anyone, but when you can, it's a pretty cool way to stay in touch.

Setting Up FaceTime

Your iPad came with FaceTime already installed, and setting it up is pretty easy. In fact, you don't have to do anything to get an account! FaceTime uses the Apple ID you created when you set up your iPad in Chapter 2, "Getting Started: Set Up and Sync Your iPad."

Because you logged in to your Apple ID when you set up your iPad, FaceTime already has that information. You just need to type in your password the first time you open FaceTime and tap Sign In. After you've done that, the only thing you need to do is add some people who can also use FaceTime to your address book. Then you're ready to make some FaceTime calls! (Learn all about adding contacts to your address book in "Using Contacts" in Chapter 5, "Talk to Me: Texting, Chatting, and Email.")

If people want to call you on FaceTime, just give them the email address you use for your Apple ID and they can call you whenever you're online.

Making FaceTime Calls

To make a FaceTime call, you need to first make sure that your iPad is connected to a Wi-Fi or 3G/4G network and then tap the FaceTime app on the home screen to launch it. Next, follow these steps:

1. Find the person you want to call in your contacts list and tap their name.

2. Tap the phone number or email address that the person uses for FaceTime.

3. FaceTime tries to make the call. If the person is online and wants to talk, they accept your call and, in just a second, you're having a video chat.

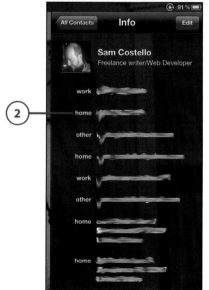

4. When you're on a FaceTime call,
   three buttons appear across
   the bottom of the screen: Mute,
   Switch Cameras, and End Call. Tap
   the Mute icon if you want to mute
   the microphone on your iPad so
   the person you're chatting with
   can't hear you. Tap it again and
   they can hear you.

5. The iPad, iPhone, and iPod touch
   models that can run FaceTime all
   have two cameras. Normally, it's
   the iPad's front camera that takes
   your picture for FaceTime, but you
   might want to show the person
   you're chatting with something
   else nearby. Switching to the iPad's
   back camera might be the best
   way to do that. Tap the Switch
   Cameras button to switch the camera they're looking through. Tap it
   again to switch back.

6. When you're ready to hang up,
   tap the End Call icon.

>>>Go Further

MAKING FACETIME CALLS WITH SIRI

Tapping someone's FaceTime name or number isn't the only way to start
up a chat. Siri can also help you. To use Siri to call someone, hold down
the Home button until Siri pops up and then say, "Call Mom," or "FaceTime
John Smith." That person needs to have a FaceTime account, and you have
to have it stored in your Contacts app. If that's the case, FaceTime fires up,
and you'll be chatting in just a minute.

Who You Can Call and Who You Can't

FaceTime is so cool that you're probably going to want to call everyone you know using it. I'm sorry to tell you, though, that you can't call just anyone. You can only call other people who have FaceTime. To use FaceTime, you and the people you want to call need the following:

- An iPad 2 or newer
- An iPhone 4 or newer
- A fourth-generation iPod touch or newer
- A Mac with FaceTime installed

Unfortunately, your friends with other tablets, cell phones that aren't iPhones, or Windows computers can't use FaceTime.

>>>Go Further

USING FACETIME OVER CELLULAR

When FaceTime first came to the iPad, it only worked when you were connected to Wi-Fi. But if you have iOS 6 and a Wi-Fi + 4G iPad, you have a new option: FaceTime over Cellular (aka 3G or 4G). This means that you can make and receive FaceTime calls anywhere you can get online, regardless of what kind of wireless network you're using. Now you never have to be out of touch. Depending on what company you get your 4G data plan from, FaceTime over Cellular might require an extra cost on your monthly plan, or changing the plan you use, so be sure to ask your parents about that if you want to use it. And, when you use it, always try to use Wi-Fi first; video calls can use up your monthly data plan quickly—and might end up costing you extra.

Answering FaceTime Calls

When someone calls you using FaceTime, you hear whatever ringtone you've assigned to FaceTime (check out "Choosing Your Sounds" in Chapter 3, "It's All Yours! Customizing Your iPad," for more info) and two buttons appear on the screen: Accept and Decline.

To talk to the person who's calling, tap Accept. If you don't want to talk to them, tap Decline.

Hold All Your Calls with Do Not Disturb

Being available for FaceTime calls is great—when you want to talk to people. But if you don't feel like talking, or if you need to concentrate on something (like homework) and don't want to be distracted, then having a FaceTime call interrupt you isn't so fun. Luckily, a feature called Do Not Disturb can help.

Do Not Disturb lets you control when you don't want to be available by FaceTime or bothered by any alert sounds from your iPad.

Enabling Do Not Disturb

Turning on Do Not Disturb when you want some peace and quiet is simple. Just go to your iPad's home screen and follow these steps:

1. Tap Settings.

2. Slide Do Not Disturb to On. As long as that slider is On, you won't get FaceTime calls and alerts won't make noise. Just make sure you remember to turn it Off when you're ready to talk again.

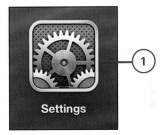

Scheduling Do Not Disturb

Using Do Not Disturb for those times when you want silence is great, but there are probably some times when you don't want to be bothered by your iPad at all, like when you're sleeping or in school. In that case, you can use Do Not Disturb's scheduling feature to automatically turn the feature on and off. To do that:

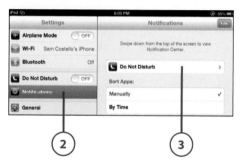

1. Tap Settings on the home screen.

2. Tap Notifications.

3. Tap Do Not Disturb.

4. Move the Scheduled slider to On.

5. To set the time when Do Not Disturb will be on, tap the From/To box and use the wheels to choose the hours you want.

6. You can make exceptions to Do Not Disturb. For instance, you can always allow calls from certain groups of contacts from your Contacts app, such as family members. To do that, tap Allow Calls From and select a group of contacts (to learn about Contacts groups, check out "Making Contacts Groups," in Chapter 5).

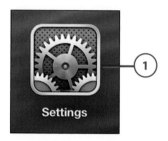

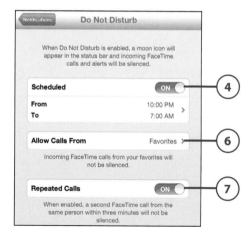

7. If someone really needs to talk to you, like in an emergency, they'll probably call right back if they don't get you the first time. Do Not Disturb is smart enough to know this. Keep the Repeated Calls slider On to allow calls through if the same person calls twice in three minutes.

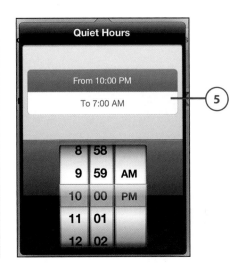

Do Not Disturb puts these settings into effect every day at the time you selected until you move the Scheduled slider to Off.

Skype: FaceTime for People without FaceTime

Just because some of your friends don't have FaceTime doesn't mean that you can't video chat with them. You both just need to get an app called Skype. Skype lets you make phone and video calls over the Internet from your iPad, iPhone, Mac, PC, or phone or tablet running Android. (This section focuses on video calls, but phone calls work basically the same way.)

You can download Skype for free from the App Store or www.skype.com, but you do need to register for a Skype account (get help from your parents to do this) and be online at the same time.

Adding Friends in Skype

In order to video chat with your friends using Skype, you all need Skype accounts. When you have them, you need to add your friends to your Skype contacts. Begin by tapping the Skype app to open it and then follow these steps:

1. Tap the + button to add a new contact.

2. Tap Search Skype Directory to look for your friends' Skype usernames.

3. Tap in your friends' names or their Skype usernames and then tap Search.

4. Find your friend in the search results and tap their name.

5. If it's your friend, tap Add Contact and they'll be saved to your contacts. Repeat these steps until you've added all your friends and family members with Skype accounts to your contacts. Then you'll be ready to chat!

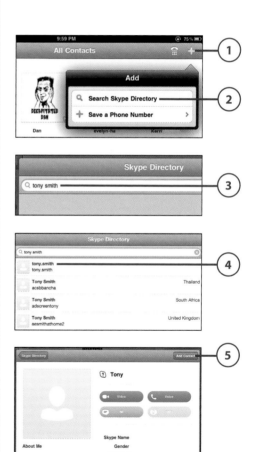

Making Video Calls Using Skype

After you've added some friends and family to Skype, you can start video chatting! To do this, you need to make sure you're connected to the Internet—Wi-Fi is best since it's unlimited, but you can use 3G/4G too. (Remember that both 3G and 4G usually have a limit on how much you can use, so make sure to get parents' permission before you use them for Skype.) To get started, tap the Skype app to open it.

1. You'll see your friends and family on the All Contacts screen. The contacts with phone icons on them can't have video chats. Look for the contacts with the green check mark at the bottom. That check mark means that person is online and available for a video chat. Tap the person you want to chat with.

2. In the contact window that pops up, tap Video to start the call. The person you're calling has to accept your call (the same is true for you; if someone tries to call you on Skype, you can either accept or decline the call). When they do, a picture of them appears on your iPad's screen.

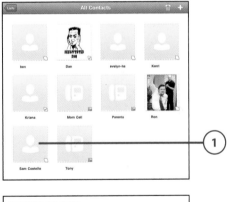

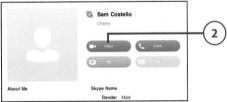

3. When you're on a Skype call, a number of icons appear across the bottom of the screen. When you tap the box with the arrow in it, the video chat window shrinks and reveals Skype's sidebar. From there, you can access your contacts or account.

4. The Chat icon lets you type messages to the person you're chatting with while your video conversation is still happening. You might use this to say something to the person you're talking to without people nearby you overhearing.

5. Tap the Camera icon to choose which of the iPad's cameras is shooting the video for the chat. You can choose either the front-facing camera above the screen, the one on the back, or no camera at all in case you want to chat but don't want the other person to see you.

6. The Microphone icon mutes your video chat so that, even if you're speaking, the other person won't be able to hear you. Mute is turned on when there's a red line through the Microphone icon and off when the line is gone.

7. Tap the Volume icon to adjust the call volume.

8. Tap the Hang Up icon to end your calls and video chats.

Be Safe: On FaceTime and Skype

When it comes to being safe on FaceTime or Skype, there's one very simple rule to follow: Don't chat with people you don't know.

Because you can see the name of the caller before you accept their call, if you don't know the person, you can decline the call. If you follow this rule, it's hard to get into unpleasant situations on FaceTime or Skype. Here are some other good rules to follow:

- Don't give your FaceTime or Skype username to strangers or people who you don't know offline.

- If someone calls from a number you know, but you don't recognize their picture when it appears, hang up.

- If something happens on FaceTime or Skype that makes you upset, uncomfortable, or worried, tell a parent, teacher, or another person you trust.

Write short documents
with Notes.

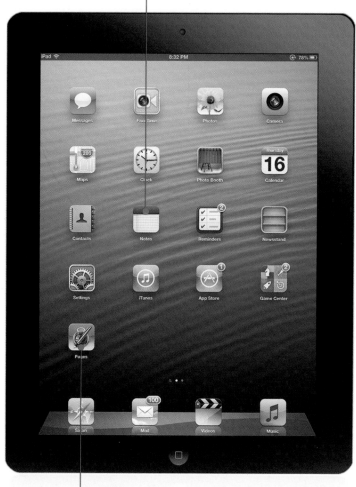

Write school papers on
your iPad using Pages.

In this chapter, you learn about some of the many ways the iPad can help you do your schoolwork, including:

- → Writing and printing on the iPad
- → Using Notes
- → Using Pages
- → Using your iPad in class
- → How to use the Internet for homework

7

Using Your iPad for School

Your iPad isn't just an awesome gadget for games, music, movies, and the Internet. It's also a powerful tool for doing your schoolwork. That might seem like less fun than some of the other stuff in this book, but if your parents bought your iPad, they'll be glad they did if you use it for school, too. From writing papers to keeping track of your schedule to doing research online, you can use your iPad in almost every part of your academic life.

Writing and Printing on the iPad

Writing on the iPad involves a lot more than just tapping on the screen when the keyboard appears. It can include wireless keyboards, hidden special symbols, and, of course, lots of useful apps.

To start writing, though, you need to decide what kind of keyboard you want to use. Two kinds of keyboards can be used with the iPad: the onscreen keyboard that pops up in lots of apps or an external keyboard. Some external keyboards connect using the Dock Connector; wireless keyboards use Bluetooth to link to the iPad.

Which Keyboards You Can Use

Even though it would be nice—and a lot easier—you can't just use any keyboard with your iPad. Most computer keyboards connect to the computer with a type of cable/connector called USB. Your iPad doesn't have a USB port. Therefore, instead of plugging your computer keyboard into the iPad, you have to get a separate one.

Remember the Dock Connector, the port on the bottom of the iPad that you plug the cable into to sync? A few keyboards plug into that and then prop the iPad up for easy typing.

Apple makes the most popular one of these keyboards. It's pretty nice, but because it's a regular keyboard—and one with a very awkward shape—it doesn't fold or bend and isn't as portable as some other options.

The other option is a Bluetooth keyboard.

Bluetooth is a kind of wireless technology that lets your iPad connect to accessories such as speakers, headphones, and keyboards. Bluetooth keyboards are cool because they're wireless, so the iPad doesn't have to be right next to the keyboard. Some of them fold up, making them easier to carry, and others come with carrying cases and mount the iPad like a laptop.

Which kind of keyboard is best for you depends on what you like, what you can afford, and where you're using the keyboard (the Dock Connector version might be better on a table, while the Bluetooth version could be better in bed or in your lap).

Connecting a Bluetooth Keyboard to Your iPad

If you choose a Bluetooth keyboard, you need to follow a few steps to connect it. Before you begin, make sure your keyboard is near the iPad; Bluetooth can only connect devices that are within a few feet of each other. Also, make sure the keyboard has charged batteries in it. Now you can follow these steps:

1. Open the Settings app on your iPad.

2. Tap Bluetooth from the options available and then, on the Bluetooth screen, move the slider to On.

3. Your keyboard (make sure it's powered on) will appear in the devices menu. Tap it.

Pairing a Keyboard

Some Bluetooth keyboards have to be put in what's called "pairing mode." This means they're ready to connect to the iPad. Check your keyboard's instructions to find out if you need to, and to learn how to, put it in pairing mode.

4. A window appears on the iPad with four numbers in it. Type them on your keyboard and then press Enter on the keyboard.

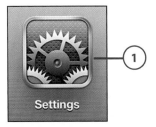

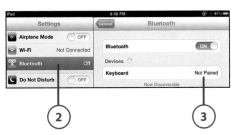

5. If everything worked, the Devices menu should now show your keyboard and read "Connected." If not, check the instructions that came with your keyboard and try again (or ask a parent for a little help).

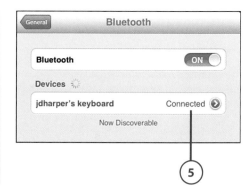

Using the Onscreen Keyboard

External keyboards aren't your only option, though. The iPad has an onscreen keyboard that can be a great option for writing. The iPad's onscreen keyboard appears in any app where you can enter text, such as Mail, Notes, or Safari. There are a few tricks about using the onscreen keyboard you should know.

Type in all caps using Caps Lock.

Hide, move, and split the keyboard.

Insert numbers and special characters.

Entering Numbers or Symbols

To enter a number or symbol using the onscreen keyboard, follow these steps:

1. Tap the number button. The keyboard changes to show numbers and some basic punctuation marks.

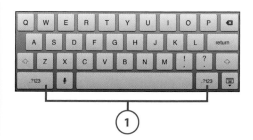

2. Here you can enter numbers along with a variety of symbols, such as parentheses, question mark, and so on. To access more uncommon symbols, tap the symbols button on the number keyboard.

3. To go back to the regular keyboard, tap the letters button. To go back to the numbers and punctuation marks, tap the numbers button (which button you see depends on which keyboard screen you're on).

Entering Accent Marks and Alternate Symbols

To write words in other languages, or use some really unusual and fun symbols, you have to tap and hold certain letters and punctuation marks. When you do this, you see lots of alternate versions. The letters that have these alternate versions are *a, e, i, o, u, c,* and *n.* The punctuation marks that have alternative versions are -, $, &, "., ?, !, ', and %.

To use an alternate version of a letter or punctuation mark, follow these steps:

1. Tap and hold one of the keys that has alternate versions. Options pop up above it.

2. To select an alternate version, don't take your finger off the screen (if you do, the options disappear). Instead, slide your finger to the option you want, and when the option turns blue, take your finger off the screen. The alternate version appears where you were typing.

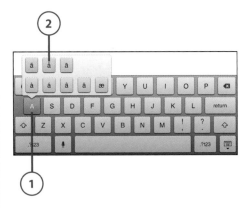

Enabling the Caps Lock

If you want to type something all in uppercase letters, the fastest and easiest way is to use Caps Lock.

- To do this, double tap the Shift (up-arrow) button on the keyboard. It turns blue. This means Caps Lock is on.

- When you want to turn Caps Lock off and start using lowercase letters again, single-tap the up-arrow button.

When the Shift key is blue, Caps Lock is enabled.

It's Not All Good

WHEN CAPS LOCK DOESN'T WORK

If Caps Lock isn't working for you, it might not be turned on in your settings. To turn it on, tap Settings and then General. Scroll down and tap Keyboard. On that screen, move the Enable Caps Lock slider to On.

Copying and Pasting Text

Copying and pasting text on a desktop computer is pretty easy: Select the text you want, click the necessary menus or keyboard shortcuts, and paste the text where you want it to go. But the iPad doesn't have menus or the same keyboard keys as your desktop, so how do you do it?

Not every iPad app handles copying and pasting exactly the same way, so there's no single way to show you how to do it. These steps show you one way. If the app you're trying to copy and paste in handles it differently, use what you learn here and try to apply it to that different process.

Begin by finding the text you want to copy (nearly every app on your iPad that lets you write, read articles, or browse the Web offers copy-and-paste functionality). After you've done that, follow these steps:

1. Tap and hold on the text you want to copy until the magnifying glass pops up. Then let go.

2. To select just one section of the text, tap Select.

Select All

If you tap Select All, all the text on the page will be selected.

3. When you tap Select, the text you tapped gets highlighted in blue. The blue highlight tells you what text is selected to be cut or copied. You can change the selection by dragging the blue dot on either side of the selected text.

4. Most apps let you choose to cut or copy the text. Cut means you'll delete the text and then paste it somewhere else. Copy means you'll make a copy to paste elsewhere, but not delete the original text. As mentioned earlier, different apps have slightly different options, but they should all at least offer copy.

5. Find the place where you want to paste the text—this could be in the same app or another app; it doesn't matter. Tap and hold until the magnifying glass appears. Then let go.

6. Tap Paste in the menu that appears.

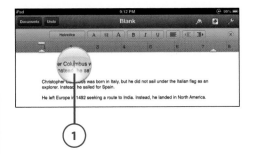

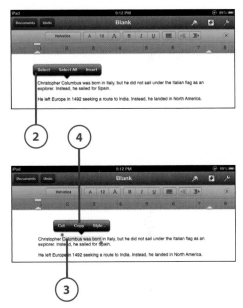

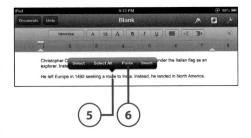

>>>Go Further

AUTOCORRECT

Not a great speller? Don't worry. The iPad has a feature called Autocorrect that automatically fixes any spelling mistakes you make. When you type a word the iPad thinks is misspelled, a little box pops up beneath it with a suggested change. To use the suggestion, tap the spacebar to make the change. If you don't want the change, tap the X next to the suggestion and then keep typing. Keep an eye on the screen when you type: Because tapping the spacebar accepts Autocorrect changes automatically, sometimes you might accept suggestions that you don't mean to and mess up what you're writing.

Syncing Documents to Your iPad with iTunes

It's easy to move documents such as school papers and e-books from your computer onto your iPad. To do that, you first have to sync your iPad and computer. After you've done that, follow these steps:

1. In iTunes, click the Apps tab to access the document-sharing options.

2. Scroll to the bottom of that screen and find File Sharing.

3. You see a list of all the apps on your iPad that can sync documents with your computer. Click the app you want to sync the document to.

4. Click Add.

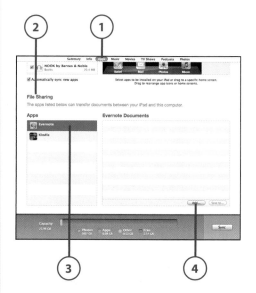

5. Browse through the window until you find the document you want to sync. Click once on the document.

6. Click Open. Repeat this for as many documents as you want to sync to that app. You can also choose other apps and repeat these steps to sync documents to them.

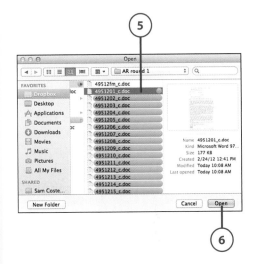

7. When you've added all the documents you want to sync, click the Sync (or Apply) button in iTunes. When the sync is complete, the documents will be on your iPad. Just tap the apps you synced them to and you can start reading them.

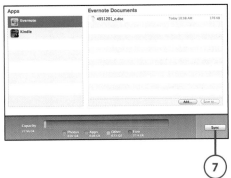

AirPrint and Compatible Printers

Just like with keyboards, printing from the iPad is a little tricky because there's no connector for printers to plug into. You can always sync or send files from your iPad to your computer to print there, but if you don't have a computer or want to print right from your iPad, you need something else: AirPrint.

AirPrint is an Apple technology that lets you print wirelessly from your iPad to certain printers. For this to work, you can't use just any old printer; you need one that's AirPrint compatible.

Because not all printers support AirPrint—not even all printers that have Wi-Fi—you and your parents need to do some research if you're thinking of getting one. The list of printers that support AirPrint is always changing, but big companies such as Hewlett-Packard, Epson, Canon, and Lexmark all make AirPrint-compatible printers.

How to Print

Just like different apps handle copy and paste differently, there's no single way to print using iPad apps. That's because apps are so different in what they do and how they look. There are a few common ways to print—such as by tapping the Action box (the square with the arrow curving out of it)—but you won't find that in every app. (Not even every app that can print works this way.) This chapter includes tips on how to print in two writing apps, Notes and Pages. Many other apps that can print work in similar ways.

Writing Apps: Notes

If you want to write something besides an email—a school paper, for instance—the only writing app that comes with your iPad is Notes. Notes is far from the only writing app available for the iPad (check out the "Writing Apps: Pages" or "Awesome Apps" sections later in this chapter for others), but it's a good tool for quickly writing down your ideas or keeping track of things. If you want to write papers for school, it might not be the best tool, but for writing short things, it's a good choice.

Creating a New Note

To write something new using Notes, begin by tapping the app to open it and then follow these steps:

1. Tap the + button to create a new note.

2. A blank note and the keyboard appears. Begin typing.

Saving Your Note

Your note is automatically saved as you type, so there's no Save button to tap.

Printing and Deleting Notes

After you've created a few notes, you can do several other things with the app. First, hide the keyboard by tapping the down-keyboard button. Then you have options such as the following:

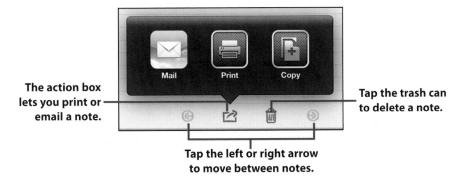

The action box lets you print or email a note.

Tap the trash can to delete a note.

Tap the left or right arrow to move between notes.

- To email, text, or print a note, tap the Action box at the bottom of the page and tap Mail or Print. When you tap Mail, a new, blank email will be created with the text of the note in it. When you tap Message, a new mes-sage with the text of the note in it is created. When you tap Print, you'll have to select your printer and the number of copies you want to print.

- To delete a note, tap the trash can icon and then tap Delete Note.

- To move between notes, tap the left and right arrows.

Viewing the Notes List

If you've created more than one note, you have two ways to see a list of all your notes so you can choose the one you want:

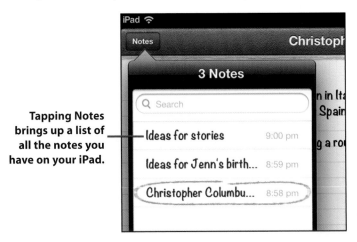

Tapping Notes brings up a list of all the notes you have on your iPad.

- If your iPad is in Portrait mode, tap Notes and then tap the note you want from the list.

To see a note, just tap it in the sidebar.

- In Landscape mode, the list of notes appears automatically in the sidebar. Simply tap the note you want to read or edit.

Writing Apps: Pages

If you want to create a document with images or charts in it, or that uses different fonts and colors, you need a more powerful app. There are a lot of good choices, but Apple makes one of the best. It's called Pages, and you can buy it at the App Store.

If you're planning to use your iPad to write papers for school, you'll probably want Pages. Not only does it offer the features you're probably used to from using programs like Microsoft Word, it has some special ones, too. For instance, it comes with document templates that allow you to write your own text while using the template's layout to create a cooler-looking paper. It can also help you drag and drop pictures, charts, and graphs. With Pages, you have the tools to create homework that really wows your teachers.

Creating a Basic Document

To create a basic document in Pages, such as a short paper, note, or story, start by tapping the Pages icon on your iPad's home screen to open the app and then follow these steps:

1. Tap +.

2. Tap Create Document to open a new document.

Documents Save Automatically

Just like in Notes, you won't find a Save button in Pages. That's because your changes get saved automatically every 30 seconds when you make them.

3. You see a selection of templates, pre-built documents designed for different uses (there are templates for letters, papers, reports, and much more). Tap the template you want to use to create your document. If you choose any template other than "Blank," there will be some text and images in it already that show you how to use it; replace those with your own writing or pictures. For a plain document, tap Blank. From here you can immediately begin typing into the new document.

Other Templates

Pages comes with lots of different templates designed for various uses. They include different styles of letters, flyers, and school papers. Experiment with the templates when you have different kinds of documents to create. They'll make it easier to create great-looking papers.

Formatting a Document

When you've begun writing a document, you'll probably want to format your text—for instance, make it bigger or smaller or change the font. Formatting can be a lot of fun and a good way to make your papers more interesting and creative looking. Be careful, though: If you're creating a paper for school, check with your teachers about what kind of formatting they like. Some teachers have very specific rules about that.

To format your documents, you need to select the text—which was already covered in the section "Copying and Pasting Text"—and then choose from the following options:

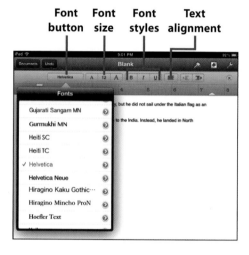

- **Font**—Tap the font button to see a list of all your font choices (the preview shows what each font looks like). Tap the arrow next to the font name to see different versions of the font. Tap the one you want to use in your document.

- **Font Size**—There are two options here: Tap the number button and then select a new font size, or tap the small A to make the font smaller and the large A to make it bigger. Tap the correct A until the font is the size you want.

- **Style**—Choices are bold (the B button), italic (the I button), and underlined (the U button).

- **Alignment**—This controls whether the text lines up on the left, right, or center of the page. Tap the button to make your choice. You can also choose Justify if you want the edges of the text to be even on both sides.

Advanced Formatting Options

When you get to be a pro with basic formatting, you might want to try some more advanced options. To access them, tap the Paintbrush button. The menu that appears offers several options spread across three tabs:

- **Style**—The default tab is Style and contains basic formatting options as well as additional styles such as strikethrough (to make text look crossed out) and pre-made styles such as title, heading, and bullet.

- **List**—The List tab contains the controls for making bulleted and numbered lists. The arrow buttons control what level of the list the selected text is on, and the buttons below control whether numbers or letters are used for each item in the list.

- **Layout**—The Layout tab changes how many columns your document has and how much space appears between lines (important when your teachers want a double-spaced paper).

Get a Word Count

If you're writing a paper for class or for your school newspaper, you'll need to know how many words your document has. To turn on Pages' word count feature, tap the wrench icon, then Settings, and then move the Word Count slider to On. The word count displays at the bottom of the page. It updates as you add or delete words.

Adding Headers and Footers

You might want to add headers and footers to the documents you create. A header is a section at the top of the page. A footer is the same thing, but at the bottom of the page. Headers are commonly used for your name or the paper's title, and footers often show page numbers. After you've set them up, they're automatically added to each page.

1. Open the document you want to add the header or footer to. It could either be a new document or one you've already been working on.

2. Tap the wrench icon.

3. Tap Document Setup.

4. The paper goes into Setup mode. To add a header, tap the Tap to Edit Header button and then type in the text you want to have in the header. Automatically insert a page number on every page by tapping Page Numbers and choosing the format you prefer. When you've created the header you want, tap the page.

5. To add a footer, tap the Tap to Edit Footer button and add the text or page number you want in the footer. When you've added what you want, tap the page.

6. When you've added a header or footer, tap the Done button to go back to writing your document with the new header or footer in it.

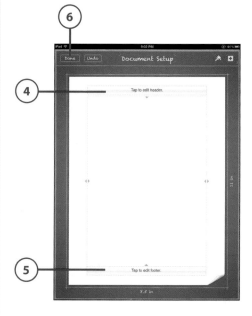

Changing Margins

Document Setup mode also lets you change the amount of empty space at the sides and top and bottom of your document. These spaces are called *margins*. It's always safe to use the built-in margins (1 inch at the edges, 0.88 inches at the top and bottom) because they're pretty standard. But if your teachers want you to use a different margin, this is where you do it. Tap the arrows at the edge of the page and drag in or out to change the side margins. Tap the arrow at the top or bottom of the page and drag up or down to change those margins. When you have them where you want them, tap Done.

Adding Images to a Document

One of the really cool things about Pages is that it's easy to add images to make your document look extra good. To do that, start by tapping the document you want to add an image to and then follow these steps:

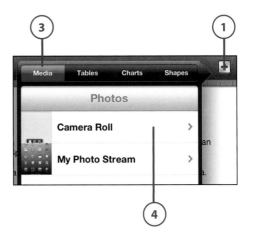

1. Tap the Plus icon.

2. The first time you do this, you have to tap OK to give Pages access to your photos (not pictured).

3. To add a photo, tap Media from the menu.

4. Tap Camera Roll (or if the photo is located elsewhere in your Photos app, choose that location). You can select any image already saved on your iPad.

5. Tap the image you want and it is added to your document.

Add Other Options

You can also add tables, charts, and shapes to your documents by choosing those options in step 3.

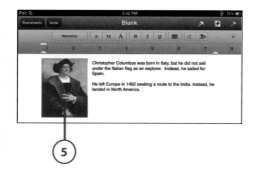

5

Formatting Images and Shapes

When you add an image or shape to your document, you can change how it looks by tweaking its size and location. To do that, first tap the image or shape and then follow these steps:

Drag selection handles to resize image.

Use the options above a selected image to cut, copy, delete, or replace an image.

Tap, hold, and drag an image to move it around the page.

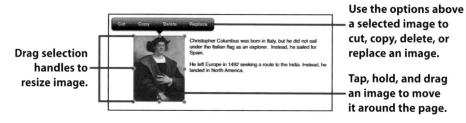

- To change the size of the image or shape, tap and hold one of the blue dots at its edge. Drag in to make the image or shape smaller; drag out to make it larger. When it's the right size, take your finger off the screen.

- To change the place where the image or shape is located in your document, tap its center and drag the image or shape to a new location. The text flows around it.

- To delete the image or shape, tap it and then tap Delete from the pop-up menu.

Formatting Tables

After you've inserted and selected a table, choose from these options:

Tap and drag the circle to move the table.

Change this number to alter the number of rows in the table.

Make a table larger or smaller by tapping and dragging the blue dots.

- Add or remove rows (the horizontal strips that make up part of the table) by tapping the rows button and then tapping the up or down arrow to choose the number of rows the table should have. Adding or removing columns (the vertical strips in the table) works the same way.

- To move the table, tap and hold it, then drag the table to a new location. Let it go when the table is where you want it.

- To delete the table, tap it and then tap Delete.

Naming a Document

The documents you create in Pages are automatically given a name based on the text in them. But you can also give them names you want so it's easier to identify them from the main Pages screen.

1. Find the document you want to rename and tap its current name underneath its icon.

2. Type in a new name.

3. Tap Done and the new name is saved.

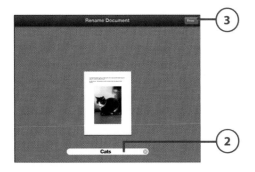

Printing a Document

To print a document in Pages, you first have to tap the document you want to print to open it. Then follow these steps:

1. Tap the wrench icon.

2. Tap Share and Print.

3. Tap Print.

4. Tap Printer to select your printer. Remember, your iPad and printer both have to be on the same Wi-Fi network for AirPrint to work—and your printer has to be AirPrint compatible.

5. Tap the + or – button to choose the number of copies you want to print.

6. Tap the Print button to start printing.

If You Don't Have an AirPrint-Compatible Printer

There's a good chance you don't have an AirPrint-compatible printer. That's okay; not that many people do yet. If that's the case, and you can't print from your iPad, you have some options, including emailing your document to someone who has a printer (more on emailing using Pages in a minute) or syncing it to iTunes if your computer has a printer connected.

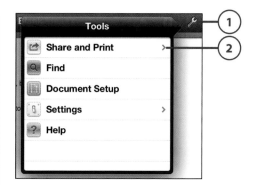

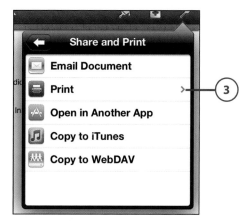

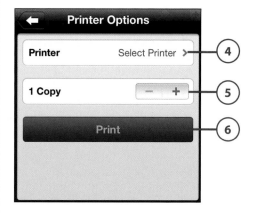

Emailing a Document

If you want to email a document you've created in Pages (for instance, to send your homework to your teacher), start by tapping the document you want to email to open it. Then follow these steps:

1. Tap the wrench icon.

2. Tap Share and Print.

3. Tap Email Document.

4. Choose what format you want to send the document in: Pages, PDF, or Word. For school papers, ask your teachers what format they want before you send. Different teachers will want you to send different formats.

5. A blank email will open with the paper attached to it. Fill out the email like you normally would and tap Send to send it.

Deleting Documents

If you want to delete a Pages document, you first have to open Pages
by tapping it on your home screen.
When you see the list of all your
documents, follow these steps:

1. Tap Edit.

2. Tap the document you want to
   delete. Pages highlights it with a
   yellow border.

3. Tap the trash can icon.

4. Tap Delete Document. This erases
   the document—permanently—
   from your iPad and, if the document is synced using iCloud, from
   all other devices where it's synced
   (so be sure you really want it
   gone).

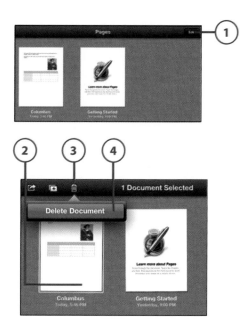

Awesome Apps

The only app for writing that comes with the iPad—Notes—is okay for writing, well, notes. But if you need to write anything longer or more complicated—and if you use your iPad for school, you definitely will—you'll want
a more powerful writing app. Pages is one good choice, but it's far from the
only one. Here are some other suggestions:

- **Daedalus Touch**—A cool word processor designed just for the iPad.
  It lets you create papers, but also helps you make and email PDFs and
  e-books. **$4.99**

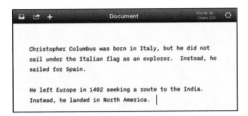

- **iA writer**—Not only does this word processor let you focus on what you're writing—and not all the buttons and options that other word processors have—it also lets you touch the screen to perform actions (such as undoing your typing with a swipe). It's really only for writing, though; if you need even basic formatting, you should use a different app. **$0.99**

- **PlainText**—A very simple program that is like writing on paper. Not only does each document look like a piece of paper, you store them in folders. You can even use it to back up your documents online. **Free ($1.99 to remove ads)**

It's Not All Good

USING YOUR IPAD IN SCHOOL

If using your iPad for school is helpful, using it *in* school should be pretty good, too, right? It probably is, but that doesn't mean you should or can use it in class.

Some schools have programs in which they have kids use laptops or iPads in class as part of their work; other schools don't. If your school doesn't have one of those programs, you should ask your teachers' permission before you start using your iPad in class. Some teachers may not mind—some might even encourage it!—but others might find it distracting or not want you to use it if other students don't have one, too.

The iPad can be a great tool to help you do homework, but ask permission before you bring it to school.

Using the Internet for Homework

If you're using your iPad for schoolwork, you'll probably use the Internet to do research for your papers. If you're going to do that, though, there are a few things you need to know.

How to Do Research Online

It might seem obvious, but doing research for your schoolwork online works pretty much the same way that finding any other information does. If you don't know where to find what you're looking for, begin by searching for it at a search engine such as Google and tapping the sites that come up in the search results. If you know of websites that have the information you want, you can also go directly to them.

Of course, online isn't the only place to do research. Your school or neighborhood library is packed full of helpful books and magazines. Ask your parents to take you there and then get help from the librarian to find what you're looking for. Libraries are full of things you can't get online at all. You never know what you'll find at them—and that's pretty cool!

Choosing Good Sources

The places you find information for your school papers are called *sources*. Books, encyclopedias, and even websites can all be sources.

Creating a website or blog is pretty easy. But because it's so easy, that means just about anybody can do it—and not everyone is an expert on the things they're writing about. When you're writing papers for school, you should use only the best and most expert sources, not just the first ones you find.

But with so many websites online, how can you figure out who's an expert? Here are some tips:

- **Be skeptical**—This means you shouldn't automatically believe everything you read. A smart way to try to figure out if something is true is to check to see whether other websites are saying the same thing about the same topic. If they are, that means it's more likely to be true.

- **Use established sources**—If you're writing about a news story, going to a big-name news website such as CNN, CBS, or NPR is good idea. They'll usually have more accurate information than the blog of a person who isn't directly involved with what they're writing about.

- **Use primary sources**—A primary source is someone with first-hand experience of a situation. For instance, if you're writing about the Declaration of Independence, quoting writing by someone who helped write it or the Declaration itself are both great primary sources. If you're writing about a person, quoting their own words is a terrific primary source.

- **Consider the source**—When deciding whose information to use in your paper, figure out who's saying it. If you're writing about biology, quoting a college biology professor is a better idea than quoting some random person with a blog but no expertise in biology.

- **Watch out for Wikipedia**—Wikipedia seems like an easy place to get all the information you need, but it's not always accurate. That's because almost anyone can change articles on Wikipedia, even if the changes they make are wrong. When using Wikipedia, find the information you're looking for and then click the little number after the sentence or paragraph you want to use. This shows you where that information came from. Go to that site to confirm the information for yourself. If there's no link, try finding the same information somewhere else to make sure it's correct.

Using Research in Your Papers

When you find something that you want to use in your paper, don't just copy and paste it. It's important to give credit to the person who wrote what you want to use. If you don't, and act like their words are your own, you're committing plagiarism, which is a form of lying. If you wrote something and someone else used it, you'd want them to give you credit, right? You should do the same for others. When you find something you want to add to your paper, do the following:

- Always make sure to put the text you're copying and pasting into your paper in quotes.

- Make sure to accurately write down who wrote the text you're quoting and where they wrote it or where you found it.

- After the quotes, put the writer and the name of their work in parentheses. Italicize the name of the work.

For example, if you're quoting something written by Ben Franklin in a book called *Ben Franklin Writes About American History* (which I made up), and the quote is "American history is interesting," you should write the following:

"American history is interesting" (Ben Franklin, *Ben Franklin Writes About American History*).

If you're getting the quote from a website, try this:

"American history is interesting" (Ben Franklin, www.benfranklin.com).

- Even if you're not directly copying and pasting something from another document, it's a good idea to give the writer credit for their ideas, as in the following example:

Ben Franklin wrote that American history is interesting (www.benfranklin.com).

- Your teachers might have another way they want you to credit the sources you're quoting. If they do, use their guidelines instead.

If you always follow these rules when you're writing your papers, you won't run the risk of getting in trouble for plagiarism and will establish writing habits that can help you succeed in school for years to come.

Keep track of your
schedule and
important dates.

See what you have
to do each day from
a single screen.

In this chapter, you find out about some of the many ways that the iPad can help you keep track of all kinds of things, from birthdays to important events to things happening at school. To learn how to do that, you need to learn about:

8

Get Organized with Calendar, Reminders, and Clock

Using Calendar

Calendar is a great app to use for school because it lets you keep track of all the important events in your life. Whether that's your friends' or family members' birthdays, when big projects or papers are due in class, or an important game or the school play, putting those dates in your calendar—and setting alerts to remind you—can be a big help. And because Calendar can sync with your computer and iCloud, even if you're not near your iPad, you never have to be far away from your important dates.

Adding Events

To add an event to your calendar, first tap the Calendar app to open it and then follow these steps:

1. Tap + to add an event.

2. Enter the name of the event (say, Dad's birthday or the last day of school) and, if you want, a location for the event.

3. Tap the date and time box to choose when the event is happening.

4. For the Start time, move the wheels until you have the right date and time. If the event is all day, like a birthday, move the All-day slider to On instead.

5. Tap the Ends box and do the same.

6. Tap Done.

7. If everything looks right, tap Done, and the event is added to your calendar.

Add Calendar Events Using Siri

Typing isn't the only way you can add events to your calendar; you can also use Siri. Hold down the Home button until the Siri menu appears at the bottom of the screen. Then speak the event you want to create. For example, you could say, "New appointment at the dentist Monday at 11," or, "New Event: Piano practice," and then answer the questions Siri asks. Save the event by tapping Confirm and your calendar is updated.

REPEATING EVENTS

If there's an event you go to regularly (say, a weekly piano lesson or sports practice), you don't have to put it in your calendar every week. Instead, just create it once and set it to repeat. Here's how:

1. Follow the first six steps for creating an event (see the previous how-to).

2. Instead of tapping Done to save the event, tap Repeat.

3. Tap to choose to have the event repeat every day, every week, every 2 weeks, every month, or every year and then tap Done.

4. Tap Done to save the event. Check your calendar for every day the event is supposed to repeat and you'll see it.

Creating Alerts

Do you ever forget to do something that you need to do? Maybe you want your iPad to remind you when an event is happening so you don't forget it? You can use alerts to do that.

1. Follow the first six steps in "Adding Events," as previously described.

2. Tap Alert.

3. You can choose to get an alert when the event happens, a few minutes before, or a day or two before. Tap the option for when you want to be reminded.

4. Tap Done.

5. Make any other changes you want to the event and then tap Done to save it. Remember, the sound that alerts you to the event is controlled by the Calendar Alerts sound in the Settings app (explained in "Choosing Your Sounds" in Chapter 3, "It's All Yours! Customizing Your iPad").

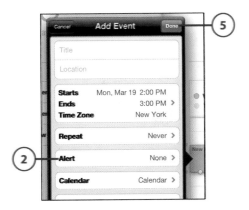

Editing Events

If you want to change something about an event you've already created, just find the event in the Calendar app and tap it. This pulls up all the event's options, and all you have to do is make your changes and tap Done to save them when you're finished.

You can also use Siri to edit or delete events. Just hold down the Home button until Siri appears and then speak the change you want to make. For example, you could say, "Cancel piano lesson on Tuesday," "Reschedule tutoring to next Thursday," or, "Cancel soccer on Saturday." Siri might ask some follow-up questions. Answer them and your calendar is updated in no time.

Deleting Events

If you want to get rid of an event from your calendar, it's very simple. Start by finding the event you want to delete. Then tap it and follow these steps:

1. If you're in Landscape mode, scroll to the bottom of the pop-up window (if you're in Portrait, you don't need to scroll) and tap Delete Event.

2. Tap Delete Event to remove the event.

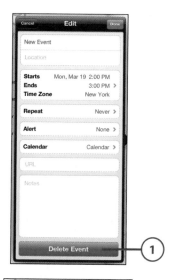

DELETING REPEATING EVENTS

If you want to delete an event that repeats, things are slightly different. Follow the first two steps, but after you tap Delete, you're asked to make a choice. If you just want to cancel the event once (say, piano practice is cancelled this week), tap Delete This Event Only. If you want to delete every single one of these events for all time (you're not going to play the piano anymore), tap Delete All Future Events.

Using Multiple Calendars

Do you want to keep a separate calendar of all your school events and your home events? How about one calendar for sports and another for birthdays? You can do that by using multiple calendars. To create more than one calendar, follow these steps:

1. Tap Calendars to view your list of calendars.

2. Tap Edit.

3. Tap Add Calendar. This adds the new calendar to your iCloud account and automatically syncs it to all your devices that have iCloud turned on, so they're all up to date.

4. Type in a name for the calendar.

5. Tap a color. All the events in this calendar will be in this color so you can tell them apart from events in other calendars.

6. Tap Done.

7. Tap Done again and you'll have a new calendar.

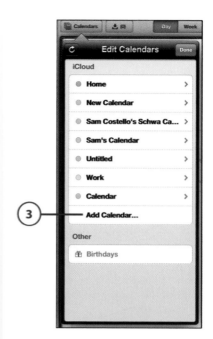

>>>Go Further

SYNCING CALENDARS AND ADDRESS BOOK FROM YOUR COMPUTER

One benefit of syncing Calendar and Address Book information from your computer is that anything you have set up in those apps transfers to your iPad. So, if you have multiple calendars on your computer, just select those when you sync (for a refresher on syncing, check out "Syncing with iTunes" in Chapter 2, "Getting Started: Set Up and Sync Your iPad") and they'll all be added to your iPad. Also, if you include people's birthdays in your Address Book, those birthdays are automatically added to a Birthdays calendar on your iPad.

Deleting a Calendar

If you have more than one calendar and want to delete one entire calendar (not just a single event), follow these steps:

1. Tap Calendars to view the list of your calendars.

2. Tap Edit and tap again on the Calendar you want to delete.

3. Tap Delete Calendar.

4. Tap the Delete Calendar button again (and remember, when you do this, you're also deleting every event in the calendar, so you better be sure you want to get rid of it). This also deletes the calendar from anywhere it's synced, like your computer or iCloud account.

5. Tap Done.

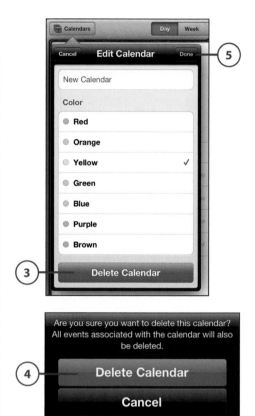

Using Reminders

Calendar is a good app for keeping track of events, but there's another app that comes with your iPad that can be a big help, too: Reminders. Reminders helps you manage all the things you need to do, such as big school projects and buying birthday presents for your relatives. Unlike Calendar, which ties events to dates, Reminders lets you create to-do lists that hang around until you complete them.

Creating Reminders

To create a reminder, start by tapping the Reminders app on the home screen and then follow these steps:

1. Tap the + button to add a reminder.

2. Type in the reminder you want to create and tap Return on the keyboard. This creates a reminder. To create another, repeat these steps again.

3. When you've done the thing the reminder is there to help you remember, tap the box next to it to mark it as done.

Add Reminders with Siri

Just like with Calendar, you can add reminders using Siri. Hold down the Home button until Siri appears and then say the reminder you want created. For instance, you can say, "Remind me to buy Dad a birthday present," or, "New reminder: take out the trash." If Siri asks any follow-up questions, answer them. Tap Confirm to create your new reminder.

More Reminder Options

The basic reminder is just a box you can check off when you're done. But reminders have options that enable them to do a lot more to help you. You can access those options by tapping the reminder you want to change; then follow these steps:

1. To have your iPad automatically alert you about the reminder, make sure the Remind Me On a Day slider is moved to On (it's there by default) and then tap the date.

2. Use the wheels to select the date and time when you want to be reminded.

3. Tap Done.

4. If you want the reminder to auto-matically repeat, tap Repeat.

5. Tap on how often you want it to repeat.

6. Tap Done.

7. Tap Show More to access other options.

8. To assign an importance to the reminder, tap Priority and then tap Low, Medium, or High.

9. To add the reminder to a to-do list, tap List and then tap the list you want to add the reminder to. (See the "Creating To-Do Lists" section later in this chapter for more information.) When you've made your choice, tap Done.

10. To add additional information to the reminder, tap Notes and enter more details.

11. Tap Done one more time to save the Reminder.

Editing Reminders

If you want to change something about a reminder you've already created, tap it and then tap any of the items in the menu you want to change. When you've made the change you want, tap Done.

Deleting Reminders

To completely delete a reminder (rather than just marking it as done), first tap the one you want to delete and then follow these steps:

1. Tap the Delete button (shown in the image for steps 9–11 of "More Reminder Options").

2. When asked to confirm, tap Delete again to finish the deletion.

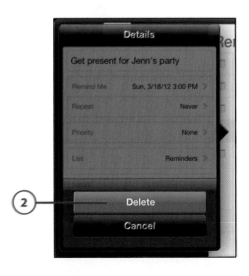

Creating To-Do Lists

If you want to stay organized by cre-ating groups of reminders—say, one for things you're doing for school, another for Boy or Girl Scouts, a third for chores—you need to make to-do lists. Start doing that by tapping Reminders to launch the app and then follow these steps:

1. Tap Edit.

2. Tap Create New List. Give the new list a name and tap Done on the keyboard.

3. When you're ready to save the new list, tap Done again.

4. To rearrange the order of your to-do lists, tap and hold the bars next to a list and drag it to the new location. Let it go to save the new order.

Awesome Apps

Reminders is a good app for doing just what it says—providing you remind-ers to do things. But it's pretty basic; if you want more advanced or powerful features, you might want to check out these great to-do list apps:

- **2Do**—This powerful, complex app can be hard to figure out, but it can also help you get super-organized. Not only can you use it to create to-do lists, but each item on that list can have an action attached to it—like a phone call or an email—as well as GPS locations or voice notes. It's an expensive app, but it's very powerful. **$9.99**

- **Awesome Note HD (+ToDo)**—This is another powerful to-do list tool. The interface is tricky, but after you get the hang of it, it can help you. Use it to create to-do lists and take notes. You can add photos, GPS locations, and other things to each to-do and sync your to-dos with other apps. **$4.99 or free 3-day trial version**

- **ToodleDo**—The basic display of the to-dos in ToodleDo is easy to understand and use. You can add reminders to each to-do, organize them into folders, and sort them in all kinds of ways. The priority system can be a little tricky, though. **$2.99**

Always Wake Up on Time: Using Alarm Clock

Have you ever slept too late and then had to rush to get ready for school on time? That feeling of being behind and needing to catch up is no fun—and you can avoid it with a good alarm clock to make sure you wake up on time. Luckily, your iPad comes with a Clock app that can help you out.

It's Not All Good

CLOCK IS IOS 6 ONLY

The Clock app comes preloaded only with iOS 6, so if you're running iOS 5 or earlier on your iPad, these tips don't apply to you. If you're in that situation, you can either upgrade to iOS 6 (remember, it's free) or get one of the many good alarm clock apps available at the App Store.

Setting an Alarm

To create an alarm, tap the Clock app
on your home screen and then follow
these steps:

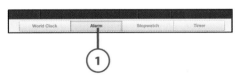

1. Tap Alarm at the bottom of the
   screen.

2. Tap + to create a new alarm.

3. If you want the alarm to repeat
   (say to wake you up every school
   day), tap Repeat and then tap the
   days when you want the alarm to
   go off.

4. Tap Sound to choose the sound
   you're woken up by. You can
   choose the sounds that come
   with the iPad or any song in your
   iPad's music library. To do that, tap
   Pick a Song and then tap the song
   you want.

5. If you want to enable snooze (a
   button you hit to sleep just a few
   more minutes), make sure the
   Snooze slider is moved to On.

6. Move the wheels to the time you
   want the alarm to go off.

7. When you've created the alarm
   and want to save it, tap Save.

Setting Alarms with Siri

You can also use Siri to create an
alarm. Hold down the Home button until Siri appears and then
say something like, "Wake me up
at 8:00 a.m. tomorrow," or, "Set an
alarm for 7:00 a.m. tomorrow." Siri
confirms the alarm has been created and you're done.

Turning Alarms Off

If your alarm normally wakes you up at 7:00 a.m. on Monday but this Monday is a holiday and you have the day off from school, then you might want to sleep in. To do that, you don't have to delete your alarm—you can just turn it off. Start by opening Clock and then follow these steps:

1. Tap Alarm at the bottom of the screen (not shown).

2. Tap the alarm you want to turn off.

3. Move the slider to Off.

Don't Oversleep!

If you've turned your alarm off, make sure to slide it back to On for the next day you need it—you don't want to oversleep!

Editing or Deleting an Alarm

If you want to change an alarm or delete it, tap the Clock app and fol-low these steps:

1. Tap Alarm at the bottom of the screen (not shown).

2. Tap the alarm you want to edit or delete.

3. Tap Edit.

4. To edit the alarm, tap it in the drop-down menu and change the parts of it you want. Tap Save.

5. To delete the alarm, tap the red icon and then tap Delete. When you do that, it completely deletes the alarm, so make sure you really want to delete the alarm.

Have Siri Do It for You

Just like with creating an alarm, Siri can delete alarms for you, too. Just hold down the Home button until Siri appears and say some-thing like, "Delete my 8:15 alarm," and Siri takes care of it for you.

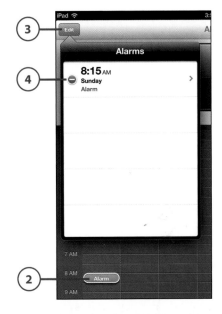

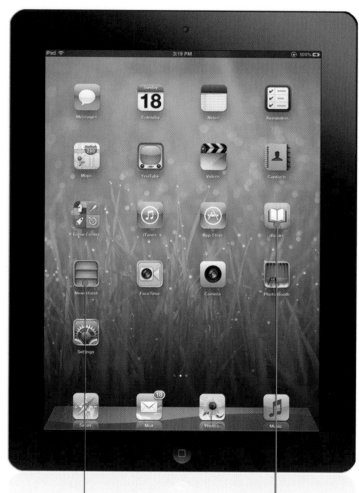

Subscribe to newspapers
and magazines using
Newsstand.

Read books on
your iPad using
iBooks.

In this chapter, you find out how to use your iPad to take a whole library's worth of books, magazines, and newspapers with you in your backpack. You learn about:

→ Where to get e-books
→ Buying e-books at the iBookstore
→ Getting e-books from Amazon and Barnes & Noble
→ Getting e-books from the library
→ Getting magazines and newspapers at Newsstand

E-books and iBooks

Whether you like to read for fun or have to read books for school, the iPad makes it easy to get all the books you need. You have tons of choices for places to get books—from online stores like Amazon, Apple's own offering called iBooks, or from many local libraries—and more books to choose from than you can find in big bookstores. And, because the books are on your iPad, they sometimes offer extras that you can't get in a printed book, like audio and video.

You can choose from lots of e-book apps, but one you might want to start with is iBooks. Like most other e-book apps, the iBooks app itself is free, but if you want to get books to read in it, you usually have to buy them.

Getting the iBooks App

The iBooks app is free. To get it, just open the App Store app that comes with your iPad. You might get a pop-up window asking you to download iBooks. Say yes. If you don't see the pop-up, search for iBooks, tap the price (free), and then tap Install. When you have it, you can dive into a lot of great books.

Where to Find and Buy E-books

There are lots of ways to get e-books for the iPad—some are free, some you have to pay for. The three major e-book stores for the iPad all have free apps, but lots of other apps and websites offer e-books, too.

You might want to check with your parents to find out if they have an e-book app they like or want you to use. If the whole family uses the same app, you can share books and accounts.

- **iBooks**—This is Apple's e-book app. It has the cool page-turning animations you might have seen. You can buy books that work with it at the iBookstore in iTunes, through the iBooks app, or at some other online stores. **Free**

- **Kindle**—This app lets you use e-books from Amazon on your iPad (or any other compatible device, such as Amazon's Kindle e-reader). To read Kindle books, you have to buy them from Amazon's website or from stores that sell Kindle-compatible e-books, not through the app. **Free**

- **Nook**—This app works pretty much the same way as the Kindle app, except it's from Barnes & Noble. The books you buy for Nook work in the app and on Barnes & Noble's Nook e-reader. Like Kindle, you can't buy books through the app here; you have to use the Barnes & Noble website. **Free**

- **OverDrive**—OverDrive is one of the most widely used apps by libraries. Instead of going with your library card and checking out a book, use this app to borrow e-books for your iPad over the Internet. **Free**

- **Project Gutenberg**—Project Gutenberg is a cool website that lets you download classic books for free. If you want Shakespeare, Dickens, or other classics, check out the Project Gutenberg website at www.projectgutenberg.org. **Free**

If none of these apps look interesting to you, the App Store has dozens of other e-book apps, some of which contain hundreds of books. Others are dedicated to just one book and include special features such as audio and video. Some e-book apps are free; others you have to buy.

After you have the iBooks app, grab some great books and start reading. Just like with everything else you download from Apple, you use your iTunes account/Apple ID to get books. If the books you want cost money, you pay for them using that account or your iTunes Allowance (read more in "iTunes Allowance: What It Is and Why Your Parents Should Give You One" in Chapter 2, "Getting Started: Set Up and Sync Your iPad").

Buying E-books at the iBookstore

To begin, make sure your iPad is connected to the Internet, tap the iBooks app from your iPad's home screen to open it, and then follow these steps:

1. Tap Store to connect to the iBookstore.

2. There are three ways to find books:

   a. Search for the name of the book or writer you're interested in.

   b. Tap More and select one from the drop-down list.

   c. Tap one of the featured items on any page. These items are usually grouped around a specific theme, such as holiday specials or particular genres, or bestsellers, such as the buttons at the bottom of the screen.

3. When you've found a book you're interested in, tap the cover to see more information about it.

4. To read a sample of the book before you buy it, tap Sample. A chapter or two of the book downloads to your iBooks bookshelf. Return to your bookshelf and tap that book to read it.

5. To buy the book, go back to the iBookstore, tap the price, and then tap Buy Book (books can also be free; in that case, tap the Free button).

6. When you've bought the book, it downloads to your library. Tap the book on your bookshelf to read it.

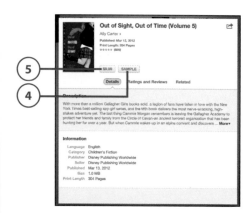

Deleting Books

If you've finished a book and decide that you don't want to keep it, you can delete it from iBooks. To do that, begin by opening iBooks and going to your library (if a book is open when the app opens, tap the center of the screen and then the Library button to go back to the Bookshelf). Then follow these steps:

1. Tap Edit.

2. Tap the book or books you want to delete. A blue check mark appears on each one you select.

3. Tap Delete.

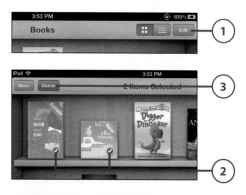

Gone Forever?

Even if you delete a book you got at iBooks from your iPad, it's not totally gone. You purchased that book and it remains associated with your account. Check out "Redownloading from iCloud" in Chapter 17, "Fixing Problems Yourself," to learn how to get it back.

4. In the pop-up window, tap Delete again and the book will be gone.

Reading Your iBook

A bunch of options let you control how the book looks when you read it. Use them to make the book look the way you prefer. After you've opened iBooks and started reading a book, you can access any of the following controls and options:

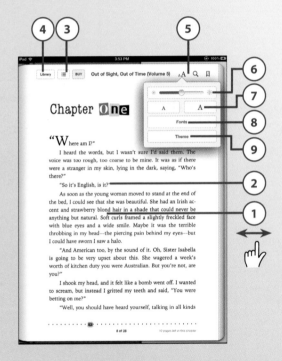

1. To move to the next page, swipe from right to left. To go back, swipe from left to right.

2. To access the options, tap the center of the screen. The options icons appear at the top of the screen.

3. Tap the Table of Contents button to view the book's Table of Contents. You can jump to any chapter from there by tapping it.

4. Tap Library to go back to your bookshelf so you can read another book.

5. To change the way the book looks, tap the icon with the two As. The next few items are the options in the drop-down that appears when you tap this icon.

6. Move the slider to adjust the brightness of the screen to something that's comfortable for your eyes. For a refresher on what adjusting the brightness of the screen can do for you, check out "Changing Screen Brightness" in Chapter 3, "It's All Yours! Customizing Your iPad."

7. Make the text bigger by tapping the big A or smaller by tapping the small one.

8. You can change what the book's text looks like by tapping Fonts and then tapping the one you want to use. Each font option previews what the text will look like.

9. To change the color of the text and the background, tap Theme and then tap your choice.

10. You can also read your book in full-screen mode, without seeing the graphics that mimic the edges of a book. To do that, move the Full Screen slider to On in the Themes menu.

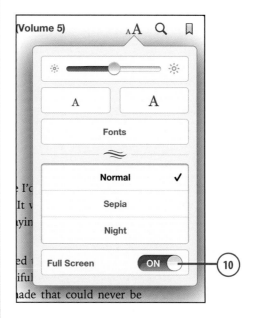

Searching in iBooks

When you're seeking a particular bit of information in a book, there's no need to flip through every page to find what you're looking for. Just use iBooks' Search tool.

1. To do this, tap the center of the screen to display the icons at the top.

2. Tap the magnifying glass and enter the text you want to search for.

3. A menu drops down to show every time the item you searched for appears in the book.

4. To jump to a particular result, tap it and you go to that page in the book.

5. If you want to go to a different part of the book, tap the magnifying glass again and tap another search result.

6. To clear the search, tap the X next to the text you searched for.

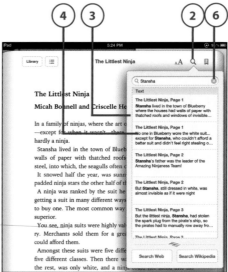

Making Bookmarks

If you come across something in an iBook that you really want to remember, or that you think you'll come back to more than once, you should create a bookmark for it. These are the digital equivalent of real bookmarks that let you mark your place in a book except that you don't need to create a bookmark to save your place when you stop reading. iBooks is smart enough to know where you stopped last and start you there the next time you open that book.

1. To bookmark a page so you can come back to it later, tap the screen so that the icons appear at the top of the screen.

2. Tap the bookmark icon to create the bookmark.

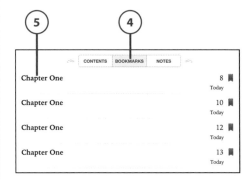

Removing a Bookmark

To remove a bookmark, just tap the bookmark icon again. The bookmark disappears.

3. To see a list of your bookmarks, tap the center of the screen and then the Table of Contents button.

4. Tap Bookmarks.

5. To jump to a bookmark, tap it.

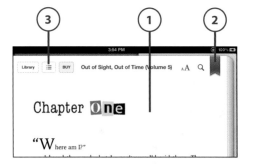

Highlighting Text

When you're reading a printed book for school and want to make sure you remember something important, you can underline or highlight it to remind yourself. You can do the same thing in an e-book using iBooks's highlight feature. To highlight text, first find the section you want and then follow these steps:

1. Tap and hold on the text you want to highlight for two or three seconds and then let go.

2. A word or section is highlighted in blue. If you want to change the highlighted section, tap the blue dot at either end and drag it until the blue highlight covers everything you want.

3. Tap Highlight in the pop-up menu to add highlighting to the text you selected.

4. Tap on the color you want the highlight to be.

5. If you want to remove a highlight, select the highlighted text the same way you did when you created the highlight. Tap the Highlight button and tap the white circle with the red line through it.

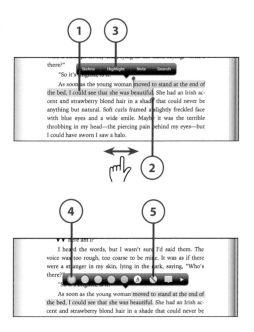

Adding Notes to iBooks

In physical books, sometimes you write in a book's margins to add your thoughts about the text. Just like with highlights, iBooks has a Notes tool that lets you make notes with your e-books. First, find the section you want to add a note to and then follow these steps:

1. Tap and hold the text you want to mark for two or three seconds and then let go.

2. A word or section is highlighted in blue. If you want to change the highlighted section, tap the blue dot at either end and drag it until the blue highlight covers everything you want.

3. Tap Note in the pop-up menu.

4. Type your note using the onscreen keyboard or a physical keyboard.

5. When you're done, tap anywhere on the page to hide the note.

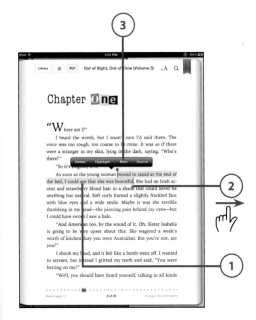

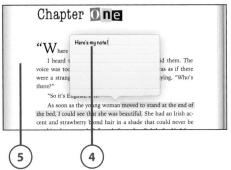

Deleting Notes, Highlights, and Bookmarks

You can delete a note by tapping it and then erasing all the text in it. The pop up disappears, although the highlight on the text remains.

If you want to delete a few bookmarks, notes, or highlights at once, tap the Table of Contents button and then tap Notes. You see a list of notes. Swipe to the right on anything you want to erase and then tap Delete.

Getting E-books from Amazon and Barnes & Noble

Even though a lot of apps offer in-app purchases to let you buy extra features or content, many don't. Two of the most important apps that don't—and ones that you might think would—are Amazon's Kindle and Barnes & Noble's Nook e-book apps.

Unlike iBooks, neither of these apps includes a way to shop for, buy, and download e-books directly to the app. Instead, getting e-books for those apps means buying at the respective website and then downloading the book.

Buying an E-book at Amazon

To buy an e-book at Amazon to read on your iPad, make sure you have the Kindle app installed, are connected to the Internet, and have launched your Safari app from the home screen.

1. Go to http://www.amazon.com.

2. When you're there, tap the drop-down menu next to the search bar.

3. Select Kindle Store to only search for Kindle books.

4. Type in the name of the book or author you're looking for and then tap Enter.

5. In the search results, tap the book you want. You go to a page full of information about that book.

6. To buy it, tap on the Buy Now with 1-Click button. If you don't have your own Amazon account (and you probably don't), you need to get your parents' permission before you buy. They need to use their existing Amazon account or create one in order to complete the purchase. (This is true even for free books.)

7. When you've completed buying the book, press the Home button on your iPad and tap the Kindle app to launch it.

8. If you're not already signed in to the app, enter the email address and password for the Amazon account you used to buy the book (probably your parents').

9. Tap the Register This Kindle button.

10. If you—or your parents, if you're using their account—have purchased Kindle e-books for other devices, you can download them to your iPad. To do that, tap the Cloud button; then tap the down arrow to download the book you want. (If you've already registered your iPad, as you did in step 8, you can choose to send the book to your iPad in step 6 and it will automatically download.)

Kindle

Buying an E-book at Barnes & Noble

To buy an e-book at Barnes & Noble to read on your iPad, make sure you have the Nook app, are connected to the Internet, and have launched the Safari app from the Start screen.

1. Go to http://www.bn.com.

2. When you're there, tap the drop-down menu next to the search bar.

3. From the list of options that appear, tap Nook Store to search only for e-books.

4. Type in the name of the book or author you're looking for and then tap Enter.

5. In the search results, tap the book you want. You go to a page full of information about the book.

6. To buy it, tap the Buy Now button. If you don't have your own Barnes & Noble account (and you probably don't), you need to get your parents' permission before you buy. They need to use their existing Barnes & Noble account information or create a new account in order to complete the purchase (even for free books).

7. When you've completed buying the book, press the Home button on your iPad and tap the Nook app to launch it.

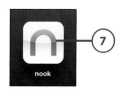

8. If you're not already signed in to the app, tap Sign In and type in the Barnes & Noble account you used to buy the book (probably your parents') and then tap the Sign In button.

9. If your new book hasn't already downloaded, tap the refresh button to update the screen, and your new e-book will download. Tap it to start reading.

Getting E-books from the Library

What if you don't want to buy every book you read? What about the old tradition of borrowing books from your local library? Can you do that with e-books? If you have the right app, the answer is yes.

The app you want is called OverDrive. Many libraries use it to let people with library cards check out e-books and read them on their iPads. OverDrive is free and just requires that you have a library card. Get it at the App Store, and then read on to learn how to get e-books using it.

Kindle Likes Libraries, Too

The Kindle app also lets you check e-books out from some libraries. Find out which app (or both!) your library supports and then you can use it to check out books for free.

Before you use OverDrive, there are two more things you need: a library card and an Adobe account. (Adobe is a company that makes, among many other things, e-book software.)

If you don't have one already, ask your parents to take you to the library to get a card. They're free and useful for borrowing all kinds of things, not just e-books. When you're there, find out if your library will let you check out e-books or if your parents have to do it for you. To get an Adobe account, have your parents go to Adobe's home page at www.adobe.com. Look for the Sign In or Create an Account button to get started.

Finding Your Library with OverDrive

After you have an account and have OverDrive installed on your iPad, launch the app from your iPad's home screen and follow these steps:

1. Type in your Adobe account information, which includes an Adobe ID and a password.

2. Tap Authorize. You should only have to do this the first time you use the app.

3. Tap Add a Library so you can add a library near you to your list.

4. Type in the city and state, or ZIP Code of the library where you have a library card.

5. Tap Search to have OverDrive search for your local library.

6. Scroll through the list of libraries and tap the one from which you want to check out an e-book.

7. Tap the library's listing. You jump to Safari and go to the library's website. Log in and continue.

Logging In to Your Library

Different libraries handle their e-book lending differently, but most of them ask you to create an account or log in to an account using your library card. Have your parents follow the instructions specific to your library's website.

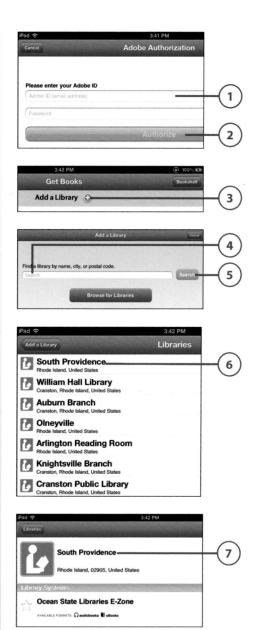

Checking Out a Book with OverDrive

After you've set up your OverDrive app with your account and your local library, it's time to start borrowing books.

1. When you're logged in, browse or search for the book you're looking for. Even if there's an e-book version of the book you're looking for, you might not be able to check it out. That's because libraries aren't allowed to lend all e-books, just some.

2. When you find the book you want to check out, you have two choices: Kindle book or Adobe EPUB e-book. The Kindle book works in your Kindle app. The Adobe EPUB e-book version works in OverDrive. Tap the Add to Cart button next to the version you want.

3. Choose how long you want to check the book out for (usually 7, 14, or 21 days) and then tap Proceed to Check Out.

4. Tap Download.

5. You jump back to the OverDrive app, where the book is downloading. To read the book, tap it. Swipe left and right to turn the pages, just like in any other e-book app.

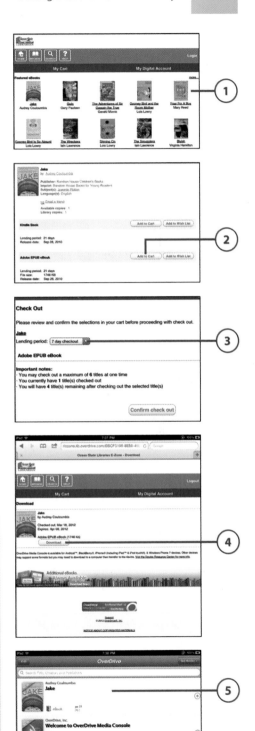

>>>Go Further

RETURNING AN E-BOOK

Just like with a physical library book, when you're done with an e-book, you need to return it to the library. There are two ways to do this. First, you can wait until the amount of time you borrowed the book for ends. The book is then automatically returned.

To return a book early, swipe across it like you're deleting it and then tap the Delete button that appears. When you do this, a message pops up that asks whether you want to just delete the book or return and delete it. Tap Return and Delete, and the book is sent back to the library.

Many libraries limit the number of e-books you can check out at one time (for instance, my local library only lets you borrow six at once), so if you're done with a book, return it and you're ready to get another.

Awesome Apps

Looking for something good to read on your iPad? There are thousands—probably millions, actually—of great options, from books to comics and more. Here are some suggestions for apps that give you a lot of choices:

- **DC Comics**—Like Batman, Superman, Wonder Woman, and other heroes of the DC Universe? You can read their adventures in this app. The DC Comics app lets you buy, download, and store individual issues of hundreds of comics right on your iPad. This way, you can take a huge comics collection anywhere you go. **Free (Comics cost $1.99 to $3.99 each)**

- **Good Reader**—If you want to read PDFs, Word documents, and other text files, Good Reader is a great option. It's one of the best document readers available for the iPad and can read tons of kinds of files that other apps can't. **Free or $4.99**

- **Marvel Comics**—Do you prefer Spider-man, Iron Man, Wolverine, or the X-Men for your comic book adventures? Then this app from Marvel Comics is for you. It works the same way as the DC app, but gives you access to the huge library of Marvel comics. **Free (Comics cost $1.99 to $4.99 each)**

Getting Magazines and Newspapers with Newsstand

Your iPad isn't just good for books; you can also use it to read magazines. Even better, though, you can subscribe to magazines and have new issues automatically download to your iPad when they come out. And because they're digital, these magazines also have audio, video, and lots of interactive features that make them more interesting and educational. The program you use to get magazines and newspapers is Newsstand, which comes preloaded on your iPad. As usual, you use your Apple ID to buy issues and subscriptions, so if your parents pay for your iTunes purchases, get their permission before you buy anything.

Buying at Newsstand

To buy a magazine or newspaper using Newsstand, you need to have the Newsstand app open (big surprise, right?). To do that, make sure you're connected to the Internet, tap the app on your home screen, and then follow these steps:

1. Tap Store to connect to the Newsstand store.

2. To find the magazine or newspaper you want to read, either tap the featured items or browse the content. When you find something you're interested in, tap it to get more information.

3. To download the app for the magazine or newspaper you want to read, tap the price and then tap Install.

4. The app downloads to Newsstand. Tap it to launch the app. Many magazine/newspaper apps come with a sample of their latest issue. Depending on whether the magazine or newspaper is free or paid, if you want to read more, you might need to subscribe.

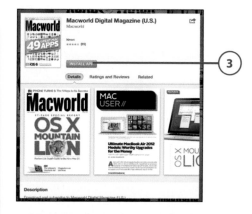

It's Not All Good

FREE APPS, PAID SUBSCRIPTIONS

Even though a lot of magazines and newspapers say they're free, it's a little more complicated than that. Just like with e-books, the apps are usually free, but to get the actual issues of the magazine or newspaper, you need to buy them one at a time or subscribe. To find out how much something costs, look at the Top In-App Purchases section on the left side of the app page under the app information.

Buying Individual Issues or Subscriptions

Remember, when you get a magazine or newspaper app using Newsstand, you're usually getting just one issue and sometimes not even that. In that case, you have to use in-app purchases to buy individual issues or to subscribe.

Each app works a little differently in terms of how you buy issues or subscriptions, so you first need to see how the app works. Most apps show you individual issues as well as a subscription, with the price listed next to each.

Tap the Buy button for either the issues or the subscription you want.

Remember, because these are in-app purchases, anything you buy gets billed to the iTunes account or iTunes allowance you use with your iPad. If your parents are paying for your purchases, make sure to get their permission before you buy.

If you buy a subscription, when a new issue is available, you tap the Download button to get and read it.

Reading Magazines and Newspapers

Because most magazines and newspaper apps are different, there's no single set of buttons or controls to read magazines or newspapers on the iPad. Because of that, there's no one set of instructions on how to use these apps. Instead, you have to learn the controls for each individual publication; many include how-to guides. Like with books, though, it's always safe to try swiping left and right or up and down to move through the app.

Deleting Magazines and Newspapers from Newsstand

To delete a magazine or newspaper app from Newsstand, follow these steps:

1. Tap and hold on the app you want to delete. Let go when the icon starts shaking.

2. Tap the X to begin deleting the app.

3. Tap Delete in the pop-up window. Remember, when you do this, you're deleting the app and all the issues you've downloaded, so make sure you really want to do this

Getting Magazines and Newspapers Back

Like with any app, you can re-install the apps for magazines and newspapers that you remove. After you do that, in some cases you can redownload the issues of the magazines and newspapers you've already bought.

>>>Go Further

DELETING ISSUES OF MAGAZINES AND NEWSPAPERS

Besides deleting the entire app for a magazine or newspaper, you can also delete individual issues. If that's what you want to do, first tap Newsstand and then the app for the magazine or newspaper you want. Find the issue you want to delete. Depending on the app, there might be a Delete button or Archive button. Tap it. If a window pops up, confirm the deletion and the issue is removed. If you want to read it again, you have to download it a second time.

Awesome Apps

Like to read magazines? Here are some suggestions for magazines that you can read on your iPad that cover all kinds of interests. Remember, all of these apps are free, but you have to buy individual issues or subscriptions.

- **Comic Heroes**—If you like comics, especially superheroes, *Comic Heroes* magazine is a lot of fun. **$6.99 per issue, $30.99 subscription**

- **FamilyFun Magazine**—Get all kinds of great ideas for recipes, activities, parties, and games in this magazine. **$2.99 per issue, $7.99 subscription**

- **Dolls' House Magazine**—Do you enjoy playing with dolls and imagining their lives in a doll-house? This magazine gives you great ideas for new doll furniture and more. **$2.99 for the app, $4.99 per issue, $39.99 sub-scription**

- **Famous Monsters**—If you like scary movies or classic monsters such as Frankenstein and The Mummy, you'll get a thrill out of this magazine. **$3.99 per issue, $23.99 subscription**

- **Guitar World**—Learning to play guitar? Then this maga-zine is essential reading. It has interviews and tons of tutorials on playing great rock songs. **$7.99 per issue, $14.99 sub-scription**

- **How It Works**—Curious about everything around you? Want to learn how different things—from science to technology to nature—work? Then this is your app. **$3.99 per issue, $17.99 subscription**

- **National Geographic Kids**—Are you interested in nature, animals, or how people live in other countries? Then check out this kids' version of the classic magazine about geography and culture. **$3.99 per issue, $19.99 subscription**

- **Papercraft Inspirations**—Making things out of paper means a lot more than folding paper airplanes. If you like arts and crafts, check out this magazine for lots of fun ideas. **$4.99 per issue, $39.99 subscription**

- **Popular Science+**—If you're interested in science and technology, *Popular Science* is one of the best magazines available. The iPad version offers all that and interactive features. **$2.99 per issue, $14.99 subscription**

- **Writing Magazine**—Do you like to write stories? Have you ever thought that you might want to be a writer? This magazine gives you tips on writing, ideas on where to send stories, and interviews with other writers. **$4.99 per issue, $39.99 subscription**

Use math to fly a
rocket to the stars.

Show off your knowledge
of American History.

iPad 📶   11:28 AM   100% 🔋

Learn Piano   Math Mago   Blaster   Draw Animals

Rocket Math   KosmicMath 4   Magic Piano   MayaCivilization

Mult Div 3-4   OrderUp Hist   Oregon Trail   US Trivia

Pluto Piano   Puzzle Map   3D CellStain   U.S. Geo

EasyBeats 2   Solar Walk   RockProdigy   VideoScience

Safari   Mail   Photos   Music

Learn about planets, stars,
and the solar system.

Apps are great for entertainment, gaming, and getting things done, but that's not all they're good for; they can also help you do better in school. In this chapter, you encounter dozens of apps that can help you excel in subjects like:

→ English/language arts
→ Math
→ Science
→ History/social studies
→ Music
→ Art
→ Foreign language

Using Your iPad in Fourth Grade

Whether you use your iPad at school as part of your lessons or you just use it at home, the iPad can be a major part of getting good grades. Hundreds of great educational apps are out there to help you do better in school and learn all about the world around you. The apps in this chapter aren't the only ones, but they're some good places to start when you want apps to help you learn.

This chapter and the following chapters suggest apps that can help you do better in school. Each chapter is divided by subject—math, science, and so on. Within most subjects, there is one featured app where you not only see screenshots, but you also find out how to use it in school and for homework.

English/Language Arts

Every school is different, but at many schools, fourth grade is when you tackle tricky topics such as grammar, phonics, and learning how to type. If those subjects aren't part of your classes, maybe you get to learn more complex kinds of words, such as synonyms and antonyms, as well as how to figure out the meaning of words you don't already know. These apps can help you with all those tasks.

Show Off That Fancy Vocabulary with Boggle

Cost: $0.99 or free demo version

To really master new vocabulary, you have to practice it. With regular use and practice of new words and language concepts, your expanded vocabulary can become a natural part of how you speak and write.

Boggle is a great word game for practicing your vocabulary. This is the iPad version of a classic board game that you might have played with your family. In it, you look at a board full of jumbled-up letters and try to create the longest words using the letters available. It's great at helping you remember words and see patterns. Play by yourself or with your friends, either on your iPad or by email.

Perfect Your Handwriting with Cursive Practice

Cost: Free ($0.99 for ad-free version)

One of the things a lot of third and fourth graders learn in their English/language classes is how to write in the fancy style called cursive. You won't use cursive all the time (unless you want to; some people prefer the looping, stylish letters used in cursive), but adults use it for formal documents and signatures.

Cursive Practice helps you learn how to write all the letters in cursive, both in uppercase and lowercase, on a virtual blackboard. Go beyond just writing letters and discover how letters connect to form words and what sentences written entirely in cursive look like. The free version of the app includes ads; the paid version removes them.

Make Grammar Fun with Grammar Games

Cost: $0.99

Sentences and paragraphs are held together by a set of rules called *grammar*. You've been learning grammar as you've learned how to speak and read, but learning the formal rules of grammar can be tough. So why not make it easier with this collection of games?

Grammar Games helps you remember rules you've learned at school, or maybe even teaches you new ones, using things like a flight control game where you have to keep airplanes from crashing by correctly identifying the parts of speech.

Write Better Sentences with SentenceBuilder for iPad

Cost: $5.99

Speaking of grammar, writing sentences that properly use all aspects of grammar can be a challenge. There are a lot of things to consider: Does the subject agree with the verb, do your plurals match, are you using the right form of verb?

SentenceBuilder for iPad helps you overcome those challenges. The app shows you pictures, and you have to create grammatically correct sentences by selecting words from a wheel. With instant feedback that helps you learn, apps like this make it more fun to learn how to write well.

Improve Your Spelling with Simplex Spelling Phonics 1

Cost: $4.99

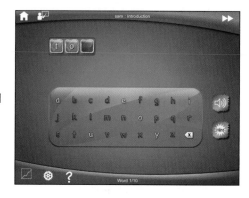

Phonics is based on the sounds and letters and words, and it is one of the techniques teachers use to help kids learn to read and write. It's how I learned to read and write, and here I am writing this book, so it can't be all bad!

Simplex Spelling Phonics 1 helps you learn more than 450 impor-
tant words—both common and unusual ones—so that you can improve your English skills. Learning phonics can help you gain the skills needed to learn all sorts of words, not just the ones in the app—and that will be useful for your whole life.

Master New Words with Dictionary.com

Cost: Free or $4.99 without ads

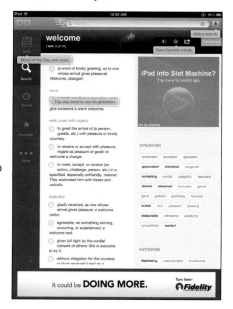

Learning new vocabulary means you'll constantly encounter words you've never heard before or have heard but don't quite know the meaning of. Skipping over those words isn't an option. You need to find out what they mean if you want to build your vocabulary. One way to do that is with an app.

When you run into these unknown words, the Dictionary.com app is a big help. Use it to look up the mean-ings of almost two million words! You can even say the word you want to look up and the app finds it for you. Besides being a dictionary, this app is also a thesaurus, a type of reference that helps you discover words related to the one you look up.

Looking Up Definitions with Dictionary.com

If you come across a word that you don't know the meaning of, you can find out its definition in the Dictionary.com app. To do that, tap the app to open it and then follow these steps:

1. Tap in the search box and type the word you want to look up.

2. The app suggests words as you type. If the word you're looking for is in the list, tap it. Otherwise, finish typing the word you want and tap Search on the keyboard.

3. On the definition screen, you see lots of information, including

   a. How to pronounce the word

   b. Multiple definitions of the word

   c. The historic origin of the word

   d. Synonyms—different words that mean the same thing. To find out more about each synonym, tap it.

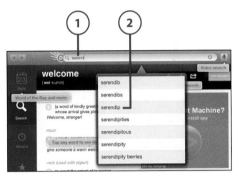

Discovering Synonyms and Antonyms Using the Thesaurus

Besides discovering definitions, the Dictionary.com app also lets you learn synonyms and antonyms (opposites) for words. To do that, tap the app to open it and follow these steps:

1. Tap Thesaurus.

2. Tap the search box and type the word you're interested in.

3. The app suggests words as you type. If the word you want is in the list, tap it. Otherwise, finish typing the word and tap Search.

4. On the results page, you see groups of synonyms and antonyms to the word you searched for. Tap the options to learn more about those words.

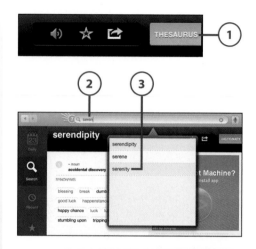

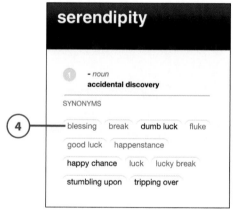

Math

Math starts getting pretty interesting in the fourth grade. This year many schools cover multiplying and dividing with bigger numbers, and learning about averages and how to add and subtract fractions and decimals. Even if your school teaches different subjects this year (which is fine—you'll learn all of this stuff by the time you get to high school!), you should find some helpful apps here.

Your Smarts Get Rewarded in MathGirl Addition House

Cost: $0.99

There are lots of things math can be used for. It can be all about space and science, but math is also important when dealing with things like flowers and houses, too.

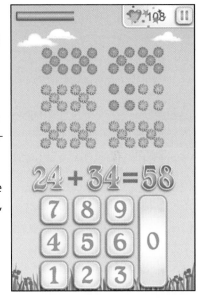

In MathGirl Addition House, you start out with a plain house. If you want to customize it, you'd better be fast at adding and recognizing patterns. If you are, you earn points that let you decorate your in-game house with new paint, doors, fences, pets, and much more. When you're done, your house shows off your smarts.

Kung Fu Learning! Math Ninja HD

Cost: $1.99

Think math is just about hitting the books? It can be, but serious studying isn't the only way to improve your skills. Sometimes you can get better at math by mastering other skills—like your ninja skills.

In Math Ninja HD, you have to protect your tree house from a carnivorous tomato and his robot henchman. (Don't know what *carnivorous* means? Get the Dictionary.com app and look it up!) On each level, you use math to defend yourself. When you beat a level, you earn points to upgrade your defenses.

Save a Falling Star Using Motion Math HD

Cost: $2.99

Just like there are many different ways to get to the same answer in math, there are also many ways to write the same number. Fractions, percentages, and decimals are important mathematical concepts, and they're actually all different ways to write the same number. Learning that, and how to use them, is key to more advanced math.

In Motion Math HD, a star has fallen out of space and landed on Earth. It wants to get home and only you can help it get there. Use fractions, percentages, and decimals to help the star find its way back to its home galaxy.

Build Spaceships by Solving Problems in Rocket Math

Cost: $0.99 or free version

Each math concept or skill you learn is a new tool you can apply to your schoolwork. If you think of your basic knowledge as a house, each new skill you master is like adding another room onto the building.

Rocket Math works in a very similar way. In it, you start with a basic rocket and you conquer levels with different kinds of math problems—from multiplication and division to fractions and decimals. With each level you pass, you earn in-game money so that you buy new components to customize your rocket.

Solve Equations in Many Ways with Math Mago

Cost: $0.99

Math isn't just about taking a series of numbers and adding or subtracting them to get an answer. To get really good at math, you need to learn how to make numbers do whatever you want.

Instead of giving you two numbers so that you have to figure out how to add them or multiply them to get an answer, Math Mago instead gives you the answer and asks you to choose two numbers to make the equation work. Learning how to solve problems in multiple ways often comes in handy in real life—you can start learning how in this app.

Testing Your Math Skills with Math Mago

To test your math skills and learn the different kinds of equations you can use to get to the same answers, tap Math Mago from your home screen and follow these steps:

1. Tap Play.

2. At the bottom of the screen, a problem and an answer displays. Pay attention to whether the problem uses addition, subtraction, multiplication, or division. When you know that, find and tap two numbers that equal the answer. The kind of problem changes each time you solve one, so make sure to look before tapping numbers. Keep doing this until you clear all the numbers from the screen.

Correcting Wrong Answers

If the numbers you tap don't solve the problem, they turn red and are removed from the boxes. Try until you select numbers that make the equation work.

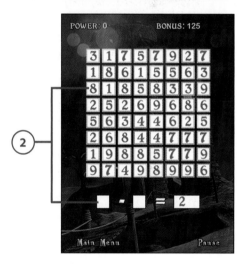

Science

Many fourth-grade science classes help you learn in two important areas. First, you learn about specific scientific topics, such as matter, energy, sound, and the solar system (though different schools focus on different topics). Second, you find out how to work and think like a scientist. You do this by discovering how to observe and analyze events, predict outcomes, design experiments, and test your ideas.

Travel to Other Planets Using Britannica Kids: Solar System

Cost: $4.99

In order to understand not just our world, but the universe that the Earth is part of, you need to study the solar system. The Earth and the other seven planets are a big part of that solar system, but there's a lot more to it as well.

Discover tons of fun information about the planets that make up our solar system with this app from the makers of the world-famous *Encyclopedia Britannica*. Not only does it offer tons of facts about nearby planets, moons, asteroids, and comets, this app also packs trivia quizzes, games, and other fun ways to learn.

Learning Gets Your Hands Dirty in Kid Science: Gross Science

Cost: $2.99

Scientists don't just sit in labs, read books, or use computers. Some of the most interesting science is done by getting hands-on with the things you're studying and experimenting with.

In some cases, doing science right means that you have to get your hands dirty with some pretty gross stuff. This app helps you learn by working with things that would gross other people out. You learn about bugs and bacteria, and even how to make mold and fake blood. That might not sound scientific, but believe me, it is.

Discover the History of the Stars with Solar Walk

Cost: $2.99

One neat thing about astronomy—the study of the stars and planets—is that you can take part in it every night. Just go outside and look at the sky and you see distant stars and planets. Apps can help you make sense of what you're seeing.

You can get great information about our solar systems and its planets, and explore it in great detail, with this app. Besides being on a cool topic, though, Solar Walk has some really great features that help it stand out. For instance, did you know that the arrangement of stars and planets changes over time? Well, with this app, you can pick any date in history and see how the planets were aligned then! That's pretty cool.

Investigate the Solar System Using Solar Walk

To start learning about the planets and stars in our solar system, tap Solar Walk from your home screen to open it, then follow these steps:

1. Tap the magnifying glass for a list of all the things you can learn more about: Planets, (man-made) Satellites, Geography, and Stars. Tap the category at the bottom of the menu first and then tap the item you want to know more about.

2. You zoom through space to your selection. When you get there, you can rotate by tapping and dragging, or zoom in to see more detail (this is especially useful with planets).

3. To learn more, tap the I button and read the information in the drop-down menu.

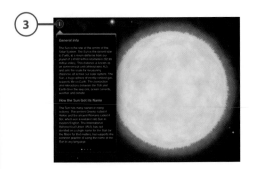

Watch Videos About Space

Solar Walk also includes some very cool, very educational animations. To watch them, tap the app to open it, then:

1. Tap the menu button.

2. Tap Movies.

3. Tap the movie you want to watch. When you're done, tap the X to go back to the main app.

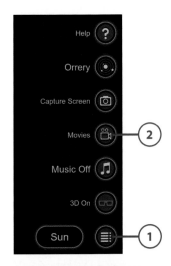

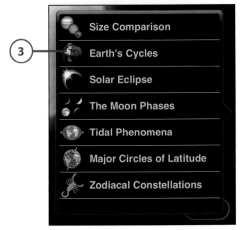

History/Social Studies

If you've ever wondered what life was like for kids who lived 100, 150, or even 200 years ago, this is the year you probably start to learn. Besides finding out what daily life was like for people in the past, many schools also teach how the government works and cover important events in American history.

History in the Right Order: American History Time Line

Cost: $0.99

History is the study of the past. There are a lot of aspects of history that you have to study to truly understand why things happened the way they did. One of the most basic things, though, is the order in which events happened. If you don't have the order straight, it's hard to get anything else right.

American History Time Line helps you keep events in order by helping you visualize when major events in American history happened. Not only will you learn, but you'll test your knowledge with games that ask you to put events in the right order and match dates with people and events.

A Roadtrip, 1800s Style: The Oregon Trail

Cost: $0.99

To truly understand history, you need to understand what day-to-day life was like for people at the time you're studying. What did they do when they got up in the morning? What was school or work like for them? What were their opinions about hot topics of their day? One of the best ways to understand these things is to put yourself in the shoes of those people.

This classic game (so classic I played a version of it in my fifth-grade computer class in 1987!) has been a hit with kids for decades. In it, you lead a group of settlers taking the Oregon Trail out west to Oregon. Along the way, you encounter the same problems that real settlers did: sickness, dangerous animals, finding food, and bad weather. This game is so much fun, you won't know you're learning. Watch out for the in-app purchases, though; they can really add up (for more about in-app purchases and why they're dangerous, check out "Watch Out for Surprise Purchases" in Chapter 16, "It's Play Time: Gaming On the iPad").

Fit the Country Together in Stack the States

Cost: $0.99 or free Lite version

In geography class, you study how countries, states, cities, and other locations are organized and related to each other. Knowing geography can help you in history, but it can also help you in day-to-day life. The more you know about geography, the easier it is to read maps and not get lost.

For instance, can you recognize states just by looking at their out-lines? Do you know each state's capital city? Can you tell people what states border the one you live in? This app helps you learn all that, and more, using a set of fun games.

Learn the Lay of the Land with U.S. Geography by Discovery Education

Cost: $6.99

Geography includes reading maps, but it's a lot more than that, too. Studying geography also means learning about different regions and cities, and what makes them unique. When you know that, you understand regions, states, and the country better—and that helps in history, social studies, and life.

This app, from the people behind the Discovery Channel TV network, combines facts and games to help you learn all about the country. From educational videos and articles to nearly 1,000 questions to test your knowledge, it can help you get to know the U.S., coast to coast.

Meet Each Region in U.S. Geography by Discovery Education

This app lets you find out all about the climate, culture, geography, and other exciting aspects of the many regions that make up the United States. But instead of just asking you to read about these regions, you can watch videos, read facts, listen to audio, and take quizzes. To start learning, tap U.S. Geography by Discovery Education app on your home screen and then do the following:

1. Tap Play.

2. Tap New User and enter your name. Then tap Next.

3. From the map of the U.S., tap the region you want to learn about.

4. When you've selected a region, you have two options: Activities or Challenges. To learn about the region, tap Activities. To take quizzes about the region, tap Challenges. I recommend starting with Activities because the Challenges test you on the information you learn in them.

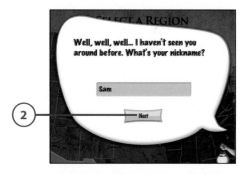

5. Tap the subject you want to learn about.

6. On the subject page, you have many options:

   a. The buttons across the top help you move between sub-jects in that region.

   b. Swipe up and down in the text area to read facts about each state in the region. Tap Listen for audio versions.

   c. To watch videos about the subject, tap one of the videos.

   d. In the center of the screen are quick quizzes that let you test your knowledge and learn.

   e. When you're ready to move to Challenges, tap the back but-ton twice.

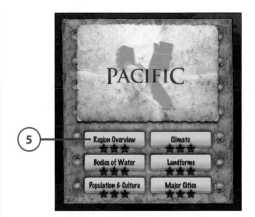

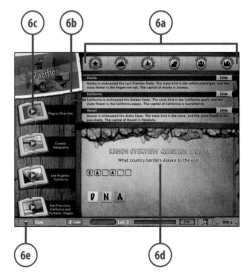

Music

Music class can teach you a lot of things. For one, you can learn how to play all kinds of different instruments in it, from violin to glockenspiel to recorder. In some classes, you might even learn how to create your own music instead of playing someone else's. Whether you want to learn how to read or write music, or just want to create your own songs, there are great iPad apps to choose from.

Play or Create Your Own Songs with DoReMi 1-2-3

Cost: $1.99 or free Lite version

There are lots of great ways to express yourself and be creative. Playing music is one of the best. Before apps, composing music meant knowing how to read music and write notes—but not anymore. Apps have made it easy for you to create songs without knowing musical notation at all.

Learn how to play other people's songs or create your own with this app that helps you improve your musical knowledge and skills. By learning how songs are created, you can start to hear the building blocks of songs and, eventually, create and record your own using the app. Watch out for in-app purchases, though—they're easy to accidentally make in this app.

Get Funky in Easy Beats 2 Pro Drum Machine

Cost: $4.99

The drums are a really fun instrument. I mean, where else are you allowed to really let loose and make a ton of noise? Unfortunately, a lot of parents don't want you making that noise in the house. But there is a way for you to make drum sounds without bothering your family.

Do you prefer hip hop or electronic music to the guitar or piano? Then you'll love this app, which is designed to help you create your own beats. Use the built-in sounds and then drag and drop them into patterns to create your own drum tracks. You can even share your beats with other people online.

Tickle the Ivories with Learn Piano HD

Cost: $1.99

Music apps can do two things for you: It can help you practice between lessons, or it takes the place of lessons entirely. If you're interested in learning to play the piano, you should check out this app.

This app is designed to teach you how to play the piano without any in-person lessons at all! Instead, use the onscreen videos and tutorials to learn both the basics of piano and how to play well-known songs, including holiday favorites. You need a piano to practice (the app doesn't have an electronic one built in), so this is best if you're already learning.

Start Reading Sheet Music in Treble Clef Kids

Cost: $1.99

Reading music can be tough—what do all those squiggly symbols mean?—but it opens up the entire musical world. If you know how to read music, you have a foundation that enables you to play all kinds of instruments and styles of music.

Start learning to read notes in this app, which bases its training on the piano. Choose from three increasingly tough levels as you get better. After you master this app, there are other apps in the Treble Clef Kids series that will help you learn even more music.

Art

Creating art is another great way to express how you feel, how you see the world, or just say something about who you are. Sometimes it's fun just to make a silly or pretty picture, too. Whether you're ready to paint a masterpiece or just throw together some fun doodles, there are lots of art apps to help you express yourself.

Finger Paint on Your iPad with Doodle Buddy for iPad

Cost: Free

Making art can be really messy. Whether you get ink all over your hands or paint on your clothes, a mess can be a sign that good art is being made (or a sign that your parents are going to get mad when they do your laundry!).

We all grew up finger-painting; Doodle Buddy helps you transfer that kind of art to the digital age—minus the mess. Use one, two, or more fingers to create pictures, and then add shapes with stamps and tens of thousands of colors. When you have something you're proud of, send it to your friends or teachers by email.

Create Fun Scenes with Kid Art for iPad

Cost: $0.99

Not all art starts from scratch. Sometimes you use existing tools such as stamps or brushes. Learning how to take advantage of the tools you have is an important step in learning how to create art.

Show off your creative side by using the included backgrounds and stamps of animals and objects in this app to create fun scenes. After you've created a scene, you can color it in however you like. This app also comes with a blank drawing space where you can start your own creation from scratch.

Draw and Color Your Favorite Animals in iLuv Drawing Animals

Cost: $2.99

One important way to learn how to draw is by tracing—taking an existing drawing you like, laying a sheet of paper over it, and then following over the lines to create a copy of the original drawing. By doing that, you can learn how the artist assembled their work.

Love animals? Love to draw? This is the perfect app for you. Draw more than 40 different animals with your fingers using the built-in tracing patterns in this art app. After you have the animal's outline, you can color in it and its habitat. Save your favorite pictures on your iPad or share them by email.

Draw a Cat with iLuv Drawing Animals

iLuv Drawing Animals comes with tutorials on how to draw 40 animals, and the app's tools let you choose what colors to use, whether you draw with a pencil or marker, and much more. Here's what you need to know to draw a cat. Begin by tapping the app to open it and then follow these steps:

1. Tap the arrows to browse the animals you can draw. Tap the cat.

2. If you want to use the pencil, choose its thickness—thin, medium, or thick—by tapping the pencil. When you've selected the one you want, tap the X to close the menu.

3. If you want to use the marker for lines or to color in your cat, tap the marker. You can choose from three line thicknesses again. The paint bucket dumps the color you choose inside any shape you draw. Swipe back and forth to see all the colors and tap the one you want. Tap the X when you've made your selections.

4. You'll see the outline of a shape on the screen. Tap the marker or pencil (whichever you want) and trace the shape to start drawing.

5. Tap the arrow to move to the next step in drawing the cat. At each step, you choose the marker or the pencil, different marker colors, or the paint bucket.

6. If you make a mistake and want to fix it, tap the eraser. Your options include erasing the entire drawing, changing the size of the eraser, and undoing or redoing your last action. If you just want to get rid of a line or two, tap the eraser you want and then swipe over what you want to erase. Tap X to close the menu.

7. When you've drawn the cat, you can save your creation. Tap the Action box and choose to save it to app's Drawing Book or the iPad's built-in Photos app. You can also email it or print it via AirPrint.

8. To draw a new animal, tap the notebook button to go back to the main list.

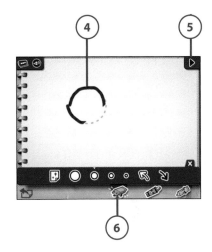

Foreign Language

Learning a foreign language can be interesting, entertaining, and helpful. Wouldn't it be great to go to another country and be able to speak to the people there in their own language? If you're starting to learn a foreign language, practice can help make you fluent. Try these apps to build your vocabulary in a number of languages.

Feed Your Brain with MindSnacks Apps

Cost: Free

Whether you have a foreign language class in school this year, want to get a head start on next year, or are just interested in learning, practicing a foreign language on your iPad can help you get ahead in school.

This series of apps is designed especially to help kids learn how to speak other languages. There are apps to help you learn Spanish, French, Italian, German, and Mandarin Chinese, and each one of them is free, although you do have to sign up for a MindSnacks account. (Get permission from your parents first.) In them, you learn languages through vocabulary practice, learning games, and listening to native speakers. In-app purchases of $4.99 add additional levels of lessons.

MindSnacks Is an iPhone App

Apps created for the iPhone can run on the iPad, but they're designed for a smaller screen. Because of that, they don't take up your iPad's whole screen. MindSnacks is one of these apps. To make it fill the full screen, tap the 2X button in the bottom-right corner. The app will be a little fuzzy looking, but it will be bigger. If you prefer the sharper, but smaller, version, tap the 2X button again.

Learn Basic Vocabulary

The first lesson in MindSnacks is free and teaches you numbers. First, the app takes you through a tutorial on how to use the app. Then, to start learning a language, follow these steps:

1. Tap Review.

2. You see the first number—zero—in English and the language you're learning. Swipe up the screen to see each number in both languages. Tap on each number to hear it pronounced in the language you're learning.

3. When you think you've learned the numbers and want to test yourself, tap Games.

4. Tap Fish Tank.

5. In Fish Tank, you're shown a number in either English or the language you're learning and two options for the number in the opposite language. Tap the one you think is right. If you're correct, you move on to the next question. If you're wrong, you get a message letting you know the right answer. You can get three answers wrong.

Adding More Lessons

To upgrade to all 50 lessons, tap the Learn More button and buy them for $4.99. As always, if your parents pay for your iTunes purchases, get their permission before you buy.

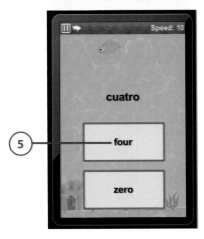

Discover fascinating parts of science by studying things like light.

Learn math in fun, new ways—like in deep-sea diving.

Become a better musician by playing along with apps.

You may have some of the same classes every year, but each year they get harder and more interesting and you learn more. The same is true with the apps in this chapter. Check out these recommendations for more-advanced apps in subjects including:

→ English/language arts

→ Math

→ Science

→ History/social studies

→ Music

→ Art

→ Foreign language

Using Your iPad in Fifth Grade

In fifth grade, your classes build on the things you learned last year and introduce you to even more exciting and challenging topics. Because your teachers expect you to do more this year, you need to make sure you're working hard and practicing all your subjects. Check out these apps that can help you get ahead in your studies.

English/Language Arts

In many schools, fifth-grade English/Language Arts is when you encounter some familiar topics, such as grammar and vocabulary, but you also start enjoying new and exciting topics, such as describing and understanding genres and different kinds of writing. Even if your school has a different focus this year, these apps should be able to help you.

Build a Bigger Vocabulary with 5th Grade Vocabulary Prep

Cost: $2.99

You really never stop learning new vocabulary words. Even as an adult, you learn new words all the time for work or from the news. Grade school is the time that you probably learn the most new words, though.

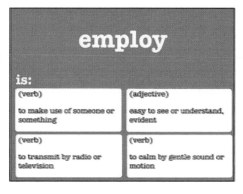

The quizzes offered by this app help you learn hundreds of new, interesting vocabulary words. Fifth Grade Vocabulary Prep lets you choose whether to see the words and match their definitions or to see the definitions and decide which word fits. There's even a teacher's version of the app, so you might end up using it at school.

Object Meets Action in GrammarPrep: Subjects and Verbs

Cost: $3.99

Grammar is so important, and can be so specialized, that you can't always use general overview apps. Sometimes, to really understand a part of grammar, you have to go really in depth.

This app is the first in a series of grammar-lesson apps, each of which focuses on a specific, important part of grammar. In this app, you learn how subjects and verbs work together to create sentences and how to make sure the ones you use agree and don't become grammatically incorrect. Knowing this is key to becoming a good writer.

Smooth Out Your Sentences with GrammarPrep: Fragments, Run-Ons, and Comma Splices

Cost: $3.99

Have you ever heard someone talk so fast and so much that it was like they were just babbling on and on? That's what your writing can sound like if you don't know how to identify and prevent run-ons and comma splices.

One way you can show that you really understand grammar and how to write well is to use complete, correct sentences. Although everyone wants to do that, sometimes pieces of sentences (called fragments) or two sentences smushed together into one creep into our writing. Use this app to find out how to stop your writing from sounding like babbling.

Write Your Own Book with Storybuddy 2

Cost: $6.99

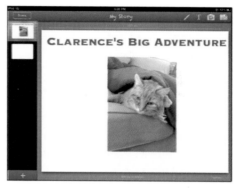

English isn't just about learning vocabulary and grammar. Sometimes it's about taking those tools and putting them to use in creating something fun like your own stories.

Storybuddy 2 lets you make your own storybooks. Begin by choosing from built-in images or importing your own pictures taken with the iPad's camera. After you do that, add pages and write the text of the story on each page. Even though the examples at the App Store are for younger kids, there's no reason you can't make something more mature. When you're done creating your story, you can share it by email.

Verbs and Vocab: iTooch ENGLISH Grade 5

Cost: $5.99 or free Lite version

There are many great apps to help you learn English in the App Store, but a lot of them aren't designed to help you in a specific grade. It's important to remember that different schools teach different things in fifth grade, but this app might match what you're learning and be a good study aid.

You'll be a grammar master after you spend some time with the more than 2,000 questions covering grammar, verbs, and vocabulary in this app. It's packed with tutorials and examples designed specifically for fifth graders, and it tracks your progress and success in each section of the app. It even includes Game Center support to let you compare your scores with other people's.

Test Your Grammar Skills

You can use iTooch ENGLISH Grade 5 to make sure you really learn the grammar lessons you've gone over at school. The better the scores you get on these quizzes, the more knowledge of grammar you'll have. To start learning, tap the app on your home screen and follow these steps:

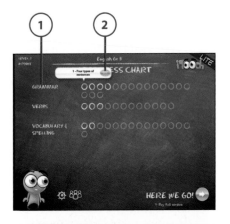

1. Choose what part of language you want to test yourself on: Grammar, Verbs, or Vocabulary & Spelling. Next to each subject are white circles. Empty ones are tests you still need to take; stars show which ones you've passed. Tap the one you want to work on.

2. In the pop-up menu, tap Go to get started.

3. There are two modes you can work in, Practice and Test. You'll be in Practice—where your answers don't count—when you start.

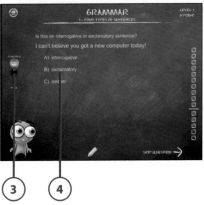

4. Read the question at the top of the screen and type the answer into a text box or tap the correct multiple-choice answer, depending on the question. The character in the bottom left tells you if your answer was wrong or right.

5. To continue, tap Next Question.

6. When you're done with Practice, tap and drag the Mode lever down to Test. Testing works the same way as Practice, except this time your answers count, so you better get them right!

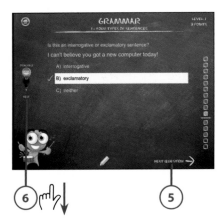

Math

In many schools, fifth grade is the time when you become very familiar with fractions, decimals, and percentages. Even if those aren't the things your school teaches this year, you'll probably find out how to solve multistep word problems, figure out the relationships between numbers, and maybe even start some basic geometry or computing with powers.

Prepare for Standardized Tests with 5th Grade Math Testing Prep

Cost: $2.99

Standardized tests are a common tool that states use to track how their students are doing and decide if they need to make changes to what's being taught. As you get older, these tests become more important: Some states require passing grades to graduate from high school. Practicing for these tests can help you do better.

A company donated 200 books to a local library. If 70 of them are fiction, what percent of the donated books are fiction?

| 20% | 30% |
| 70% | 35% |

If you live in a state that uses standardized tests each year, you might want to try out this app. It covers all kinds of math: decimals, division, fractions, probability, and word problems. And, because there's a teacher's edition of it, you might use it in school to prepare for those tests.

Learning Games in Epic Math HD

Cost: $1.99

Putting your math skills to the test doesn't have to mean quizzes and multiple choice tests. It can also mean games that you want to play over and over—and the more you play them, the more you'll know.

Instead of taking the traditional textbook approach to teaching

you math, Epic Math HD features a storybook that you can read and interact with to learn. This app also packs in a number of mini-games and helps you learn how to add, subtract, multiply, and divide very large numbers. When you get questions right, you earn points that you can use to buy prizes in the game.

A Whole New Kind of Math: Fractions App by Tap to Learn

Cost: $0.99

Fractions are numbers that let you represent parts of a whole. Some fractions that you've probably already run into include ½ and ¼. Understanding what those fractions mean isn't hard. But what if you need to add them together or multiply them?

Master fractions by taking them out of the world of abstract math and start using them in day-to-day life. This app lets you take everyday objects such as pizzas and candy bars and touch the iPad's screen to create fractions of them. When you think you've learned the lessons, you can test your skills with quizzes.

Geometry, Graphs, and Game Center: iTooch MATH Grade 5

Cost: $5.99 or free Lite version

Just like the version of this app for English, it's helpful to have an app designed specifically for the subjects you're likely to learn this school year.

Go beyond just learning about fractions in this app—it includes more than 4,500 questions on topics such as graphs, statistics, estimating, and geometry. One really neat feature of this app is that it integrates with Game Center (more on this in the "Using Game Center" section of Chapter 16, "It's Play Time: Gaming on the iPad ") so you can share your scores and achievements with your friends and classmates.

Solve Equations Under the Sea with Lobster Diver HD

Cost: Free

Knowing how to use fractions in day-to-day life is easy for ones like ⅛—just look at a pizza and its slices. Figuring out how to handle ⅜ or ⁵⁄₁₆ or even ⅘ is a lot trickier, but it's also important.

In Lobster Diver HD, you're a deep-sea diver who's hunting for tricky sea creatures such as lobsters while trying to avoid electric eels. The only way to do it, though, is by using math. You use fractions, different ways to show the same numbers, and other math techniques to complete the dives and haul up your catch.

Show Your Work on the Virtual Chalkboard in MathBoard

Cost: $4.99

In the old days, kids your age didn't have iPads or computers to use in school. In fact, they didn't even have paper notebooks. Instead, they used slates, tiny blackboards that they wrote on with chalk. Although slates aren't super high-tech, they do offer you scratch space to figure out math problems by showing your work.

Doing math on your iPad using this app is just like writing on a chalkboard. It can randomly generate quizzes of up to 250 questions so you don't have to take the same test over and over. In addition to just taking quizzes, if you need tips to figure out how something works, try the Problem Solver tool.

Customizing Your Questions

When you use MathBoard to review your math lessons, you can match the kinds of questions you're asked to what you've covered in school. This way, you can just work on things you've learned, but also add new topics later. To customize the questions you get, tap MathBoard on your home screen and then follow these steps:

1. If this is your first time using the app, enter your name in the pop-up window so MathBoard can track your results. Tap Save.

2. Tap Operator Types in the Settings box. This lets you choose whether you just want addition and subtraction or if you want to add multiplication, division, squares, cubes, or square roots to the questions. Tap the box next to each option you want to add.

3. Swipe up to Problems. Here, you can choose how many problems are in your quizzes, how they're displayed (vertical or horizontal), and whether they're multiple choice or not. Tap each item and make your selection.

4. Swipe up again to Number Range. Here, you can limit the kinds of numbers in your quizzes to what you've studied. For instance, if you haven't studied how to multiply three-digit numbers, you probably won't want to be tested on them. Tap the arrows next to minimum and maximum and make your choices (you can ignore the other options for now).

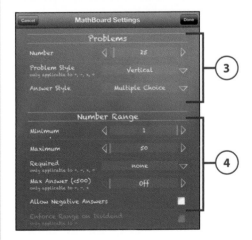

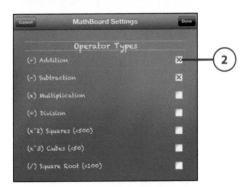

5. Swipe up to Equation Types. This section lets you decide what kind of problems you get—basic ones or ones where you solve for variables. Tap the box next to the kind you want and then tap Done to save your settings.

Testing Your Skills with MathBoard

With your settings chosen, it's time to start learning!

1. Tap Play.

2. A problem will appear on the board, with a set of answers beneath it (if you picked multiple choice answers, that is). If you know the answer, tap it.

3. If you need some room to work out your answer, you can draw in the empty space at the bottom. To make that area bigger, you can either tap Expand or tap and drag the three lines at the center of the space.

4. When you've worked out the problem and want to make the space smaller so you can answer the question, tap shrink or tap and drag the three lines down.

5. When you select your answer, MathBoard tells you if you're right or wrong and then gives you your next problem.

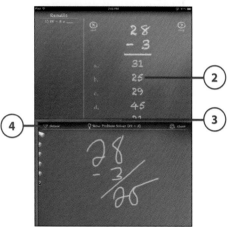

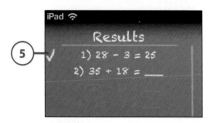

Science

In many schools, fourth-grade science was about far-away things such as planets and stars. In those schools, fifth-grade science comes a lot closer to home—in fact, it even takes you inside your own body. This year, you may learn about how light works, about the cells that make up our bodies (and all other living things), what goes on inside these cells, and what germs are. If your school focuses on different topics this year, check out Chapters 10, 12, and 13 for other suggestions.

Discover the Secrets of DNA in Cell and Cell Structure

Cost: $2.99

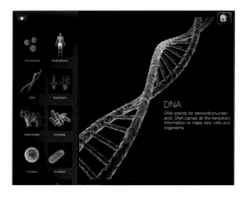

Understanding biology—the study of life—requires learning about the building blocks of life. Those building blocks take lots of forms, but one of the most important, and diverse, is the cell. All living things are made of up cells and the more you know about cells, the more you know about life itself.

Learn about cells, DNA, and other significant, microscopic structures in Cell and Cell Structure, an app designed for middle school science students. This collection of interesting 3D models of cells and HD videos on various topics presents the lessons with beautiful illustrations, and tests what you've learned with quizzes. The information is advanced, but you'll be able to use this app in school for years.

Find Out How Lasers Work in Bobo Explores Light

Cost: $4.99

Some of the most fundamental things about our world—things we take for granted and maybe don't even think that much about—are crucial and fascinating topics to study in science. The more you learn about these concepts and processes, the better you understand how the world works.

One of those things, light, does a lot more than just help us see. It also helps plants to eat and grow, changes how things look at sunrise and sunset, and powers lasers. In Bobo Explores Light, you learn all about light from more than 100 pages of material, plus videos, animations, and 3D holograms you can move by touching the screen.

Learn About Lightning

To start discovering all the amazing properties of light, and some of the really unexpected ways that it affects the world, tap Bobo Explores Light on your home screen and follow these steps:

1. On the main screen, tap Start reading to start from the beginning or Table of Contents to choose where you start.

2. If you chose Start reading, tap the arrow button at the bottom-right until you get to Lightning. If you chose Table of Contents, swipe up to put Lightning in the frame and tap it to begin reading.

3. On the main page of each section, there are three options across the top of the screen. Tap them to read them. These sections often have fun little surprises. Tap the heading to see what happens. To close these sections, tap the name at the bottom of the window.

4. To move to the last or next subjects, tap the arrows at the bottom-right corner. To go back to the table of contents, tap the round swirly button.

History/Social Studies

Your history/social studies class this year continues to help you understand how historical events fit together and influence each other. At many schools, this also includes special sections on important parts of American history, such as slavery and the Civil War as well as the Constitutional amendments that resulted from it. If your school studies something else this year, though, check out some of the other chapters to see if there are apps that match your classes.

Relive the War with The Civil War Today

Cost: $5.99

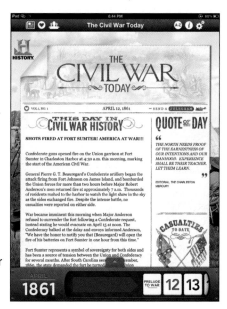

In Chapter 4, I said that understanding what people's daily lives were like in the past was an important part of understanding history. This app lets you experience the Civil War unfolding just the way people at the time did—one day at a time.

The Civil War lasted for five years—an amount of time equal to how long it will take you to go from fifth grade to halfway through high school. To understand what it was like to live through that, The Civil War Today updates itself every day with information about what was happening on the same day 150 years ago during the Civil War. That means it will have new information every day until April 2015! Read articles from newspapers at that time and from letters and diaries, see photos and videos, and much more.

See How the Country Developed with History: Maps of the United States

Cost: $7.99

If you know your American history, you know that the country didn't start out made up of 50 states and covering a huge part of the continent. Instead, it started out as 13 colonies on the East Coast. To understand how the country went from there to where it is today, you need to understand the country's expansion.

One great way to learn how the United States developed throughout its history is by consulting maps that show how things changed. This app includes tons of different kinds of maps, from geographic to military, wealth distribution to street maps, to those that show routes of travel and exploration.

LineTime: World History Timeline HD

Cost: $2.99

A single timeline tells you what order historic events happened in. Multiple timelines, though, help you understand how events relate to each other, how history unfolded in different regions at the same time, and what trends have been important.

This app lets you experience not just American history, but world history, arranged on a timeline. You can scroll through a timeline for the past 2,000 years and, when you find an event that interests you, tap to read articles about it. If you have a specific interest, though, you can also create custom timelines based around certain kinds of events or locations.

Meet Our Leaders in American Presidents for iPad

Cost: $3.99

The history of our country has been shaped by many people and many forces. Some of the most important people were the 44 men who occupied the White House as president. (Well, not every president lived in the White House. Do you know why?) Learning about them helps you learn more about the history of the country.

From George Washington to Barack Obama, this app is packed with information about every president in the history of the United States. Read biographies of each president, check out paintings or pictures of them, take quizzes, and learn about their important actions and other key events on a timeline. A map reveals how the United States developed over time, showing the states and territories at different historical points.

Meeting a President

To get to know America's first president, the man some people call the father of our country, tap American Presidents for iPad on your home screen, and then follow these steps:

1. Swipe the screen left and right to see each president in chronological order, as well as important events on a timeline across the bottom of the screen. Because George Washington was our first president, he's first on the list. To learn more, tap him.

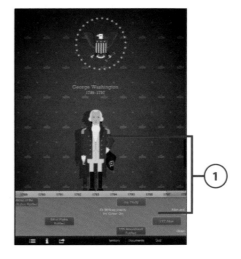

2. At the top of page, you see the years George Washington was president and some quick facts about him. To read about his life and presidency, swipe the text up.

3. To see paintings of Washington, tap Gallery. Swipe left and right to see the available paintings (and, for more recent presidents, photos).

4. To see a painting full size, tap it. Tap the X that appears in the upper-right corner to close it.

5. To hide the gallery again, tap the article.

6. To go back to the list of presidents and the timeline, tap the back arrow.

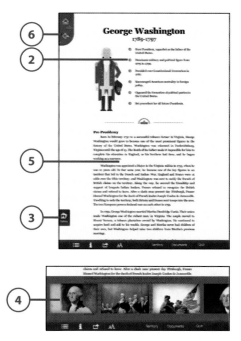

Music

Music apps for the iPad cover a wide range of options. Whether you want to learn the finer points of music theory (the ideas behind how songs are composed), just play some songs (whether you know an instrument or not), or get better at an instrument such as the guitar, these apps can be a big help.

Fine-Tune Your Ear for Music with EarMan HD

Cost: $7.99 (expansions are $0.99 each)

To become an expert musician, you need to have a finely trained ear, one that can hear notes clearly and identify them. That skill not only enables you to write music, but also lets you improvise (play songs that you make up as you play them), and jam with other people.

EarMan offers 105 lessons that help you learn music by ear, including intervals, octaves, and more. It also reinforces your knowledge by using musical notation as part of the training. Buy the app and then add on expansion packs using in-app purchases.

Make Beautiful Music without a Piano in Magic Piano

Cost: Free

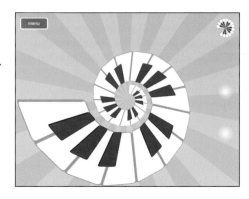

Making music isn't only something you do in school or lessons. Sometimes it's just something you do because you enjoy it or because it makes you feel great.

If you've ever wanted to do that playing the piano, but haven't known how, Magic Piano might be for you. This app won't teach you how to play exactly, but it does help you play along with your favorite songs in no time. Whether you choose piano keys or a more unusual interface, in Magic Piano you tap rays of light to make notes. Play along with 45 included songs, play duets with users over the Internet, or record your playing and share it.

Drag and Drop Composing: PatternMusic MXXIV

Cost: Free

In some ways, composing music is just a process of taking symbols that translate to sounds and arranging them in an order or pattern that creates music that sounds good. But what if those symbols you used weren't notes? Could you still make music?

In this app, the answer is yes. You create your own music in this app, but you don't use any instruments you've ever seen before. Instead of making songs using an onscreen piano, guitar, or drum, in PatternMusic you drag and drop icons for different instruments into place to create patterns from them and add voices. It might seem a little complicated at first, but stick with it.

Start Your Path to Superstardom with Rock Prodigy: Guitar

Cost: $29.99 (Extra lessons cost $0.99–$3.99.)

If you love music, there are three things you have to do to get better at your instrument: practice, practice, practice. Lessons are key, too, but the more you practice, the better you'll get.

Want to learn to play the guitar? All you need is a real guitar and this app (well, and all of that practice and hard work, too). Rock Prodigy: Guitar includes two lessons that show you the basics of playing the guitar and help you learn to play a song right away. When you play along with the app, it gives you feedback about where you're doing well and where you need to improve. In-app purchases let you add on songs by famous musicians such as Johnny Cash.

Preparing to Rock

To use Rock Prodigy, you need a guitar and to set it up for use with the app. Start by tapping the app to launch it; then tap on the kind of guitar you have: acoustic or electric.

If you have an acoustic guitar, sit near your iPad so its microphone can pick up your playing and then plug headphones into the iPad so you can hear the lessons.

If you have an electric guitar, you can either put your iPad near your amp or unplugged guitar, or get an adapter that lets you plug the guitar cable into the iPad. There are a number of these available; ask your parents about getting one.

When you're set up with either kind of guitar, tap the arrow button to continue.

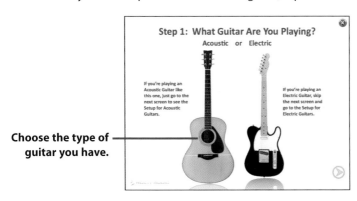

Choose the type of guitar you have.

Playing Your First Tune

Now that you're set up, it's time to start learning.

1. Tap the lesson you're interested in. If this is your first time using Rock Prodigy, start with Lesson 1. Otherwise, you start where you left off.

2. You see a brief description of the lesson you're about to take. Tap Play.

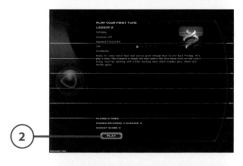

3. A voice explains the lesson and what you're supposed to do. Tap the screen to reveal the options for the lesson, including the ability to slow the music, loop it, and tune your guitar.

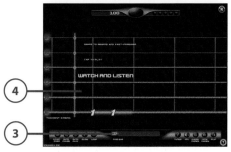

4. The notes you're supposed to play appear on the screen as numbers on the strings of the guitar. The number tells you which fret of the guitar you should hold down. The string that the number is on tells you which to press. Play along with the numbers as they come up on the screen, and you'll be playing a real rock song in no time!

Art

As your art skills improve, you're going to want to use more powerful and creative art apps. Those apps could be like blank canvases that you draw or paint on, lessons that help you improve your skills, or even tutorials that show you how to make art that doesn't exist on your iPad. Check out these tools for expressing yourself—and one for learning about one of history's most interesting painters.

Your Art Comes Alive in DoInk Animation & Drawing

Cost: $4.99

Have you ever wanted to make your own cartoons? It's a natural step to take after you've created drawings or characters you like. But what does it take to transform your still drawings into animations that move?

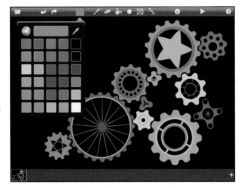

Bring the art in your imagination to life with this app that lets you create drawings, paintings, and—this is very cool—animations. It has tons of pre-made shapes, color palettes, and reusable items. When you've created something you want others to see, share it on social media or via email.

Discover an Important Artist by Visiting Frida's World

Cost: $2.99

Learning how to make art is one component of a good art education, but it's not the only one. To be a good artist, or just to appreciate the paintings, drawings, and other art you see, you need to understand the people who made the art: the artists.

Frida was a smart and funny girl growing up. She went to high school in Mexico City. For many, that was a big city, but for Frida's imagination, it was not. Her own world was so much bigger! She rode a bike to school and carried a backpack that contained butterflies, dried flowers, crayons, and books from her dad's library. It was magic!

Learn all about the life and art of the important and influential twentieth-century Mexican painter Frida Kahlo in this app. Read this at your own pace or have the app read the book to you. After you've learned all about Frida, you can take that inspiration and apply it to the included coloring book.

Draw Your Favorite Characters with Manga Art Academy HD

Cost: $0.99

To learn to draw, you need a lot more than sharp pencils and blank pieces of paper. It requires good instruction from other artists, and a lot of hard work and practice. And if you want to draw in a particular style, you need training from someone skilled in it.

In Manga Art Academy HD, you learn how to draw in the manga/anime style. This app, taught by professional manga artist Mark Crilley, offers more than 100 text and video tutorials that teach you all aspects of drawing manga/anime. Watch Crilley draw different elements of characters and follow along on paper to create your own drawings.

Create More Than Art Using Sketches 2

Cost: $4.99

What you can create in art apps is only limited by your imagination. An app might come with brushes, pencils, and markers as its basic tools, but that doesn't mean that the art you make with it has to be limited to drawings or paintings.

Sketches 2, another tool for creating sketches and graphics, proves that. This app comes with pre-made shapes, clip art, and brushes, so you have a head start on your art. One especially interesting feature is the ability to import images from the Maps app to create great-looking directions. Save your images as high-resolution files for printing or share them on online.

How to Make Origami

Cost: Free

Even though a lot of art apps are about drawing and painting, that's not the only kind of art—or art app—out there. There are also apps that help you learn how to take every-day items and make them into pieces of art.

Origami is a style of art from ancient Japan in which you take pieces of paper and transform them into tiny works of art. With just a few simple folds, your paper is transformed into a shape, a snowflake, or even an animal. In How to Make Origami, you get step-by-step instructions on how to fold paper to make different projects. And, when you know how to do this, as long as you have a piece of paper, you're able to make art almost anywhere.

Foreign Language

Whether you've been studying a foreign language for a little while now or are just getting started, you need to first learn basic vocabulary and then move on to more advanced topics. Those advanced skills and lessons include learning to read and speak the language you're studying. These apps can help.

Living Language—French for iPad and Spanish for iPad

Cost: Free ($19.99 in-app purchase)

Improve your French or Spanish with these apps from Living Language, a company that has offered foreign language instruction since the 1940s. Each app offers vocabulary, grammar, games, and more, over three levels—beginner, intermediate, and advanced. You get the first 11 lessons free; an in-app purchase gets you the other 35 to complete the set. There's a separate app for each language, so make sure to get the one for the language you're studying.

Ana Lomba's French/Spanish for Kids: The Red Hen

Cost: Free

These fun collections of classic stories helps you improve your reading, speaking, and listening of French or Spanish. One app is for French, the other for Spanish. Read the stories in French, Spanish, or English, or listen to a native speaker read them to you. But watch out; don't accidentally download the French-Chinese or Spanish-Chinese versions by mistake!

Reading the Red Hen in French

Reading the Red Hen in French and Spanish involves the same set of steps. Here's how to read it in French:

1. When you first launch the app, you can choose whether you want to read it and hear it in English or French. Tap the Play button for the language you want.

2. You move to the first page of the book. You can read the text at the top right.

3. To hear the text being read to you, tap Listen.

4. To switch the text and narration to French, tap Français.

5. To move to the next page, tap the Next Page button.

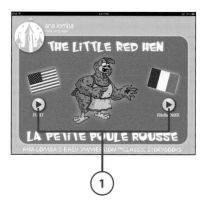

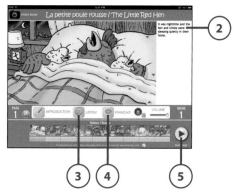

Test your brain with
tough logic puzzles.

Learn how to
type quickly
and accurately.

Express your
creativity with
painting apps.

Sixth grade is full of interesting new things to learn and great new experiences. In this chapter, you're introduced to some apps that might be useful to you in school or at home for your sixth-grade work in subjects like:

→ English/language arts

→ Math

→ Science

→ History/social studies

→ Music

→ Art

→ Foreign language

Using Your iPad in Sixth Grade

Even though you study many of the same subjects in sixth grade that you did in fifth, you're going to be learning a lot of new and exciting things in your classes. Apps can help you in the classroom or when you're doing your homework. The apps listed here aren't the only ones you might want to try, and they might not line up with the exact things your school covers (don't worry if they don't; that's normal and there are great apps for your school's classes, too), but check them out for help in your studies.

English/Language Arts

As you enter sixth grade, what you learn in English/language arts gets even more interesting. There's still vocabulary, but the words are more sophisticated and unusual. Grammar is still part of your work, but it leads to reading and writing more complex and interesting things—including reading with a deeper understanding than ever before.

Augment Your Terminology Using 6th Grade Vocabulary Prep

Cost: $2.99

You have to keep building your vocabulary. Every school year you encounter hundreds—maybe thousands—of new words, and you need to learn them all! The more of them you learn, the more you'll know, the more mature you'll sound when you speak or write, and the better prepared you'll be for high school and college.

is:

pester

(noun)

character

the beginning of a story

exposition

befriend

Just like with the versions of this app you used in earlier grades, this app helps you learn hundreds of new vocabulary words relevant to the schoolwork you do in sixth grade. Test your knowledge with word and definition quizzes. Show your teachers and parents how well you're doing by emailing them your results.

Cite Your Sources with EasyBib for iPad

Cost: Free

Including other people's writing in yours shows that you understand and can build on existing ideas; it's a sign of getting better as a writer. As you start writing more complex papers that use other people's ideas, you have to start learning how to reference the books, articles, and websites you mention in your writing. One way is to use a bibliography.

EasyBib for iPad helps you create bibliographies by taking a picture of a book's barcode with your iPad's camera or searching for the book's name in the app. After you've created your bibliography, you can add it to your paper and give credit to the people whose ideas helped shape yours.

Meet a Small Mark with a Big Role in GrammarPrep: Using Commas

Cost: $3.99

Just because something's small or easy to overlook doesn't mean that it's not important. Take an atom: It's so small that you need a powerful microscope to see it, but it's a building block of the world. Commas might look very small, but the role they play in English grammar and writing is huge.

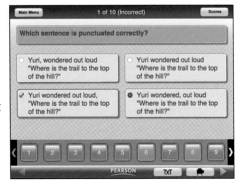

Learn when to use commas, and when not to, in the tests and quizzes offered by GrammarPrep: Using Commas. It also offers videos and podcasts so you can watch the tutorials come to life. With information designed for use by college students, this app will be useful for years. (There are other apps in the GrammarPrep series, so if you find this one useful, check out the others.)

Train Your Fingers in TapTyping

Cost: $3.99 or free Lite version

Ever watched someone who doesn't know how to type try to write on a keyboard? Seeing them search for each key and write so slowly can be frustrating—for them and for you. If you know how to type, you can use your computer or iPad to express yourself faster.

This app not only helps you learn how to type, but does so using special courses about U.S. history and using the book *Alice in Wonderland*—you end up learning two things at once! The free version of TapTyping comes with a few basic lessons, but you can buy more advanced topics—and most of the tests, really—in the app for $0.99–$3.99. It's worth knowing, though, that this app only helps you learn to type on the iPad's onscreen keyboard, not external ones.

Sink Language Errors with Zombie Grammar Force

Cost: $0.99

Grammar is about a lot more than where to put punctuation or how to make subjects and verbs agree. It's also about understanding what the parts of speech are, what words are which parts of speech, and when to use them.

When it comes to this kind of learning, what else comes to mind? It must be zombie pirates

and cannons (that's what I thought of, at least). In Zombie Grammar Force, a ship full of zombie pirates is headed for your land and you have to defend yourself. Unfortunately, your cannon can't sink their ship because clouds are in the way. Each time you answer a grammar question right, though, a cloud disappears. When they're all gone, fire away and move on the next level.

Reviewing Parts of Speech

You can get a refresher on the parts of speech used in Zombie Grammar Force.

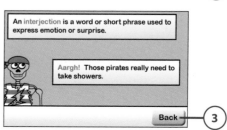

1. Tap the i button whenever you see it, and on the screen that appears, tap Next.

2. Tap the part of speech you want to learn more about.

3. Read the definition and example and then tap Back.

4. Choose another part of speech or tap Next. Tap Next again to go back to the game.

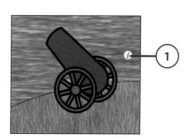

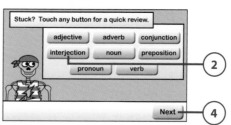

Math

Your math class this year builds on things you've done in the past—such as word problems and percentages—but also adds a few exciting new things. For instance, have you ever seen an equation that has a letter in it instead of just numbers (for instance, 3+X=7)? Those letters are called *variables*, and in many sixth-grade math classes, you learn how to solve problems that use them—and lots of other things, too. Even if those topics aren't taught this year, there are still useful apps for you in this section.

Prepare for Your State Tests Using 6th Grade Math Testing Prep

Cost: $2.99

The standardized tests used to track your progress come around every year, so it's only natural that apps that help you prepare for them show up in each chapter, right?

Use this app to prepare for the standardized tests you're taking this school year to show that you're learning what you're supposed to. It's the sixth-grade version of an app I recommended for fourth and fifth grades, too. The topics it covers include statistics, probability, percentages, and critical thinking.

Real-Life Math: Math Snacks HD

Cost: Free

Just like math can be serious or interesting or fun, it can also be really, really silly, as you'll learn in Math Snacks HD.

Learn all kinds of math with this collection of fun, animated videos. Each video teaches you about different math principles using fun stories, including how ratios can ruin a date or sink Atlantis, and how proportions and units can be important to kings and queens (aka rulers). The Math Snacks website offers even more fun lessons and quizzes.

Find the Math in Stories with Math Word Problems Grade 6

Cost: $2.99

Math comes in many forms, and not all of them include plus or equal signs. Just as often, math comes hidden in words or stories. Understanding how to identify and solve word problems is crucial to being able to use math in your day-to-day life.

Word problems teach you two really important skills: whatever math is involved in each problem, and just as important, learning how to pick out what information is valuable from among lots of irrelevant data. This app is packed with word problems that not only help you learn ratios, functions, probability, geometry, and other math, but also help you figure out what details you're presented with are worth paying attention to.

Do Better Math in Your Head in Mathemagics

Cost: $2.99

There are two ways to really prove that you know your stuff when it comes to math: solve problems really quickly and do it without using paper. The more math you can do in your head, the faster you can go and the more challenging and interesting problems you can tackle.

Mathemagic helps you get quick with your answers and teaches you to start doing complex math in your head. As you learn these tricks and take the quizzes in the app, you can share your scores and compete with your friends for the best one using Game Center.

Solve Problems with Logic Using MathLands

Cost: Free ($1.99 upgrade adds more features)

Problem solving means a lot more than just figuring out what X stands for in X+4=7. It means taking what you know about math and applying it to situations you encounter in real life, and it's one of the most important skills you can develop.

In MathLands, you develop problem-solving skills that are based on logic and an understanding of numbers. But instead of doing this using boring problems, you're faced with challenging games, comic-strip word problems, and exciting puzzles. Now, the next time you need to get four kids across a ravine using two parachutes, you'll know what to do!

Science

The scientific events and theories you study in many sixth-grade science classrooms are really, really big. Whether it's the sun or the stars, earthquakes or the movements of the Earth's tectonic plates, thermal (heat) energy or ecosystems, you go deep into some of the most powerful and most exciting parts of science. If these topics aren't taught at your school this year, check out some of the other chapters for apps that might match up with what you're learning.

Get Close Without Getting Burned: 3D Sun

Cost: Free

Earth and the planets near it are all part of the same solar system, the name given to a group of planets that all orbit the same sun. At the center of this system is the Sun.

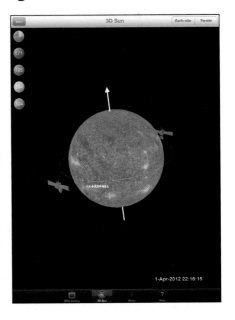

You probably know that the Sun is basically a gigantic ball of fire, so big and so hot that it has been burning for millions of years and can warm the Earth even though it's almost 100 million miles away. But did you know that there's actually a lot more than fire happening on the Sun? From solar flares to sunspots, this app can help you stay up to date about what's happening on the sun with alerts and tons of amazing, beautiful photos from NASA.

Learn About Walking on the Moon from Buzz Aldrin Portal to Science and Space Exploration HD

Cost: $1.99

Who better to learn about space from than a person who's actually been there? In this app, you can head back into space with former astronaut Buzz Aldrin, the second person ever to walk on the moon.

It includes photos from every aspect of the U.S. space program throughout history, live NASA videos, news about space and space exploration, and Buzz Aldrin's own writings about his experiences in space. You can't do much better than learning about space from one of the few people in the world who has actually been there.

Discover the Stars Right Above You in Distant Suns 3

Cost: $9.99

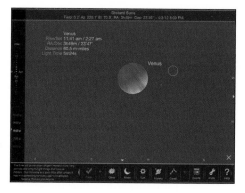

When you're interested in astronomy (the study of planets and stars), there are more stars and planets than anyone could learn about in an entire lifetime. In this app, you can go beyond just our solar system to explore more than 300,000 stars and suns throughout space.

Not only can Distant Suns 3 help you learn about all those stars by seeing telescope images of them, you can also read the stories behind the constellations. But the coolest feature of the app uses the iPad's built-in Location Awareness to figure out where you are and show you the stars that are right above you in the sky so you can know what you're seeing when you look up.

Shake Things Up with iQuakeMini

Cost: $0.99

Although major earthquakes cause tremendous damage and are big news, did you know that there are actually many earthquakes every day? You don't have to be scared, though; most earthquakes are never felt by humans.

As you learn in this app, most earthquakes are very mild, or happen in unpopulated areas. But our scientific instruments record them and, if you have this app, you can find out about them. You can learn about where they happen, their magnitude, and much more. The free version of this app delivers the basics, but if you want to really learn about what's shaking, buy the in-app upgrades.

Find Where the Nearest Volcano Is in Britannica Kids: Volcanoes

Cost: $4.99

Speaking of things that are hot and full of fire, this app from *Encyclopaedia Britannica* helps you learn all about volcanoes—and there's a lot more to learn than you might expect.

Besides shooting molten flame into the air, did you know that some islands are formed by undersea volcanoes spewing molten rock up from the ocean floor? That rock cools in the water and hardens into land. Besides that kind of information, this app includes articles, tons of great photos, games, puzzles, and even a map that helps you locate active and dormant volcanoes around the world. Are there any near where you live?

Discovering Individual Volcanoes

To see which volcanoes are near you and learn about them:

1. Spin the wheel at the bottom until you reach Map.

2. In the map section, you can tap a volcano icon to see its name.

3. Tap the arrow in the pop-up to learn more.

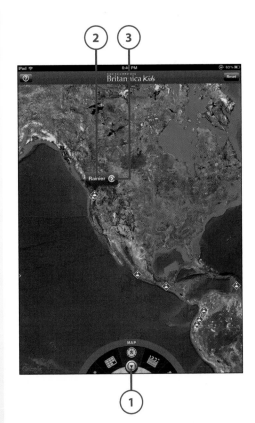

4. On the page about the volcano, you see a photo and a small description. If the icons across the bottom are lit up, you can tap them for more information.

5. Tap the jigsaw piece to play the jigsaw puzzle game.

6. Tap the squares for the Magic Square game.

7. Tap the map to see the volcano on a map.

8. Tap the document to read about it.

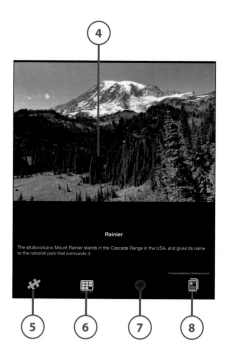

History/Social Studies

You look far into the past and far outside the U.S. in many sixth-grade history/social studies classes. You might study ancient civilizations in Egypt and Rome, and learn about the importance of primary documents—parts of the historical record written by people living through the events. Even if these aren't the topics your school covers in sixth grade, you might enjoy these educational apps.

From Gladiators to Emperors in Britannica Kids: Ancient Rome

Cost: $4.99

One of the ancient world's great civilizations was Rome, which had an empire that spanned Europe at the same time that Egypt dominated Africa (more on Egypt in a few pages). Rome inherited some of the traditions and learning of the Greeks who

preceded them, and in turn the U.S. has been influenced in many ways by Rome.

In this app, you learn all about gladiators and Roman mythology, Julius Caesar and Roman culture, and how the ideas and institutions of ancient Rome influence things like our government and laws. Just like with the Egypt app, the app includes articles, quizzes, photos, and maps.

Track Thousands of Years with Chinese History Timeline

Cost: Free

On the other side of the world, but at the same time that Egypt and Rome ruled Africa and Europe, China was a major power in Asia. It was one of the most advanced ancient civilizations, but it's one that a lot of Americans don't know much about.

In this app, you learn about the history of ancient China using a timeline featuring maps and links to relevant Wikipedia articles. You discover that ancient China was so advanced, it invented fireworks, paper, and gunpowder long before they existed in Europe. In some timeline views, you can also compare what was happening in ancient China to other parts of Asia at the same time.

Discover the Foundation of Our Country in Constitution and Federalist Papers

Cost: Free

Understanding where to find and how to use primary sources is a key part of learning history and how to think like a historian. Primary sources are not only important documents, but they often tell us a lot about the people who created them, what was important to them, how they thought, and what they were trying to do.

When it comes to primary sources, few documents are more important to United States history than these. The Constitution created the foundation for how we live today, more than 200 years after it was written, and the Federalist Papers urged adoption of the Constitution. Together, along with the articles included in this app, you start to understand why the Constitution was written the way it was and what it meant both then and now.

America's Founding Document: Declaration for iPad

Cost: Free

When it comes to understanding the founding of the United States, there's probably no better primary source document than the Declaration of Independence. Besides the Constitution, America's most important document might be the Declaration of Independence, which the colonists used to announce that the 13 colonies would no longer be a part of England and would instead be their own country.

In Declaration for iPad, you can read the Declaration of Independence, see images of the original document, and read about the men who created it and, as a result, helped create America. There's also a companion app, Constitution for iPad.

Thrilling Tales in the Myths and Legends of Ancient Greece and Rome—AudioBook

Cost: $2.99

To understand ancient Greece and Rome, you need to understand their belief systems and their religions. One of the best things about studying those civilizations is getting to learn about their fascinating, fearsome, and funny gods, myths, and legends.

From Hercules and his 12 heroic labors to the winged horse Pegasus, from Apollo (the god of hunting and archery) to Zeus (who threw lightning bolts at people who made him angry), Greek and Roman legends contain some of the most interesting, colorful characters in all of world mythology. Myths and Legends of Ancient Greece and Rome not only helps you learn about them, but it includes classic art showing them and audio versions of their stories.

Find Fun in the Past with World History Games

Cost: Free

Some people think of history as a subject that's all about reading dust-covered books or faded old maps. That's part of it—and I say that's part of what makes it a great subject; I love seeing and using those old documents—but it's not all.

Learning about the ancient world is also a lot of fun with this app. It includes more than 100 different games—from arcade games to word jumbles to puzzles—on topics throughout world history. Test your knowledge of ancient Rome, Africa, or Asia, or tackle modern topics such as World War II and learn more by reading the included articles.

Much More Than Mummies—Britannica Kids: Ancient Egypt

Cost: $4.99

The ancient world was dominated in different places and at different times by a number of fascinating civilizations. One that still captivates average people and scholars alike today is ancient Egypt.

From the mysteries of the pyramids to the challenge of deciphering hiero-glyphics to mummies' curses, ancient Egypt is one of the most fascinating and important ancient civilizations. In this app, you learn all about the rulers, culture, nature, and religion of this nearly 3,000-year empire. The app includes articles, photos, games, puzzles, and maps designed specifically for 8 to 12 year olds.

Reading Articles About Egypt

To start learning about Egypt, tap the app on your home screen. Use the callouts on the figure to navigate the main articles screen.

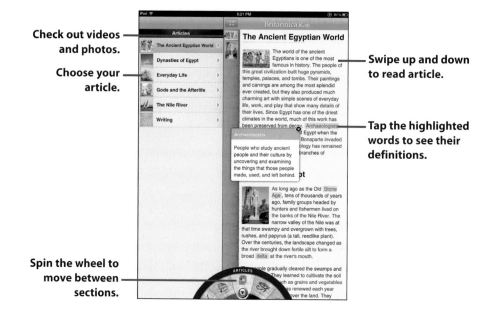

Check out videos and photos.

Choose your article.

Swipe up and down to read article.

Tap the highlighted words to see their definitions.

Spin the wheel to move between sections.

Music

A good musician is a lifelong student and always practices and tries to learn new things about music. An important part of having that knowledge is incorporating it in your playing. These apps are designed to help you take what you already know and put it to use. Use them to create, record, and share your own songs.

Learn at Your Speed with Amazing Slow Downer Lite

Cost: Free

One way to become a better musician is to learn how to play your favorite songs. You discover all kinds of theory, techniques, and styles by playing the music you like the best. If you've got a good ear for music, you might be able to figure out how to play songs by hearing them—if they would just slow down so you can work out certain sections, that is.

This app lives up to its name and helps you do just that. It takes any song on your iPad and slows it down to as much as one-quarter its original speed so you can work out each note and chord. And it does that without distorting the music so you can be sure you're playing it right. The free version plays the first quarter of any song. To upgrade to a version that can play full songs, make the $14.99 in-app purchase.

Make Music and Podcasts in GarageBand

Cost: $4.99

Music apps on the iPad aren't just about learning how to play. Sometimes, they're also about giving you the tools to create amazing-sounding music.

Get an entire band and recording studio in your iPad with this app. GarageBand is a powerful tool for making and recording music, or making your own podcasts and sharing them on the Web. You can use the built-in instruments—from piano to guitar to drums and far beyond—to create songs and then add professional-sounding effects to them. If you already play certain instruments, you can even plug them into your iPad and have GarageBand record your playing. If you like to make music, you'll love GarageBand—and will use it for years to come.

Improve Your Playing with Pianist Pro

Cost: $4.99

Piano practice can mean a lot of things—running through scales, going over hand positions, playing full songs—but whatever you include, practice is crucial if you want to improve.

This isn't an app that teaches you how to play the piano, but if you already know how, or are learning, you'll love practicing and creating new songs with it. Not only can you play Pianist Pro like a regular piano just by tapping on the iPad's screen, it's packed full of cool sound effects. Save the music you play on it as CD-quality songs and listen to it on virtually any device that plays digital audio.

Play the Classics in Virtual Sheet Music

Cost: Free

As you get better at your instrument, challenging yourself to learn more sophisticated music becomes important to your improvement. To do this, especially if you're learning to read music as part of your lessons, you might want to play using sheet music.

In Virtual Sheet Music, you get the sheet music for more than 50 classic compositions by Beethoven and many others. Not only does the app offer sheet music, but its page-turning features are designed to let you use it while you play or practice. You can buy additional sheet music to add to your collection through the app's built-in store (remember to get your parents' permission, though).

Downloading and Playing Sheet Music

To get the sheet music for a classic song and learn how to play it, tap the app to open it and then follow these steps:

1. Tap Library.

2. In the drop-down menu, tap VSM Catalog.

3. You can choose to search for a song or composer, or browse by composer, instrument, price, or other categories. Tap your choice.

4. Swipe up and down to view the sheet music available in the category you chose.

5. Tap the sheet music you're interested in.

6. To hear the song, tap Play. To download free sheet music, tap Download. To buy sheet music, tap Add to Cart. To download both at the same time, tap Download All Media.

7. When you've downloaded or purchased the sheet music, tap View to see it.

8. Tap the right arrow at the bottom of the page to begin.

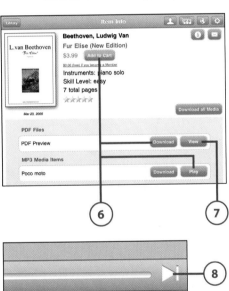

9. Swipe right to left to move through the pages. At the last page, swipe left to right back to the beginning to go back to the page for the music.

Art

Just like with music apps, this year the apps you might want to use for art are more powerful and can help you create even-better-looking pictures. Because these apps are more powerful, they're also harder to use. But stick with them and they'll be important parts of your artistic palette for a long time.

Step Up to the Art Table in Drawing Pad

Cost: $1.99 (in-app purchases of coloring books for $0.99–$1.99)

One aspect of making art that many artists enjoy is surveying their tools. This app simulates the experience of sitting down at an art table with markers, brushes, and crayons scattered all over the place and creating something new and exciting on a blank piece of paper.

In Drawing Pad, you choose from a ton of different ways to draw and color, add stickers to your images, or even import photos taken with the iPad's camera and draw on them. When you have a great drawing, you can save it to your iPad, share it using email and social media, or print it using AirPrint.

Create Dazzling Designs with Meritum Paint Pro

Cost: $1.99 or free Lite version

One of the things that's pleasing about painting is how tactile it is, how you can feel the paint on your hands and control it with your fingers. When you're painting on actual paper instead of on the iPad, you can dip as many fingers in the paint as you want and smear them all over your paper.

With Meritum Paint Pro, you can do the same thing when you paint on your iPad. Not only that, it lets you paint with up to five colors all at once for rainbow strokes. You can also pick groups of colors that look great together, and the app even lets you change how the lines you draw with your fingers look by tilting the iPad.

Professional-Level Art Tools Using SketchBook Pro for iPad

Cost: $4.99

The quality of the some art apps for the iPad is amazing. There are apps you'll buy now that can work just as well for you in grade school and for professional artists. SketchBook Pro is one of them.

It is one of the most widely used art apps; it's even used by professional artists. It comes with more than 60 prebuilt brushes, pencils, and pens that you can use to create sketches and drawings. Each one of these can be changed and tweaked to suit your vision. When you're done, save your designs to your iPad or sync them to your computer (see the "Syncing Documents via iTunes" section in Chapter 7, "Using Your iPad for School," to learn how to do this).

Choosing a Pencil, Brush, or Marker

To create a picture in SketchBook Pro, the first thing you need to do is select what you want to draw with—a pencil, pen, brush, or marker. To do that, open the app and tap the Brush icon, and then you can choose from the customizations shown in the figure.

Preview the tool you're creating.

Change the line thickness setting.

Adjust the opacity setting.

Choose your colors.

Select from different pencils, markers, brushes, etc.

When the preview shows a line thickness, shape, and color that you like, tap the background to start creating.

Foreign Language

As you progress in learning a foreign language, you continue learning vocabulary, but you also start reading more advanced writing and having more interesting conversations. Check out these apps for lessons on how to have these conversations in lots of different languages.

Spanish/French in a Month HD

Cost: $3.99 or free limited versions

If you're trying to learn how to really speak a language like its native speakers do, especially if you have a trip coming up, you might need to take a different approach to learning it. Vocabulary lessons might not cut it; you might need to start trying to have conversations right away.

As the name of these apps lets you know, they're designed to help you learn enough French or Spanish to have conversations in just a month. They take a different approach to learning a language than other apps—they help you learn to speak first and then have you learn the technical aspects of grammar and verb declensions and all the rest later.

Other apps in this series help you learn how to speak Hebrew, Italian, German, Korean, Russian, Japanese, and Chinese. Each app focuses on just one language, so make sure to choose the one you're interested in learning.

Learning Basic Vocabulary

To learn some basic Spanish vocabulary, get Spanish in a Month from the App Store and tap it to open it. Then follow these steps:

1. Tap Lessons.

2. Tap Lesson 1.

3. You see a list of all the words you'll learn. Tap Go to begin the lessons.

4. The app shows you six pictures with the words for them in Spanish, and pronounces them for you. When all six have been shown, the app repeats one of the words. Tap the picture of that word. When you have matched all six, you move on to the next lesson.

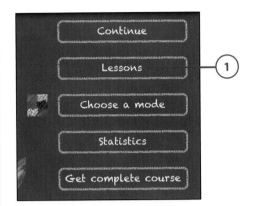

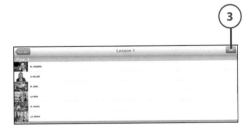

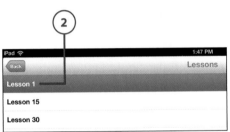

Take great notes and prepare to write homework papers.

Find out what it's like to be a scientist with apps.

Become a whiz at more advanced math.

Learn about the ancient world.

In this chapter, you're introduced to more sophisticated and challenging apps, apps that help you start to prepare for high school— which is only two years away. These apps cover subjects including:

→ English/language arts
→ Math
→ Science
→ History/social studies
→ Music
→ Art
→ Foreign language

Using Your iPad in Seventh Grade

Do you have favorite subjects in school or particular parts of those subjects that fascinate you? You can learn more about them with the articles, videos, quizzes, and games in the apps discussed in this chapter. These apps are just a small sample of everything at the App Store that you might find useful for school. Not every school follows the same learning plan, so your seventh-grade classes could cover different topics. If so, don't worry; other chapters in this book have lots of great app suggestions that might fit your classes. And you can always search the App Store. With hundreds of thousands of apps there, you're sure to find something great!

English/Language Arts

Get ready to read and write more interesting, challenging, and complex things than ever before. Many seventh-grade English/language arts classes not only teach you cool kinds of language that you haven't used before, such as idioms and similes, but they also help you learn to write better school papers and stories.

Level Up Your English Skills in Grammar Up

Cost: $4.99 or free edition

At this point, you've been studying grammar for years, but there's always more to learn. In fact, as long as you're writing, you learn new forms of grammar. At some point, you know all the basic rules, but every time you write, you use those rules in different ways to say what you want exactly how you want to say it.

This app helps you master grammar with more than 1,800 multiple-choice questions to test your grammar skills in advanced concepts such as causative verbs, gerunds, and conditionals. Start getting ready for high-school English—and be prepared when you get there in a couple years—with this app.

Understand How Stories Work Using Literary Analysis Guide

Cost: $3.99

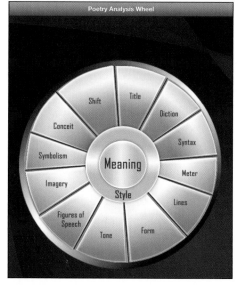

When a writer creates a story or poem, an essay or book, he is trying to make you think or feel a particular thing. You know whether he's succeeded if you have a strong reaction to what you read. But knowing why he succeeded is another matter. To understand that, you need to understand the building blocks of what he wrote.

Every story—every sentence and paragraph, really—is made up of many parts of language. Understanding what those parts are, and how they fit together to create good writing (or don't fit together and result in something bad!), is crucial to becoming a skilled writer. This app helps you learn how to analyze the things you read and write for the quality of the writing.

Organize Your Thoughts with Outliner for iPad

Cost: $4.99

There's a lot more to writing than just having something to say and possessing the vocabulary and mastery of grammar to say it well. You also need clearly organized ideas. All of those things add up to good writing.

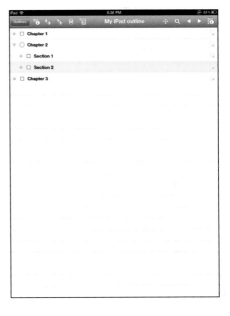

One major technique many—maybe even most—writers use to organize their ideas is outlining. When you outline, you create a list of everything you want to write about and then organize those ideas into related groups and order those groups in ways that make sense and help you make your point. Outliner helps you create great outlines for simple tasks and complicated ones. It even helps you track your progress as you work.

Crossword-Style Competition: Scrabble

Cost: $9.99

Showing off your ever-increasing vocabulary isn't just something you do in writing or when you speak. It can also be the key to success in some games.

Scrabble is my favorite word game, and if you enjoy English class, it will probably be yours, too. In it, you try to create words using the letters you have and those that other players have already used during their turns. Soon enough, the board looks like a crossword puzzle. Each letter is worth a different number of points, and placing letters on different parts of the board can multiply the value of your letters or words. It can provide hours of fun, and no two games are the same. This app brings the classic Scrabble game to your iPad and lets you play against friends online.

Take Better Notes with Evernote

Cost: Free

No one can remember every single idea they have. This is especially true if they're writing something that's very long or is heavily researched with a lot of sources. For that, you need to take notes. And, when you're taking notes on the iPad, you need an app.

Evernote is my favorite note-taking app. In fact, I use it for all kinds of writing. Whether I'm researching an article or a book, planning a short story, or writing something longer, all my ideas and plans start in Evernote. With it, you can type notes into your iPad (including images, audio clips, and maps) and organize them into folders. Because Evernote is also web-based, you can access your notes anywhere you can get online using any device with a web browser, whether or not it has the Evernote app. There's also a spin-off called Evernote Peek that you can use to create your own flashcards to help you study.

To use Evernote, you first have to have an Evernote account. This is, as mentioned earlier, because the information you store in Evernote is synced to a web-based account that lets you to access it on your iPad, other devices running the app, or web browser. You wouldn't want to go without your notes! After you have an account (get permission from your parents first), you're ready to make some notes!

Taking Notes with Evernote

Using Evernote to take notes is very simple, but if you want to keep good, organized notes, there are a few things to do after you're in Evernote.

1. Tap New note at the bottom of the screen to create a blank note.

2. Tap the Title: field and give the note a title that describes what this note is about.

3. By default, all of your notes are stored in one notebook. Notebooks are collections of notes on the same subject. It's a good idea to organize your notes this way so you don't lose track of your ideas. To create a new notebook, tap the arrow at the end of the Notebook: field.

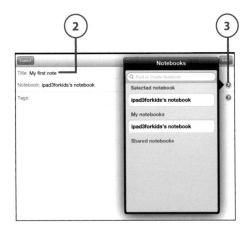

4. Type the name of the new notebook you want to create into the text box.

5. Tap Add to create the new notebook.

6. Tap the empty note and the Notebook: field should show the name of the new notebook you just created.

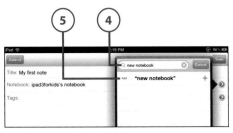

7. Tap into the main body of the note and start typing. The buttons across the top let you format your note.

8. When you've finished writing your note, tap Save.

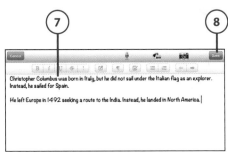

9. To see the note in its notebook, tap the Notebooks tab at the top of the screen.

10. Tap the Notebook you saved it in.

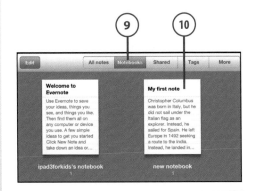

11. The notebook opens, with all of the notes in it at the top of the screen. Tap the note you want to read or edit and it appears below.

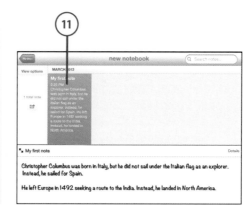

Math

Sometimes when you're studying math, you might get frustrated and ask yourself, "When am I ever going to use this stuff?" That question is answered in seventh-grade math. You study a lot of topics, but in many schools some of the most fun ones—which are also the ones you'll use most in day-to-day life—include algebra and geometry.

From Algebra to Statistics: 7th Grade Math Testing Prep

Cost: $2.99

Bad news if you hate standardized tests: They're back this year (and you take them every year through the eleventh grade). By seventh grade, you've prob-ably gotten pretty used to the annual ritual of taking standardized tests to show what you're learning in key subjects. Whether you like those tests or hate them, you still have to take them this school year, so why not prepare for them and do well?

This app is just like the versions for previous grades, except it helps you pre-pare for the tests you face in seventh grade, with topics such as algebra, criti-cal thinking, exponents, negative numbers, and scientific notation.

Find Out When You'll Use This Stuff with Elevated Math

Cost: Free (In-app purchases of additional lessons cost $1.99)

One complaint that you may hear from your friends—or you may even say yourself—when the going gets tough (or boring) is, "When are we ever going to use this stuff?" It turns out that you'll probably use math all the time. (I'm a writer and I use it way more than I ever expected.)

This app helps you learn algebra (and a lot of other math topics) with its fun questions, and it shows you why you should learn math in a series of videos that explain where you'll use math as an adult. It comes with two free lessons—to learn more, you need to buy other lessons via in-app purchase.

Monkey Math: Middle School Math Pro 7th Grade

Cost: $0.99 or free introductory version

There haven't been any math games in this chapter so far, but that doesn't mean that math gets any less fun as you move up to new grades. Don't worry; there are still lots of fun ways to learn.

In Middle School Math Pro 7th Grade, you have one simple goal: help a monkey climb down some ladders. The goal might be simple, but the way you do it isn't: answering math questions. Each time the monkey comes to a new ladder, you need to solve a problem—using negative numbers, absolute value, fractions, and scientific notation—to help it climb down. Compare your scores with your friends using Game Center and email your stats to your teachers.

Multitouch Math: Algebra Touch

Cost: $1.99 or free version that offers the first five lessons

In one common way to learn algebra—problems that have variables such as x or a instead of numbers—teachers tell students to envision rearranging the equation to make it less confusing. On paper, that means rewriting the equation. But not on the iPad.

Algebra Touch helps you master the subject by taking advantage of the iPad's touchscreen to let you move variables and numbers to different parts of the equation to solve problems. Test yourself on algebra topics such as order of operations, prime numbers, variables, and substitution.

Learn Order of Operations

Order of operations is a mathematical principle that helps you know what order you should solve complicated math problems in to ensure you get the correct answer. Along with many other topics, Algebra Touch helps you learn order of operations. To do that, tap the app on your home screen and follow these steps:

1. Tap Explain to start learning.

2. Read the information in the pop-up window. It explains a number of mathematical principles that are required to understand order of operations.

3. You can solve the problems in the center of the screen by tapping and swiping the numbers. To add, subtract, multiply, or divide two numbers, first tap the symbol between them and then drag one number onto the other. This solves the problem.

4. When you've done that, tap Next in the pop-up window.

5. After you've gone through the examples and learned the topic, tap Practice.

6. Use the lessons you've learned to solve the equations. If your answer is correct, you see a check mark and two buttons. Tap Another Problem? to continue practicing your math.

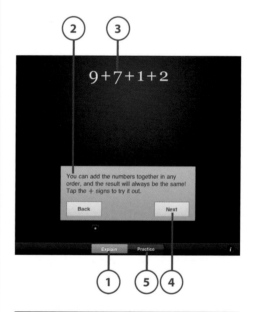

Science

You study a lot of things in science classes throughout your years in school, but one of the most frequent and most interesting topics is life itself. That's a big focus of many seventh-grade science classes. From studying the cells that make up plants and animals, to the genes that our parents pass to us that give us our hair color and our height, to how species have evolved over time, this year you probably learn a lot about the mechanics of life in all its forms. If your school teaches other topics in seventh grade, check out other chapters for apps that match your classes.

See Cells How Scientists Do in 3D Cell Simulation and Stain Tool

Cost: Free

If you're interested in science, and maybe becoming a scientist when you're older, it's a good idea to start learning some of the tools and techniques that scientists use in their research. One technique that biologists use a lot is cell staining, where you add a dye to a cell to highlight certain areas or structures.

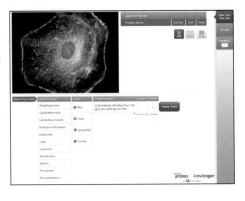

3D Cell Simulation and Stain Tool is a pretty advanced app, but if you're really into understanding how cells work and what all of their parts do, you'll enjoy it. You can choose to either inspect 3D versions of cells—rotate them by touching the screen or watch videos about them—or stain virtual cells to examine them the same way scientists do.

Go from Egg to Adult in a Life Cycle App

Cost: $0.99

The cycle of life is one of the most important things to learn in biology. It shows how processes repeat themselves and how the many different biological systems that make up the world are related to each other—even when they don't seem to be.

A Life Cycle App—which was partially created by high school students in Texas—can help you learn about the cycle that living things go through, from egg to fertilization to juvenile to young adult to adult. You also learn about cycles related to water, rocks, oxygen, and plants.

Get Under Your Skin Using Powers of Minus Ten—Cells and Genetics

Cost: $1.99

Understanding that things that can appear simple are actually complex is an important part of learning to think like a scientist. That knowledge helps scientists know when to ask questions that deepen our understanding of the world or discover new things.

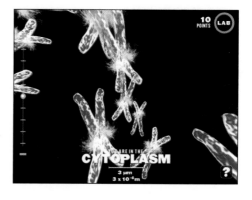

Powers of Minus Ten lets you go deep—very deep—into some-

thing you see all the time: your hands. This app helps you understand how they work using appealing 3D illustrations that let you dive into the structures that make up your hand. Go even deeper by exploring the cells in each part of your hand, right down to the atomic level.

Meet the Beautiful Building Blocks of Life in the Elements: A Visual Exploration

Cost: $6.99

Elements are building blocks of the natural world, and each one has its own properties and ways to combine with other elements to create things we're all familiar with. For instance, combining two hydrogen atoms with one oxygen atom creates water. Getting to know the elements and their properties helps you prepare for some really exciting explorations of biology and chemistry.

This app offers the most beautiful representation of the elements and the periodic table I've ever seen. Not only does each element on the table have an illustration, but tapping the illustration brings up a high-resolution image that you can rotate to inspect more closely and lots of detailed information about that element. You'll find this app useful in middle school, high school, college, and beyond. It's almost 2GB, though, so make sure you have a lot of storage room for it and that you download it over Wi-Fi, not 4G.

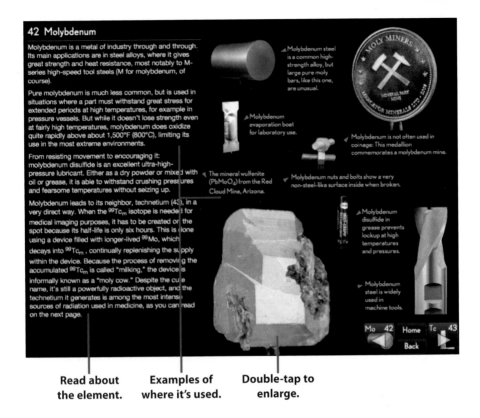

42 Molybdenum

Molybdenum is a metal of industry through and through. Its main applications are in steel alloys, where it gives great strength and heat resistance, most notably to M-series high-speed tool steels (M for molybdenum, of course).

Pure molybdenum is much less common, but is used in situations where a part must withstand great stress for extended periods at high temperatures, for example in pressure vessels. But while it doesn't lose strength even at fairly high temperatures, molybdenum does oxidize quite rapidly above about 1,500°F (800°C), limiting its use in the most extreme environments.

From resisting movement to encouraging it: molybdenum disulfide is an excellent ultra-high-pressure lubricant. Either as a dry powder or mixed with oil or grease, it is able to withstand crushing pressures and fearsome temperatures without seizing up.

Molybdenum leads to its neighbor, technetium (43), in a very direct way. When the $^{99}Tc_m$ isotope is needed for medical imaging purposes, it has to be created on the spot because its half-life is only six hours. This is done using a device filled with longer-lived ^{99}Mo, which decays into $^{99}Tc_m$, continually replenishing the supply within the device. Because the process of removing the accumulated $^{99}Tc_m$ is called "milking," the device is informally known as a "moly cow." Despite the cute name, it's still a powerfully radioactive object, and the technetium it generates is among the most intense sources of radiation used in medicine, as you can read on the next page.

Molybdenum steel is a common high-strength alloy, but large pure moly bars, like this one, are unusual.

Molybdenum evaporation boat for laboratory use.

Molybdenum is not often used in coinage: This medallion commemorates a molybdenum mine.

The mineral wulfenite ($PbMoO_4$) from the Red Cloud Mine, Arizona.

Molybdenum nuts and bolts show a very non-steel-like surface inside when broken.

Molybdenum disulfide in grease prevents lockup at high temperatures and pressures.

Molybdenum steel is widely used in machine tools.

Mo 42   Home   Tc 43   Back

Read about the element.   **Examples of where it's used.**   **Double-tap to enlarge.**

History/Social Studies

Remember how sixth-grade history/social studies focused on the ancient world—Egypt and Rome and other major civilizations of that time? In many seventh-grade history classes, you'll pick up the story of history after those civilizations begin to decline and as new ones take the center of the world stage. If your history class covers different topics, that's OK; there are surely apps for those, too.

Discover Mexico's Ancient Rulers in Britannica Kids: Aztec Empire

Cost: $4.99

Did you know that the country just south of the U.S.—Mexico—has been home to a number of important, interesting empires over the last few thousand years? Learning about these ancient civilizations right next door can help us understand both history and today's world.

The dominant civilization in Mexico in the fourteenth to sixteenth centuries was the Aztec empire. You learn all about this impressive civilization—from its leaders and religion to its culture—in this app. Not only are there educational articles and maps, but the app also offers quizzes, puzzles, and games to both help you master new concepts and test what you've already learned.

Discover the Power of Reason in the Enlightenment 101: The TextVook

Cost: $4.99

The world in which we live today started to take shape during a period in the 1600s–1700s called the Enlightenment. Understanding the Enlightenment not only helps you understand the history of that time, but it also gives you insight into the ideas that influence the way we think and live today.

The Enlightenment, which took place across the U.S. and Europe, applied the power of reason to nearly every part of life, from religion to science, art to philosophy. In this app, not only can you read articles about important people, events, and ideas from the Enlightenment, but you can also watch fun animations about them, too.

Sail Uncharted Seas in European Exploration: The Age of Discovery

Cost: Free

The age of exploration—the period in which European countries sent sailors throughout the world to find new territories and wealth—was a fascinating and important time because the explorers and their crews, who set sail from Europe, truly didn't know what they'd find when they next set foot on land. The decisions they made back then have shaped our world ever since.

With European Exploration: The Age of Discovery, you can find out what it was like to have led voyages of exploration. In it, you start from Europe and gradually discover parts of the world, and different features of those places, just like real explorers did. And, just like real explorers, you have to be careful during your expeditions to make sure your boats don't sink!

Encounter the Lost Mayan Civilization

Cost: $0.99

Long before the Aztecs ruled in Mexico, the Mayan empire dominated that country and parts of Central America from thousands of years B.C.E. to a few hundred years before Columbus reached North America. Learning about the Maya helps you understand what life was like in North America at the same time that Rome dominated Europe.

In this encyclopedia of the Mayan civilization, you learn all about the civilization, its people, and its history through articles and photos of important locations and cultural artifacts.

Experience Europe's Rebirth in Renaissance History 101: The Animated TextVook

Cost: $4.99

If the Enlightenment was the time period that shaped the world we live in today, the Enlightenment was shaped, in part, by the period that came before it: the Renaissance.

After the fall of the Roman Empire, Europe lost many of its cultural and scientific achievements. It began to re-create them during the Renaissance (the French word for *rebirth*). From the 1300s to the 1600s, Europe drew on its Greek and Roman heritage to revitalize arts, science, math, and religion. Learn all about this exciting period from articles and animations on important figures such as Shakespeare, Galileo, and Leonardo da Vinci.

Tour the Globe Using the World by National Geographic

Cost: $3.99

One mark of being well educated is that you're knowledgeable about many different parts of the world and have some idea of what makes those places unique. Of course you can't travel to every country and won't have time—even in college—to study every one, but you can learn from people and organizations whose job it is travel the world and write about it.

Whether you want to understand where one country is in relation to another, or want to go deep in learning about one specific place, this app by National Geographic can help. Besides articles, the app includes tons of beautiful photos, flags for each country, and an interactive globe that you can move using the iPad's multitouch screen.

Music

Whether you have a few years of practice under your belt or are just learning how to make music, there are apps that can help. Whether you want to become better at playing songs you already know or want to create your own, these apps are great musical collaborators.

Learn Songs at Your Own Speed with Capo

Cost: $19.99

Like Amazing Slow Downer Lite in the last chapter, Capo is a great companion if you want to learn how to play the songs in your iPad music library by ear—that is, by listening to and figuring them out.

Capo lets you slow down songs without changing how they sound so you can figure out how each section of the song works and then learn to play it at your own speed. It can also help you isolate particular parts of songs by removing the vocals or choosing the left or right speaker for playback. You need to know how to play music just by hearing it—there are no notes or instruction in this app—but if you can do that, this app is a great tool for you.

Become the Life of the Party Using djay

Cost: $19.99

Did you know that there are adults whose full-time jobs are being DJs? They work at dance clubs combining songs into mixes that make people want to dance and have a great time. If being the life of the party and controlling what music gets played sounds like fun to you, you might want to check out djay.

This app can turn you into a DJ by putting all the tools you need right on your iPad's screen. djay lets you use the songs already on your iPad to play music, record your mixes, add sound effects, and even scratch records using the onscreen record icons. If you really hit the big time, you can even hook up your iPad to a full-fledged sound system with some accessories.

Compose Electronic Masterpieces Using Looptastic HD

Cost: $14.99

These days, being a musician doesn't just mean knowing how to sing or play the guitar, piano, violin, or other instrument. Thanks to the amazing apps out there, some musicians go to their concerts with nothing more than a laptop or iPad and then use that to make music.

Do you love hip hop or electronic music? Create your songs using the more than 900 pre-made loops that come with Looptastic HD. Take those loops— and the drum, instrument, and sound effects parts they have—to compose songs that you love. You can also import and export your own loops. When you have a song you're proud of and want to share it, you can post it to the online song-sharing service SoundCloud.

A Comprehensive Tune-Up: Guitar Toolkit

Cost: $9.99

Most guitar players carry a lot of equipment with them in their guitar bags. From spare strings to extra picks, electronic tuners to chord charts, their bags can get pretty full. If you play guitar and have an iPad, though, you can leave a bunch of those things at home (though not backup strings; you should always have some of those).

Guitar players will find tons of useful tools and tips in this app. Want to learn different groups of chords or hear what each one sounds like? Guitar Toolkit has that. Need to tune your guitar? The app can help. Want a metronome to help you keep time? Guitar Toolkit offers that, too. The app even updates itself to work for you if you're a left-handed player. For a guitar player, this app has it all.

Tune Your Guitar Using Guitar Toolkit

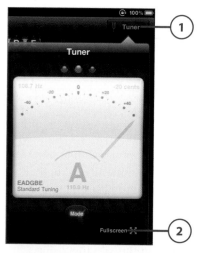

For the music you play to sound right, your guitar needs to be in tune. Each time you play it, it will go a little more out of tune, so you'll need to adjust it every so often. Here's how:

1. Open the app and tap Tuner.

2. For the easiest view of the tuner tool, tap Fullscreen.

3. Next, get ready to play your guitar, but don't hold down any of the strings. Play the string you want to tune.

4. The app hears the note using the iPad's microphone. It shows what note you're playing on the screen. Red bars mean that the string is out of tune. Green bars mean it's in tune. Keep playing the string and turning the knobs on the head of the guitar until the green bars are lit.

Art

As you've learned, the iPad is a great tool for helping you be creative. But more than that, it's also very helpful when it comes to learning about the great artists of the past. Some of the apps in this section help you learn art history using the work of some of history's greatest artists.

Get Painting Using ArtStudio for iPad

Cost: $4.99

Ready to create art using the same tools that professionals who use the iPad do? Then ArtStudio is an app you should check out (you should check it out if you're a beginner, too—it comes with useful tutorials for newbies). Paint and draw using 30 different pre-made brushes (or ones you create yourself), add text to images, and choose from dozens of special visual effects to give your creations zest. You can save your creations to your iPad, email them, or save them in Photoshop format and export them to a desktop or laptop computer for final tweaks.

A Bucket of Paintbrushes in One App: Brushes 3

Cost: Free

This powerful painting app for the iPad is a great tool for realizing your visions as digital paintings. It comes with 19 pre-made brush styles, lets you paint on one layer and then change its transparency so what's underneath shows through, and lets you share your creations online by saving them directly to Flickr. Another cool feature is that the app records your creation of a painting step by step and can replay it, so you can watch your own creation come to life one stroke at a time. Brushes has been used by professional painters to create high-profile magazine covers, so you'll be in good company when you use it!

Meet the Masters in Monet HD and Other Apps

Cost: $0.99

Art is about a lot more than just creating your own work. Many great artists are also great students of art and art history. Knowing the important works of the masters who have come before you helps make you a better artist. In this app, you can learn all about the work of the French Impressionist painter Claude Monet. The app features a tremendous collection of Monet's work from throughout his life, and it includes details about each painting, including when, where, and how it was painted, and where you can see the original today.

Monet isn't the only great painter who has an app devoted to him. The same developer has created similar apps for important artists like Vincent Van Gogh, Vermeer, Leonardo Da Vinci, Winslow Homer, Frida Kahlo, Mary Cassatt, Titian, and dozens of others. Each app includes similar information about the artist and pictures of their paintings. The apps are sold separately and cost $0.99 each.

Discovering Monet's Water Lilies

Monet painted many subjects and themes in his career, but his series of paintings of water lilies is one of his most famous and sought-after (a single painting from it sold for more than $70 million in 2008). The Monet HD app is packed full of his water lily paintings and information about them. To learn more, tap the app on your home screen and follow these steps:

1. Swipe up until you see the Water Lilies heading.

2. Tap Water Lilies.

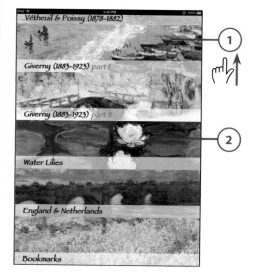

3. You see one painting from the Water Lilies series. At the bottom of the screen is the painting's title, the year it was made, the materials used to paint it, and where the painting is currently on display. To see the next painting, you can either swipe left to right or tap the arrow at the bottom of the screen.

4. To see a slideshow of the paintings in this section, tap the play button.

5. If the W icon is lit up, you can tap it to read an article about the paintings or period from Wikipedia. Tap Done to return to the painting gallery.

6. To return to the main menu to investigate other periods of Monet's life and work, tap Main.

Foreign Language

Depending on the school you go to and the grade you're in, the number and kind of foreign language classes you can take changes a lot. Although some schools offer just French and Spanish, at other schools or in later grades you might have the opportunity to learn other modern languages such as Italian or German, or ancient ones such as Latin. The wide variety of language apps on the iPad is especially helpful if you want to learn a language that your school doesn't offer; just get an app and start studying!

Veni, Vidi, Vici: Latin Phrases

Cost: $1.99

Because no one speaks it anymore, learning Latin may not seem very useful, but it was one of my favorite foreign languages to learn in school. Knowing Latin helped me understand ancient history and improved my knowledge and use of English (tons of English words have their roots in Latin). Latin is also useful to know if you're interested in religion or law.

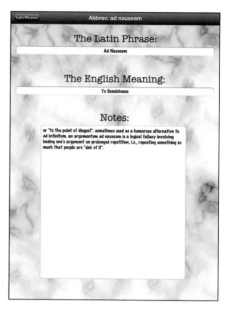

If you're taking Latin in school, check out the Latin Phrases app, which helps you learn more than 1,500 common—and not so common— phrases. Wow your friends and teachers with your knowledge of these fun, unusual sayings, or use them to do better in Latin class at school.

Living Language Apps

Cost: Free (Purchase the full course in-app for $19.99)

These apps have already shown up in this book for their French and Spanish versions, but they have apps for many other languages, too.

With lessons from Living Language, a long-established foreign-language education company, you can improve your grasp of a number of foreign languages. In the free versions of these apps, you get 11 lessons on speaking the language you're studying, including vocabulary- and grammar-building exercises, dialogues, and games. The full course is 46 lessons; you need to buy the other 35 lessons via in-app purchase to get the full set.

Languages covered in these apps include Chinese, German, Italian, and Japanese. Each app teaches a single language, so make sure to download just the one you want to learn.

Learn Up to 30 Languages with Language Coach

Cost: $9.99

As you learn more words in other languages, you'll be surprised how often you find that words that mean the same thing in different languages are pretty close to each other. Because there are similarities across languages, if you already know one foreign language, it can sometimes be easier to learn another.

Go way beyond just learning one or two languages with this app, which can help you get to know as many as 29 languages! From Spanish and French to Arabic, Chinese, or Farsi, you find them all in this app. Not only can you learn vocabulary in all of these languages, you can improve your pronunciation by hearing words and phrases spoken, and you can see cartoons illustrating common words and phrases that you might need to use in certain situations, such as at the airport.

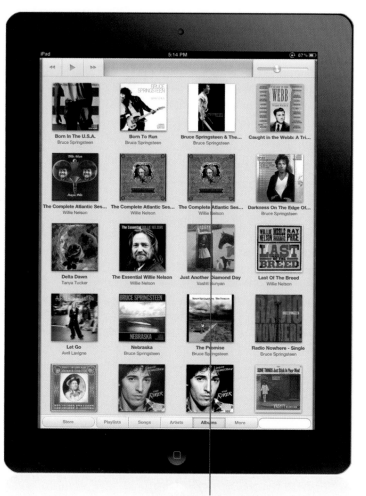

Bring thousands of your
favorite songs with you
wherever you go.

In this chapter, you learn all about where to get—and not get—music for your iPad. You also find out how to use the app that stores, organizes, and plays your songs: Music. The topics in this chapter include:

→ Getting music for your iPad
→ Using the built-in Music app
→ Making and using playlists
→ Protecting your hearing
→ Awesome apps

Rock Out: Music on the iPad

With all the cool Internet, chat, and FaceTime features on the iPad, don't forget that it's also a great music player! Whether you want to listen to your own music or stream songs over the Internet, the iPad puts thousands of your favorite songs right at your fingertips.

Getting Music for Your iPad

There are many things to keep in mind when looking for music for your iPad, such as whether it costs money, is it a download that you keep or a stream that you just listen to, and do you want to choose songs or listen to the radio? Luckily, there are a lot of options for where you can get music: CDs, online music stores, and apps are just some of the most common ways.

Ripping CDs

Even though the iPad doesn't have a slot to put a CD in, you can still play the songs from almost any CD on it. To do this, you have to use a computer to convert the CDs you have into MP3 or AAC files (this is known as "ripping" a CD) and then sync them to your iPad. To rip a CD, launch iTunes on your computer and then follow these steps:

1. Put the CD you want to rip in your computer's CD/DVD drive.

2. Depending on your iTunes settings, iTunes should automatically begin ripping the CD. If it doesn't, click the CD icon in iTunes.

3. Click Import CD.

4. When iTunes is finished (it take a few minutes to rip a CD), the songs are in your computer's iTunes library. To add the songs to your iPad, just sync. For a reminder on how to do that, check out "Setting Up and Syncing Your iPad" in Chapter 2, "Getting Started: Set Up and Sync Your iPad."

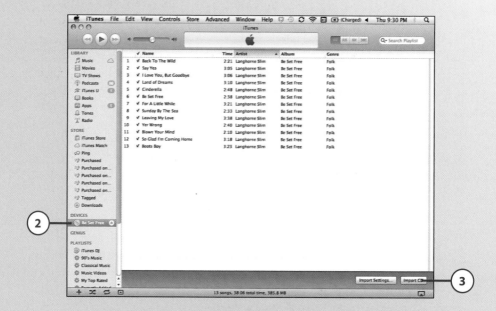

It's Not All Good

ONLY RIP YOUR OWN CDS

You should only rip CDs that you or your family own. Although it's possible to rip your friends' CDs, you shouldn't. Musicians get paid when people buy their CDs; if you rip a CD that you didn't pay for, musicians don't get paid—and that's not fair. They worked hard to make the CD, and making music is their job, so they should get paid for it.

iTunes and Other Online Music Stores

Aside from ripping CDs that you own, you can also ask your parents about buying songs at online music stores such as the iTunes Store or Amazon.com. Here are a few good music stores for iPad owners:

- **iTunes**—This is the main music store for all Apple products (including the iPhone and iPod). Your iPad comes with an iTunes Store app built in that lets you start shopping for music with just one tap. Songs at iTunes cost $0.69–$1.29, and albums cost about $7.99–$15.99. You need an iTunes account to buy the songs (you and your parents set one up back in the "Getting an Apple ID" section of Chapter 2, right?). When you buy a song, it downloads right to your iPad.

- **Amazon**—Amazon has about the same number of songs as iTunes and pretty much the same prices. One big difference is that Amazon puts music on sale more often, so if you pay attention, you can get the music you like for less than at iTunes. Just like with e-books, you need an Amazon account to buy here. You can't buy music from Amazon on your iPad; you need to buy it on your computer at www.amazon.com/mp3.

- **Google Play**—Google Play is a lot like Amazon. It also has a large selection and offers sales. You can download music from it, but one neat feature of Google Play is the ability to store your music on the Web, so that you can listen to it anywhere you have a web browser. (You can do this with Amazon, too.) There are apps that let you listen to your Google Play or Amazon songs right on your iPad, but to buy music, you have to use http://play.google.com/store/music.

- **Spotify**—Spotify isn't really a store; instead, it's kind of like the radio. You search for the song or album you want to hear and listen to it over the

Internet. If you want to use Spotify on your iPad, you need to pay $10 a month, which gives you unlimited listening, no ads interrupting the music, and the ability to listen to songs even when your iPad isn't on the Internet. You need your parents' permission to get a Spotify account, but if you have it, you can sign up at http://www.spotify.com.

Apps

A lot of apps give you free music. Most of them won't let you save the music they give you; instead, you use them to stream songs over the Internet to your iPad, much like listening to the radio (some of these apps *are* radio stations). Because you're streaming the music, you need to be connected to the Internet to use them. Even though you don't own the songs you hear in these apps, you can still listen to a ton of free tunes with them. Check out "Awesome Apps," later in this chapter, for some recommendations.

It's Not All Good

FILE-SHARING SERVICES

Another way to get free music is from file-sharing services such as LimeWire and BitTorrent. But even though free music may sound appealing, you shouldn't use file-sharing services.

First, they're not safe. Your computer can get viruses and other bad programs from using them. Second, in the vast majority of cases, it's stealing. You're getting music without paying for it, and the musicians who made it aren't getting paid either. This is no different from going into a store and just taking something and walking out without paying for it. You can do it, but you shouldn't, and there are severe penalties if you are caught. Some people who downloaded music from these services have been sued by record companies for thousands of dollars. There are ways grown-ups use these services responsibly, but unless your parents are showing you how to use them, just stay away.

Using the Music App

When you've added music to your iPad, there's no need to get a new app to listen to it. Just like with email, web browsing, and video chatting, your iPad comes with a built-in music player app. That app is called Music.

Playing Music

To play music on your iPad, tap the Music app to launch it and then follow these steps:

1. You see your music categorized by Album. Tap the album you want to listen to.

2. If you want to just listen to one song, tap that song. If you want to listen to the whole album, tap the first song and let it play.

3. To get rid of the song window, tap on the background of the app.

4. If you want to see your music organized in other ways, such as by artists or songs, you can tap the buttons along the bottom of the screen.

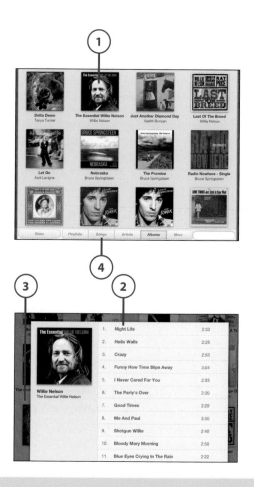

Music App Options and Controls

When music is playing, the row of buttons across the top of the app control the music, volume, and other features. Here's what they do:

- **Play/Pause/Forward/Back**—These are the most basic controls. To go to the last song you heard, tap the arrow that points left. To skip to the next song, tap the arrow pointing right. Tap the big button in the middle to pause a song and tap it a second time to start playing it again.

- **Album art**—You can tap the little square album so it enlarges to fill the screen. Tap the cover to show the controls, or tap a second time to hide them. When the cover is filling the screen, tap the arrow in the bottom left to go back to the last screen or the three lines in the bottom right to see all songs on the album.

- **Repeat song**—Like a song so much that you want to hear it over and over? Tap the button that looks like two arrows chasing each other to repeat the song. Repeat is on when the button is black. Tap it a second time to repeat the song just one time. Tap it one more time to turn repeat off.

- **Move forward/back in the song**—The long bar with the orange line in it lets you skip forward to another part of a song or hear a certain part again. It also shows how much of the song has played and how much is left. Tap and drag the orange line to move around in the song. When you let it go, the song starts playing at that point in the song.

- **Shuffle**—If you like to listen to songs in random order, tap the Shuffle button. It looks like two arrows crossing over each other. The button is black when it's on and white when it's off.

- **Genius Playlist**—Your iPad creates this playlist starting with what you're currently listening to. It adds other music to the playlist that it thinks will sound good together.

- **Volume**—Use this slider to control the volume (the right side of the slider is louder). You can also adjust the volume with the up/down button on the right side of the iPad.

- **Store**—To move over to the iTunes Store app to buy new music, tap the Store button.

Album art   Repeat song   Drag to move forward or backward in a song   Shuffle music   Genius playlist

Play/Pause

Drag to change volume

Store button   Choose how to sort music   Search

- **Bottom buttons**—Use the buttons along the bottom to choose how you see your music. Want to see it sorted by the name of the song? Tap Song. Tap Artists to see a list of all the different musicians and bands.

- **Search**—Want to search all the songs on your iPad? Tap in this box and type the song, artist, or album you're looking for.

Shuffling All Your Songs

If you want to shuffle all the songs on your iPad for a mega-mix, tap the Songs button at the bottom of the app. Tap the Shuffle button to turn on the Shuffle feature. Then tap the Play button, and rock on!

>>>Go Further

PLAYING MUSIC USING SIRI

Tapping the songs or albums you want to hear is only one way to play music on your iPad if you're running iOS 6. If you've got that version of the operating system, you can have Siri play music for you. Here's how:

1. Click and hold the home button until Siri pops up.

2. Tell Siri what you want it to play. Some examples of the kinds of music commands Siri understands are:
   - "Play song 'Crazy.'"
   - "Play Willie Nelson."
   - "Play some rap."

3. Siri will begin playing the music you asked for.

4. When music has started playing, Siri can also control that. Hold down the Home button to activate Siri and try commands like "pause" or "stop."

Making and Using Playlists

Do you want to put together a collection of your favorite songs in the order you like best? Want to make a mix of songs for a trip or to celebrate an event such as a birthday? Then you need a playlist. Here's how to make and edit one.

Making a Playlist

To make a new playlist, you first have to tap the Music app to open it. Then follow these steps:

1. Tap Playlists to begin creating a playlist.

2. Tap New to create a new playlist.

3. Give your playlist a name.

4. Tap Save.

5. A list of all the songs on your iPad pops up. Find a song that you want and tap the + next to the song to add it to the playlist. Repeat this for every song you want to put in the playlist.

6. When you've added all the songs you want, tap Done.

7. You see your playlist. You can delete songs by tapping the red icon and then Delete.

8. Rearrange the order of the songs by tapping and holding the three lines next to a song and dragging it to a new place in the list.

9. Add more songs by tapping Add Songs and choosing songs from your iPad, just like you did in step 5.

10. If you like the playlist you've made and want to keep it, tap Done to save it.

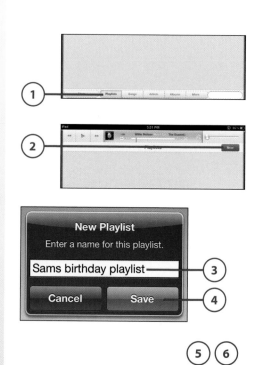

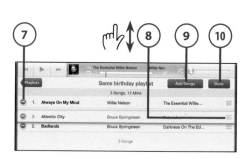

Syncing Playlists from Your Computer

The Music app isn't the only place you can make playlists. You can also create them in iTunes on your desktop or laptop computer. If you've done that, you can add those playlists to your iPad by syncing. For a reminder of how to sync, check out "Setting Up and Syncing Your iPad" in Chapter 2.

Deleting a Playlist

When you don't like a playlist anymore, the event you made it for has passed, or you just want to freshen things up, you can delete playlists. When you do, you're deleting only the playlist, not the songs in it, so you don't have to worry about losing your music.

1. To delete a playlist, display all your playlists by tapping the Playlist button in the Music app.

2. Tap and hold on the playlist you want to delete until an X appears on it.

3. Tap the X and the playlist is deleted. Make sure you really want to delete it, though—after you tap that X, the playlist is gone for good.

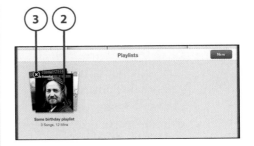

Listen Carefully: Protecting Your Hearing

You can hurt your hearing if you listen to music or TV too loud. Your parents probably warn you about this kind of thing all the time—and they're right. That might not seem very serious now, but you don't want to be wearing your grandmother's hearing aid when you're in college, do you?

Your iPad is a great music player, but you have to be careful about how you use it. If you're playing music through the iPad's speaker, there's not much to worry about—that speaker can only get so loud. But if you're listening to music through headphones, here are four things you can do to protect your hearing:

- **Not so loud!** This might seem obvious, but loud music is a very common source of hearing loss in young adults. Try to keep your iPad's volume at 75% or less of the maximum—and never listen to your iPad as loud as it can go.

- **Use the Volume Control setting.** It can be hard to remember to pay attention to your iPad's volume when you're enjoying a song, so let a setting called Volume Control do it for you. Volume Control sets a limit on how loud your iPad can get. To use it, just go to the Music section of the Settings app and tap Volume Limit. Move the slider to the middle of the line and then tap Lock Volume Limit. Your iPad asks you to create a four-digit code. Now, whenever you want to go past the limit, you have to remember that code.

- **Don't listen too long.** Giving your ears a break can help keep them from getting damaged. Every time you listen for an hour, take a 10–15 minute break.

- **Ditch the earbuds.** Your iPad comes with Apple's trademark white earbuds, but they're actually not that good for your hearing. Because the earbuds go right inside your ears, they're closer to your eardrums and can cause more damage. Get headphones that fit over your ears, instead of inside them.

Awesome Apps

Here are some great apps that you can use to listen to music, sports, and radio on your iPad for not much money (another reason to have an iTunes Allowance!) or even for free. Search for them at the App Store.

- **iHeartRadio**—You can listen to more than 750 live radio stations from across the U.S. with this app. It basically turns your iPad into a radio that works over the Internet and lets you listen to stations from far, far away instead of just those in your local area. **Free**

- **NPR for iPad and Music**—This is actually two different apps from the same organization. The NPR for iPad app helps you stay up to date on important news and events. It also gives you news articles to read, NPR podcasts, and the ability to listen to NPR stations from all over the country. The NPR Music app focuses just on podcasts, music, and live concerts. **Free**

- **Pandora and Last.fm**—These two apps take radio to the next level because they let you be the DJ. Instead of listening to a radio station created by someone else, they let you choose a song or musician you like and then play other songs that are similar so you can discover new music that you like. Pandora lets you listen to 40 hours a month for free, but Last.fm is unlimited. **Both are free**

- **Shazam and SoundHound**—Ever heard a song that you love but you don't know its name? These apps can help. Next time you're in that situation, just launch one of them, hold your iPad up to the nearest speaker, and, if you have an Internet connection, they tell you what the song is called, who sings it, and where to buy it. Kind of like magic, huh? **Shazam is free; SoundHound is free or $6.99 for a version without ads**

Use your iPad like a giant
camera and take detailed,
colorful pictures.

Switch between
the iPad's two
cameras.

Move one slider and
your iPad transforms
into a video camera.

The iPad's video and photo features give you ways to watch movies, take photos, and record your own videos. In this chapter, you find out about:

→ Watching videos from YouTube or iTunes

→ Using the iPad's cameras and apps

→ Using the Photos app

→ Being safe with photos and videos

→ Awesome apps for photos and videos

Lights, Camera, Action: Videos and Photos

Your iPad is a great tool for watching movies and TV shows anywhere you go (imagine how much more bearable summer car trips with your family will be when you have your favorite TV shows with you), but it does a lot more than that. Thanks to its two cameras and big screen, it also lets you create your own movies and take your own photos. Whether you're taking a picture of your friends, sending a video using Messages, or watching a cool new movie that you've rented from iTunes, your iPad makes using photos and videos easy.

Watching Videos from YouTube or iTunes

There are a lot of places online where you can watch videos, but two of the biggest are YouTube and iTunes. On YouTube, you can watch videos that people and companies post of all kinds of things, from people falling down to pets doing funny things to music videos and more. On iTunes, you can rent or buy movies and TV shows to watch on your iPad.

It's Not All Good

YOUTUBE ON IOS 6

If you're running iOS 6 on your iPad, you can skip the next few pages, which teach you how to use the built-in YouTube app. You can skip it because on iOS 6, the YouTube app doesn't exist. Apple had an agreement with Google, which owns YouTube, to include the app for a certain amount of time. When that time ended, the companies didn't renew the agreement and the YouTube app went away.

That doesn't mean you're locked out of YouTube, though. You can always watch videos at www.youtube.com and Google has released its own free YouTube app that you can get at the App Store.

If you have iOS 5, though, you still have the built-in YouTube app, so keep reading!

Finding Videos at YouTube

Enjoying videos at YouTube could hardly be easier on the iPad. That's because your iPad comes with a YouTube app preinstalled. To use it, first make sure you're connected to the Internet and then launch the YouTube app from your iPad's home screen.

When the app opens, it shows some featured items. To watch one of them, tap it. There's also a Search field that you can use to find specific videos.

There are a number of other ways to find YouTube videos, including searching for

- **Top Rated**—Tap this to see the videos that other YouTube users have given the most "thumbs up."

- **Most Viewed**—To check out the most popular YouTube videos, tap this.

- **Favorites**—If you've marked any videos as your favorites, tap this for a shortcut to them. To favorite videos, you have to have a YouTube account. You need to be 13 to get one, so check with your parents.

Tap a video to watch it.   **Search for a specific video.**

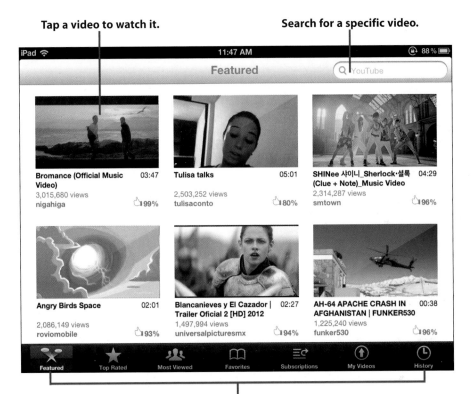

**User the options at the bottom of the
screen to look for specific types of videos.**

- **Subscriptions**—If you've subscribed to a regular series of videos, tap this
  to see the series and episodes.

- **My Videos**—If you've posted videos to YouTube, here is where you'll find
  them.

- **History**—Tap this to see a list of the YouTube videos you've watched
  recently.

Watching Videos at YouTube

When you find a video you want to watch, tap it to stream it to your iPad and then follow these steps:

1. To watch the video, tap the Play button. If you're using your iPad in Portrait mode (when the iPad is taller than it is long), you see a number of options.

2. Tap Add to save the video to your favorites.

3. Tap Share if you want to email or tweet a link to this video.

4. Tap Like or Dislike to place your vote for the video.

5. Tap Flag if you think the video you're watching is offensive or in some way breaks the law.

6. Tap enlarge to see the video in a larger size.

7. If you liked the video and want to watch others that are like it, tap Related and then tap another video.

8. Tap More From for other videos uploaded by the same person. Tap one to watch it.

9. Tap Comments if you want to leave a comment about the video.

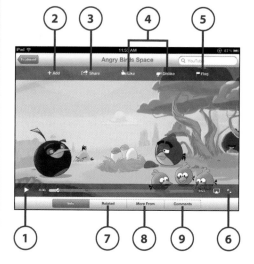

FULL SCREEN

When you tap the enlarge button, the YouTube video gets bigger, but it doesn't fill up the iPad's whole screen. You still see black bars along the top and bottom of the video. If you want to see the video in widescreen mode, turn the iPad to Landscape mode (where the iPad is longer than it is tall) and tap the Expand button. Now you can watch a large, great-looking, full-screen video.

Getting Movies from iTunes

YouTube is a great place to find short videos, but you're not going to find the latest blockbuster movies there. If you want to watch those, or other movies that you could see in the theater or on DVD/Blu-ray, one place you can go is iTunes.

iTunes lets you buy your favorite movies and store them on your iPad so you can watch them any time you want. It also lets you rent them for a lower price if you just want to watch them once.

Whichever you choose, remember a few things:

- Because both renting and buying costs money, your iTunes Allowance is charged or you need to ask your parents' permission before you buy or rent. You can learn more about setting up an iTunes Allowance in Chapter 2, "Getting Started: Set Up and Sync Your iPad."

- Movies you can watch on your iPad are really big and take a long time to download. Don't try to download them over 4G; that takes forever and you'll use up your monthly data quickly. Only buy or rent movies over Wi-Fi.

- Movies being big doesn't just affect your downloads; it also limits the number you can store on your iPad. A full-length movie can take up 1GB or more, whereas a song is usually 4MB to 8MB (1GB equals 1,024MB, so it takes a lot of songs to equal one movie). You can keep a lot fewer movies on your iPad than songs, e-books, or photos.

- You can rent or buy some movies from iTunes, but others only have one option or the other. When you tap a movie you're interested in, you can see which kind it is.

- Movies at iTunes have ratings just like movies at the theater. If your parents only let you see movies with certain ratings (for instance, no movies with R ratings), pay attention to that and follow their rules.

Buying or Renting Movies

The choice between renting and buying a movie has to do with more than just what the movie costs. If you bought the movie, it's yours forever. If you rented the movie, you have up to 30 days to watch it before the rental ends and the movie disappears from your iPad. After you start watching the movie, you have to watch the whole thing in 24 hours or else the rental ends and the movie disappears.

To rent or buy a movie, connect to Wi-Fi, launch the iTunes app from your iPad's home screen, and then follow these steps:

1. Tap the Movies button to go to the movies section of the iTunes Store.

2. You have three ways to find movies:

    - **Search**—Tap in the search box and enter the name of the movie you're looking for.

    - **Genre**—Tap the More button and then tap the type of movie you want to see, such as Adventure or Sci-Fi & Fantasy.

    - **Featured**—Tap one of the featured movies to learn more about it.

3. When you've found a movie you want to rent or buy, tap it to get more information. In the window that pops up, you see how much

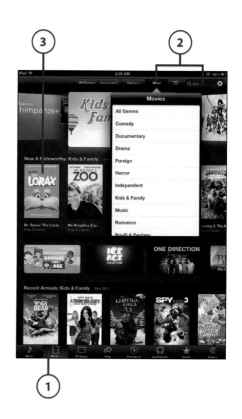

it costs to rent or buy the movie, whether you can get it in high-def, and information about the movie and the people in it.

4. To watch a movie's trailer, tap the Theatrical Trailer.

5. If you decide you want to rent or buy the movie, first decide if you want it in HD by tapping that option. If you're going to watch it on an HDTV or on the third-generation iPad, choose HD. Otherwise, you can choose SD (standard).

6. Decide if you want to rent or buy the movie. Tap the price for the option you want and then tap Buy Movie or Rent Movie. You might be asked to enter your Apple ID. Enter it and the movie starts downloading.

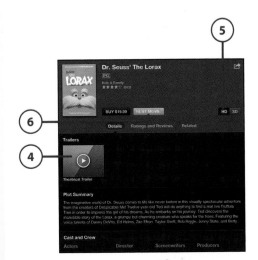

iTunes Works, Too

The iTunes app on your iPad isn't the only place you can rent or buy a movie or TV show. You can also use the iTunes program on your desktop or laptop computer. Finding and buying or renting movies through iTunes works basically the same way. After you've downloaded movies there, you can watch them on your computer or sync them to your iPad to watch while you're on the go.

Buying TV Shows from iTunes

Buying TV shows from iTunes is a lot like buying movies. (What about renting, you might be asking? Check out the section after this for the answer.) To do it, connect to a Wi-Fi network, tap the iTunes app to open it, and then follow these steps:

1. Tap the TV Shows button.

2. You have three ways to find the shows you want to watch:

    *   **Search**—Tap the box and type in the name of the show you want.

    *   **Genre**—Tap More and then pick the kind of show you want to watch, such as Animation or Kids, from the list.

    *   **Featured**—Tap one of the featured TV shows to learn more about it.

3. When you've found a show you're interested in, tap it to get more information. When you do this, sometimes you just get information on that particular episode of the show. Other times, you get details of the whole season of episodes or a set of seasons. If you get multiple seasons, tap the season you're interested in to get a list of episodes.

4. When the list of episodes comes up, you have a bunch of options. You can buy the episodes in that season all at once. To do that, tap the price and then tap Buy Season Pass.

5. You can choose to buy the episodes in high-def. If you're going to watch the show on an HDTV or the new iPad, pick HD. Otherwise, you can choose SD.

6. You can also choose to buy just one episode at a time. To buy a single episode, tap the price next to it and then tap Buy Episode.

7. To watch a preview of each episode, tap the screenshot next to the listing for that episode.

8. You might be asked to enter your Apple ID/iTunes account. Enter it, and the show starts downloading. Remember, just like with movies, buying a TV episode is charged either to your iTunes Allowance or your parents' iTunes account. If you don't have an iTunes Allowance, be sure to ask your parents before you buy.

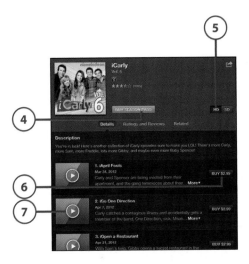

It's Not All Good

YOU CAN'T RENT TV SHOWS

Renting movies on your iPad is affordable and convenient. So renting episodes of TV shows should be just as good, right? Unfortunately, no. Apple doesn't allow you to rent TV shows from iTunes; you can only buy them. This isn't terrible, though, because most shows only cost a couple of dollars.

Watching the Movies and TV Shows You Got from iTunes

After you've rented or bought a movie or TV show from iTunes, you'll want to watch it. To find your purchase, you need to use the Videos app, which you can launch from your iPad's home screen. Then follow these steps:

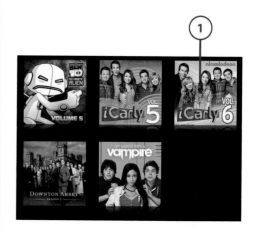

1. You see a list of all the videos you have on your iPad. Tap the one you want to watch.

2. Some more information about the video appears. If it's a TV show, you get a list of all the episodes you have downloaded from that season. Tap the video you want to watch or tap the Play button and it begins playing.

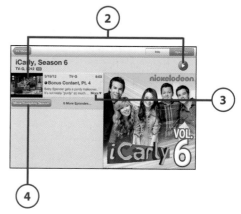

3. To read a longer description of the episode, tap More.

4. To jump to the iTunes Store to buy more episodes of this show or another, tap Show Complete Season.

Using the iPad's Cameras and Apps

The iPad is good for watching movies, but right above the screen that plays those movies is a camera, which means that your iPad can also take pictures. More than that, it can record videos.

Even though the two cameras on the iPad might look the same, they're not. The one above the screen that faces you when you use the iPad takes low-resolution pictures and video. The camera on the back takes higher-quality video and photos. Neither camera is as good as the cameras on the iPhone or standalone digital cameras, but they're both good enough for FaceTime (as you read about in Chapter 6, "Get Ready for Your Close Up! It's FaceTime!") and for taking photos or videos and sharing them with your friends and family.

Taking Photos

Taking photos with your iPad is simple. It all starts with opening the Camera app from your iPad's home screen and then following these steps:

1. The iPad's entire screen becomes like a camera's viewfinder. Whatever you see on the iPad's screen is what will be in your picture. Move the iPad so that you see what you want to take a picture of.

2. When you have your picture lined up perfectly, tap the Camera button. The photo you just took is saved to your iPad.

3. To view the photo, tap the tiny image of the photo in the bottom corner. This opens the Photos app and shows you the picture.

Tap this button to switch between the front- and rear-facing cameras.

Emailing Photos to Your Friends

Got photos you want to share with your friends? You can send them by email or using Messages. To learn how to send them using both of those apps, check out the "Sharing Pictures and Video" section later in this chapter.

Zooming In for Photos

When you use a standalone digital camera or the camera on a phone, there's often a zoom feature that lets you get closer to the image and get more detail in your picture. The iPad's back camera (but not the front one) has a zoom feature. To use it, tap the Camera app to open it and then follow these steps:

1. Tap the screen with your thumb and pointer finger together. Spread your fingers apart to pinch out.

2. A bar appears across the bottom of the screen. The more you pinch out, the more the camera zooms in. You can also drag this bar back and forth to adjust the zoom level.

3. To zoom back out, pinch your fingers in toward the center of the screen.

4. When you have the zoom where you want it, tap the Camera button to take the picture.

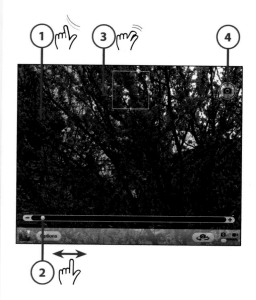

Focusing the iPad's Cameras

Another trick of using the iPad's cameras involves focus. Using the focus tool, you can make one part of your photo sharp and clear while the rest is fuzzy. This can help make the thing you're taking the picture of stand out. You can use focus with both the front and back camera. To use this feature, tap the Camera app to launch it and then follow these steps:

1. Move the iPad's screen to show the thing you want to take a picture of.

2. When you have the picture the way you want it, tap the item you want to focus on. A blue square appears where you tapped. That's where the focus will be (it might be hard to see on the iPad's screen, but it will be there in the picture).

3. If you want to move the focus, tap again somewhere else. If you're happy with that, tap the Camera button to take the photo.

›››Go Further

TAKING A SCREENSHOT

Did you know that you can also take pictures of what's on your screen at almost any time? These pictures, called screenshots, let you save things like game high scores or funny moments. To take a screenshot, press and hold the home button. Then press the power button once—do it fast or else Siri will pop up instead. The iPad's screen flashes, and you hear a camera sound. Check out your Photos app; the most recent photo is your screenshot.

Recording Video

The same cameras you use to take photographs are the ones you use to record videos with your iPad. In fact, you even use the same app! To record video, tap the Camera app to launch it and then follow these steps:

1. Move the slider from under the camera icon to under the video camera icon.

2. The Camera button changes to a red dot. When you want to start recording video, tap it.

3. You know you're recording video because the red dot blinks, and a timer appears onscreen that lets you know how long you've been recording.

4. When you're done recording the video, tap the blinking red dot again.

5. To view your video, tap the small version of it, just like you did with the photo in the earlier how-to. You can play the video in the Photos app.

Using Photo Booth

Your iPad comes preloaded with a fun app called Photo Booth. Photo Booth lets you apply all kinds of special effects to pictures to create cool, silly, and strange images. And after you've created them, you can share them with your friends. Tap the Photo Booth app from your iPad's home screen and follow these steps:

1. The screen is split into nine boxes, each one showing what a photo would look like with a different special effect applied to it. Tap the box that has the special effect you like.

2. You can tweak and change nearly all the special effects. For instance, if you choose Light Tunnel, you can move the location of the tunnel by tapping and dragging it. You can also make the tunnel smaller or bigger by pinching in and out.

3. Tap the Switch Cameras button to change which of your iPad's cameras Photo Booth is using.

4. After you've played with the special effect and created just the image you want, tap the Camera button to take the photograph.

5. When you've taken the photo, it appears on the screen in a small strip along the bottom. The pictures stay on the screen in this strip until you delete them. To see one of the pictures you've taken, just tap it.

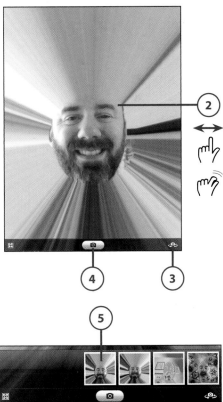

Modifying Effects

Tapping and dragging to move the location of the effect, and making them bigger or smaller by pinching, works in nearly all the effects. The only ones where it doesn't are Thermal Camera and X-Ray.

Deleting Photo Booth Photos

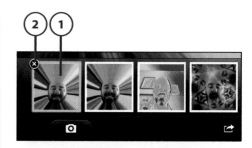

If you'd rather delete a photo than share it, open Photo Booth and then follow these steps:

1. Tap the photo you want to delete.

2. Tap the X that appears on it.

3. Tap Delete Photo. To delete more than one photo at a time, tap the Action box, select the photos you want to delete, tap Delete, and then Delete Selected Photos.

Using the Photos App

The Photos app is the place where everything you do with the iPad's cameras gets stored. Whether you're taking photos, recording videos, or making silly faces in Photo Booth, every time you tap the Camera button, the photo or video you take is saved in Photos.

Viewing Your Photos

Looking at the photographs you've taken with your iPad's cameras is simple. Open the Photos app from your iPad's home screen and follow these steps:

1. You see a screen full of small versions of your photos. You can swipe up and down to see more photos.

2. When you find one you want to see at full size, tap it.

3. Swipe from right to left to see the next photo. To see the previous one, swipe left to right.

4. Tap the screen and then tap Photos to go back to the list of photos.

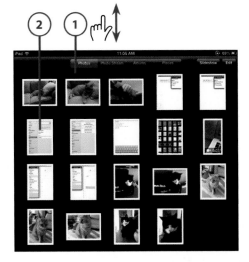

Watching Your Videos

Watching the videos you have in Photos is similar to looking at photos. To begin, tap the Photos app and then follow these steps:

1. Find your videos on the overview screen. You can identify them because the video camera icon and their length appear on the small version. Tap the one you want to watch.

2. Tap the Play button in the center of the screen or the one at the top to watch the video.

3. Tap and drag the bar at the top of the screen to move backward and forward in the video. The video starts playing again wherever you let go of the bar.

4. Tap the screen and then tap Photos to go back to the list of photos and videos.

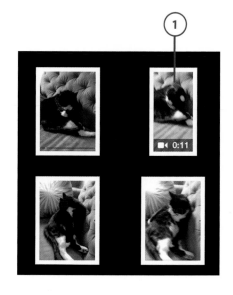

Deleting Photos

You're going to take a lot of photos
and videos that you don't want to
keep. That's just the way it is with
photography. Even professionals take
way more pictures than they end up
using. To delete photos or videos,
start by tapping Photos and then follow these steps:

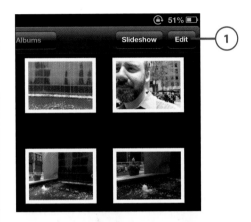

1. On the overview screen, tap Edit.
   (In iOS 5, tap the Action box
   instead. The other steps are the
   same.)

2. Tap each photo or video you
   want to delete. A blue check mark
   appears on the ones you select.

3. Tap Delete.

4. Tap Delete Selected Photos.

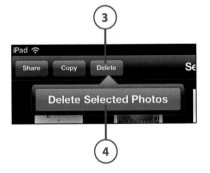

Deleting One Photo or Video at a Time

You can also delete photos and videos one at a time. In that case, tap
the photo or video to view it and
then tap the screen to bring up the
options. Tap the trash can icon and
then tap Delete Photo or Delete
Video. The video will be gone.

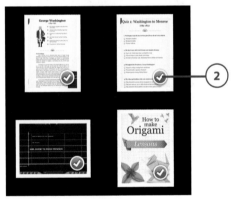

Working with Photo Albums

Unless you change things, all your photos and videos are stored in the same photo album—Camera Roll. That makes it easy to know where everything is all the time, but you might want to store similar photos and videos together in their own albums. For instance, you might want all family photos in one place, all photos of your friends in another, and videos from your school plays or sports in a third.

For that, you need to know how to create and work with new photo albums.

Creating a New Album

To create a new album, start by tapping the Photos app to open it and then follow these steps:

1. Tap Albums. If you haven't created an album before now, all you see here is the Camera Roll album.

2. Tap +.

3. Give your new photo album a name.

4. Tap Save to create the album.

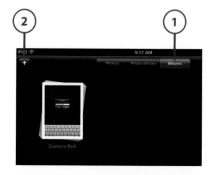

5. Decide what photos or videos
   from Camera Roll will go in the
   new album. Tap each photo or
   video you want to move. A blue
   check mark appears on them to
   let you know you've chosen them.

Photo Album Options

If you want to add all the photos in Camera Roll to your new
album, tap Select All Photos. You
can also leave a photo album
empty for later use. Do that by
tapping Done.

6. Tap Done when you've selected
   all the ones you want to move.

7. The new album—with the selected photos and videos in it—is
   created. Tap it to view the photos
   and videos you put in it.

Select Photos and Then Create Album

You can also choose the photos
first and then create an album
after, if you want. Tap the Edit box
(or, in iOS 5, the Action box) and
select the photos you want to add
to the new album. Then tap Add
To and Add to New Album. Give
the album a name, tap Save, and
the new album is saved with the
photos in it.

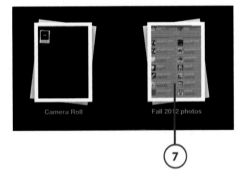

Moving Photos to Photo Albums

After you've created new photo albums, you can add pictures or videos to them anytime you want. Open the Photos app from your iPad's home screen and follow these steps:

1. Tap Camera Roll.

2. Tap the Edit button (or, in iOS 5, the Action box) in the upper-right corner of the screen (not pictured).

3. Tap the photos or videos you want to move. A blue check mark appears on each one you've selected.

4. Tap Add To.

5. Tap Add to Existing Album (in iOS 5, tap Add to Existing Photo Album).

6. Tap the photo album you want to move the pictures or videos to. The photos jump to it.

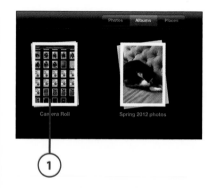

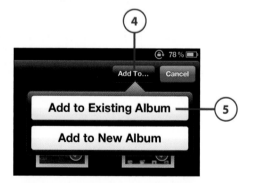

Deleting Photo Albums

Sometimes you decide to reorganize your photos and videos and, when you do, you want to delete some photo albums. To do this, tap Photos to open it and then follow these steps:

1. Tap Albums.

2. Tap Edit.

3. Tap the X that appears on the album or albums you want to delete. You can delete any albums you created, but you can't delete Camera Roll.

4. Photos asks if you really want to delete the album. An important thing to know here is that *deleting an album doesn't delete the photos in it.* They just move back to the Camera Roll, so feel free to delete albums.

5. The photo album you selected is deleted. Tap Done.

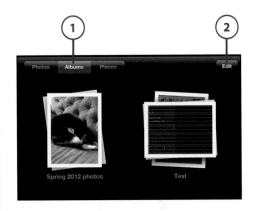

Sharing Pictures and Video

Having photographs and videos on your iPad is great for remembering fun times or for laughing over with your friends and family. But what if you want to share those memories or laughs with friends and family who don't live close enough to see them in person? Then you need to use the Internet to share them.

Sharing by Email

Email is one of the easiest ways to share your photos or videos with other people. To do it, begin by tapping the Photos app to open it and then follow these steps:

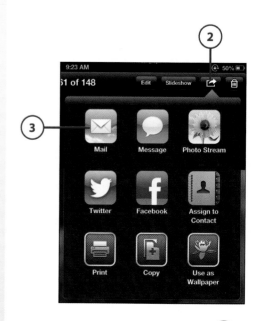

1. Tap the photo or video you want to share.

2. Tap the Action box to open it.

3. Tap Mail.

4. A new email opens with the photograph or video attached to it. Fill out the email like you normally would—by addressing it, adding a subject line and message, and so on—and then tap Send.

Sharing More Than One Photo at a Time

You can also share more than one photo or video in a single email. To do so, tap Edit (or the Action box in iOS 5) from the main Photos app screen and tap each photo you want to email. A blue check mark appears on the photos you've selected. Tap Share and Mail.

It's Not All Good

EMAIL SIZE

There's almost always a limit on the size of the email you can send through the email accounts you have set up on your iPad. The limit is there to prevent someone from sending 100 pictures at once and clogging up the computers that deliver email so no one else's messages can go through. Don't send more than three or four pictures or one or two short videos in one email.

Sharing with Messages

Sometimes you need to share something right away and email isn't fast enough. In that case, you might want to use Messages. Messages is great for texting and chatting, but it's also a great way to give your friends and family who have iPads or iPhones a glimpse into where you are or what you're doing right now. For more about Messages, check out "Using Messages" in Chapter 5, "Talk to Me: Texting, Chatting, and Email."

To share using Messages, tap the Photos app to open it and then follow these steps:

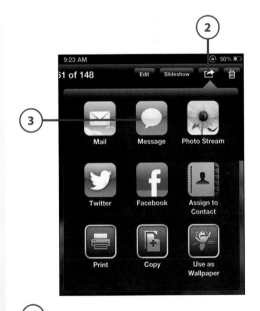

1. Tap the picture or video you want to share.

2. Tap the Action box to open it.

3. Tap Message.

4. A new message appears with the photo or video in it. Address the message like you would any other normal message.

5. Enter any text you want to include.

6. Tap Send when you're ready to send the message.

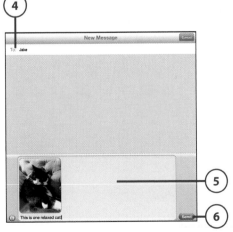

Send One Image at a Time

Just like with emails, you can send more than one photo or video in a message, but because people might be getting them on their cell phones, and cell phones often download things more slowly than computers, it's better to send one at a time. And don't try to send long videos; they take too long to download and use up the recipient's monthly data plan.

It's Not All Good

DON'T SHARE ON TWITTER OR YOUTUBE

Email and Messages aren't the only ways that your iPad has to share photos and videos. The Photos app includes YouTube for videos, Facebook (in iOS 6), and Twitter as sharing options. You probably like watching YouTube videos, so it might be tempting to post some of your own there. Same thing for Twitter or Facebook: It can be a lot of fun for talking to people, and sometimes people post their photos. But, for now at least, you shouldn't post your photos or videos to any of those sites. Sharing photos and videos can be fun, but there can be a lot of downsides, too. If you want to do this, talk to your parents to get their permission and see if they think it's okay for you to do.

Be Safe: With Photos and Videos

Sharing pictures and videos online with your friends and family is a lot of fun, but there are some rules you should follow to keep yourself safe and to keep from hurting other people's feelings:

- Never send photos of yourself, your friends, or your family to people you don't know in real life, even if they ask you to. If someone asks you to send them your picture, tell your parents right away.

- Never send your photos or videos to someone who you know only online, even if it feels like you really do know them. Again, if someone asks, tell your parents.

- If a stranger or someone you only know online sends you a photo or video, don't open it, or only open it when your parents are around.

- Don't take embarrassing pictures of yourself, your friends, or your family and then share them or post them online. Nobody likes to be embarrassed, especially where so many people can see.

- Don't post mean pictures or videos of people online to make fun of them. That could hurt their feelings, and you wouldn't like it if they did that to you.

- After you share a photo or post it online, it's out of your control. That can mean that something you thought was fun to post now will bother you or someone else later, but you might not be able to do anything about it. So, before you post or share anything, make sure to consider the consequences.

Awesome Apps

The basic apps for photo and video that come with the iPad are great for doing things that are, well, basic. But if you want to get really cool—by creating photos or videos that look old, or have special effects, or get shared in different ways—you should check out these awesome apps.

For Photography

- **Adobe Photoshop Express**—Photoshop is the program that professional photographers use to transform their raw images into beautiful finished photographs. Photoshop Express is the iPad version. It lets you rotate images, add special effects, tweak the colors and brightness of your images, and much more. **Free**

- **Color Splash for iPad**—Have you ever seen those cool pictures that are all black and white except for one part of the picture that's in rich, lively color? Color Splash helps you create that kind of picture. It takes any picture on your iPad, makes it black and white, and then lets you paint colors onto it using your finger. Save your creations on your iPad or share by email. You can also print your pictures or send them as postcards. **$1.99**

- **FX Photo Studio HD**—FX Photo Studio is a powerful app like Photoshop Express except that it offers more features and options. It comes with hundreds of prebuilt styles you can apply to your pictures to make them black and white, look like they were taken with vintage cameras, look like x-rays, and much more. Each image style has different settings that you can tweak so no two pictures ever look the same. **$1.99**

- **Pocketbooth**—Pocketbooth takes the classic photo booth (not the app, the box that you sit in to have your picture taken) experience and puts in on your iPad. With it, you hold your iPad still and the app takes four quick pictures of you and your friends. Then it saves the pictures on a strip, one picture on top of the other. You control special effects on the pictures, how long the app waits between each one, and much more. Share these neat vintage-style pictures by email. **$0.99**

For Making Videos

- **8mm HD**—8mm HD does for video what apps such as FX Photo Studio HD do for photos. When you use this app, you can take video that looks like it was recorded using old-fashioned cameras that were common in the 1920s, 1960s, or 1970s, or that has all kinds of special effects that make it look cool. Your iPad videos have never looked as good as they do when you take them with 8mm HD. **$1.99**

- **iMovie**—Want to take a video you've recorded on your iPad and make it look like a real, professional movie? Then you need iMovie. Not only does iMovie let you cut out parts of the recording that you don't like, but it lets you rearrange scenes, add music from your music library and sound effects, apply special effects, and even put text onscreen for your movie's title and stars. **$4.99**

For Watching Videos

- **Cartoon Network**—Do you ever watch the shows on the Cartoon Network? From *Ben 10* to *Thundercats*, *Generator Rex* to *Looney Tunes*, Cartoon Network is packed full of great cartoons—and so is this app. It's a free way to watch your favorite Cartoon Network shows you might have missed, or you just want to see again. To watch all of its videos, your parents have to check to make sure it works with your cable company, but if it does, it's your ticket to a ton of great cartoons. Even if it doesn't work with your cable company, there are still some videos you can watch. **Free**

- **Netflix**—You know Netflix: The company sends DVDs to your house or lets you stream videos over the Internet to your TV, DVD player, or video game system. Well, now you can add your iPad to the list of devices where you can watch your favorite shows and movies. If your family has a Netflix account, just grab this app and you can watch Netflix wherever you are. Make sure to connect to Wi-Fi and not 4G, though. Streaming this much video really uses up your data plan. **Free**

Compare your scores with other players worldwide or challenge your friends head-to-head in your favorite games using Game Center.

In this chapter, you learn that the iPad isn't just for homework and music, email, and chatting (though I bet you knew that). It's also an awesome device for playing video games! In addition to just playing games yourself, the iPad lets you challenge friends over the Internet and compare your high scores against people all over the world. In this chapter, you learn about the following topics:

16

→ Getting games

→ Using Game Center

→ Being safe on Game Center

→ Awesome Apps

It's Play Time: Gaming on the iPad

From its big, beautiful screen to its thousands of great games, from Internet features designed for gaming to the ability to control games by tilting and moving, the iPad was born to be a great gaming machine. By learning how to take advantage of its gaming features, you can make your friends who don't have iPads jealous.

Getting Games

You can play two types of games on the iPad: apps and web-based games. Just like with any other app that works on the iPad, you get games through the App Store app that comes installed on your iPad. Web-based games can be played using the Safari app, although there are some limits on what games work on the iPad.

It's Not All Good

ONLINE GAMES

As mentioned in the section "Why Some Sites and Videos Don't Work" in Chapter 4, "Surf's Up! Using the Internet," the iPad doesn't run a technology called Flash, which is used for many videos and online games. Because of that, you can't use an iPad to play any game that needs Flash to work—and, unfortunately, this blocks you from playing some of the most popular online games.

If there's an online game you want to play, it's worth trying to play it on your iPad to see if it works. If it doesn't, check the App Store—a lot of web-based games have app versions that work on the iPad.

It's no fun to be blocked from playing certain games because the iPad can't run them, but luckily you can find tons of great games at the App Store that will keep you entertained for a long, long time.

Downloading Games at the App Store

Getting games at the App Store works pretty much the same way you get any other kind of app. To download some great games, open the App Store from your home screen and follow these steps:

1. Tap More.

2. Tap Games, and then tap All Games.

3. On the main games page, you have a number of options. If you want to search for a specific game, enter its title into the search field.

4. Tap See All to browse a list of games in categories like New and Noteworthy, What's Hot, and Top Apps.

5. If one of the featured games interests you, just tap it to go directly to its page. Every game's info page contains screenshots of the game and reviews by other people who have played it.

6. To download the game, tap Free or the price, if you have to pay for it. Then tap Install App (if it's free) or Buy App (if it's paid). Just like when you buy anything at iTunes, if it costs money, either it will be charged to your iTunes Allowance or you should ask your parents' permission before you buy.

Apple ID

You may be asked to enter your Apple ID. Log in and your new game begins downloading right away.

IPAD JOYSTICKS AND CONTROLLERS

Even though the iPad's multitouch interface and motion-awareness technology make controlling games easy and fun, for some games you'll want to use the old classics—joysticks and controllers. Lucky for you, there are a lot of options: Some controllers, such as the Atari Arcade, plug into the iPad's dock connector; others, such as the ION iCade, connect using Bluetooth; and others, such as the Fling joystick, sit right on the iPad's screen. iPad game controllers can cost anywhere from $10 to $50 or more.

Watch Out for Surprise Purchases

In-app purchases are items you can buy inside apps that give you extra content, features, or tools to use in the app. iPad games are full of in-app purchases, sometimes when you don't even realize that's what they are. Usually, however, games tell you specifically if you are about to spend money with messages like the one shown here.

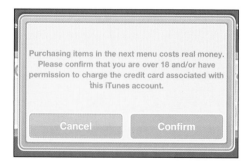

Some of the most common kinds of in-app purchases for games are extra gold or currency for your character to spend, new costumes or abilities for your character, or access to extra levels. These things are really attractive, and might even help you get past difficult parts of games where you're stuck, but you have to be really careful not to buy a lot of things for your games unless you mean to.

Making in-app purchases isn't so bad if you have an iTunes Allowance. In that case, you can make purchases until your allowance is used up for the month.

The only real downside to that is that you might spend money you didn't mean to and thus won't have it to spend at iTunes for the rest of the month.

What's worse, though, is when you use your parents' iTunes account to buy things. In that case, you could accidentally spend $20, $50, or even $150 without realizing it and cost your parents a lot of money. That's why you have to watch out for in-app purchases. Fortunately, many games warn you before you buy.

Using Game Center

Only one gaming app comes preinstalled on your iPad, but it's a useful one: Game Center.

Game Center isn't a game, and it doesn't help you get better at any of your games. Instead, it's a tool that helps you use the Internet to get the most out of the games you play on your iPad. Game Center lets you connect with your friends online, compare your high scores against all Game Center users worldwide, track the tasks and goals (called Achievements) you've completed in each game, and challenge other users to head-to-head matches of your favorite games.

Getting a Game Center account is probably the easiest thing you'll have to do in this book. To get one, you don't have to do anything at all. Your Apple ID is your Game Center account! Just tap the Game Center app on your iPad's home screen to open it, sign in, and you'll be ready to start playing.

Game Center Works with Macs, Too

Game Center originally only worked on iPads, iPhones, and iPod touches—not anymore. Thanks to Mac OS X 10.8 (aka Mountain Lion), Mac users now have the ability to use Game Center, too—though not all games that work on Mac work on the iPad and vice versa. So, if you or your friends have Macs running OS X 10.8, you can see all your achievements and high scores, and you can challenge friends to play your favorite games on both iOS and the Mac.

It's Not All Good

GAME CENTER COMPATIBILITY

Game Center is a pretty cool technology, but not every game uses it. The people who make each game have to decide to include Game Center features in their apps for you to be able to track your scores or challenge your friends using it. The only games you can use with Game Center are ones that have the Game Center icon on their pages in the App Store.

One of the best features of Game Center is that it lets you challenge other people over the Internet to play games. It's a completely different experience from playing games by yourself.

For this to work, you have to have a game that supports this capability. Not all iPad games, not even all Game Center–compatible games, let you challenge other players head-to-head; only some do. Games that do support it talk about that feature in different ways. They might call it multiplayer, online, head-to-head, challenge, or versus mode. You'll need to check your favorite Game Center games to see if they let you play against your friends.

Adding an Existing Photo to Your Game Center Account

You can add a photo to your Game Center account to make it easier for your friends to find, and challenge, you. If you want to do this, get your parents' permission first. Your parents might not want you to post pictures of yourself online. If they say it's OK, or if you want to post a picture of your pet or a graphic, you can add a photo by tapping Game Center to open it and make sure you're signed in. Then follow these steps:

1. Tap the photo icon.

2. Tap OK in the window that pops up to continue.

3. If you have a photo or picture already on your iPad that you want to use, tap Choose Photo and then tap Camera Roll.

4. Tap the photo you want to use.

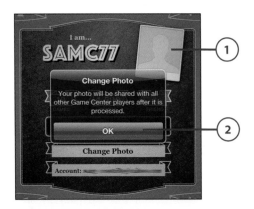

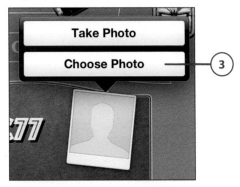

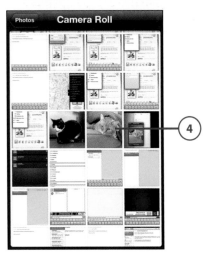

5. You can move the photo by tapping and dragging.

6. Zoom in on the photo by unpinching.

7. When the photo looks the way you want it, tap Use.

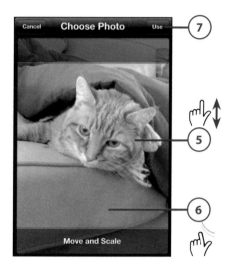

Connecting with Friends

Game Center lets you play games head-to-head over the Internet with your friends and family. In order to do that, though, you first have to connect to those friends on Game Center. (For those of you whose parents let you use Facebook, this is a lot like "friending" to connect with people on there.) To connect to your friends, tap the Game Center app to open it and then follow these steps:

1. Tap Friends.

2. Tap Add Friends.

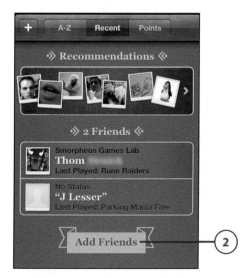

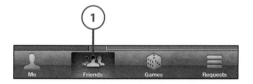

3. Enter the email address used by the person you want to friend on Game Center or their Apple ID. You can also enter their Game Center username or tap the + icon to select someone from your Contacts app.

4. Use the included friend request message or write your own.

5. When you're ready, tap Send. Your friend receives an email (if you choose their email in step 3) or a message through Game Center (if you choose their Game Center nickname) notifying them of your request. They can then decide to accept or reject your request.

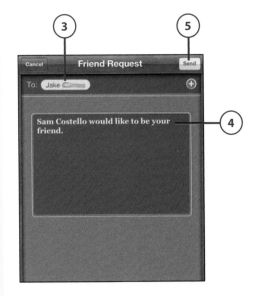

Handling Requests

When other people send you friend requests through Game Center, you get emails or Game Center notifications letting you know. To accept or reject the friend requests, open Game Center and tap Requests. On that screen, you see all the friend requests you've been sent but haven't yet done anything with. Accept or ignore the requests as you want, and you can start playing against your friends right away.

Checking Your Scores and Achievements

Every time you're connected to the Internet and play a Game Center–compatible game on your iPad, Game Center keeps track of your scores and achievements and posts them to your account. To check out your progress, tap the Game Center app to open it and then follow these steps:

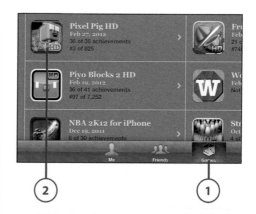

1. Tap Games to see a list of all your compatible games.

2. Tap the game for which you want to see your scores and achievements.

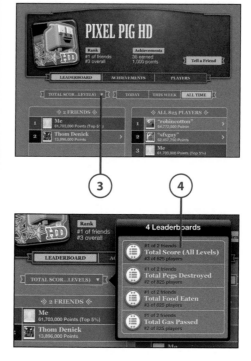

3. On the main screen, you see where you rank compared to your friends and against all players. To see how your scores in particular sections or versions of the game stack up, tap the category menu next to the date.

4. Tap one of the options that appears. These options are always specific to the game you've selected.

5. To see all your achievements within the game, tap Achievements. Not all games have achievements, so you might not see this option every time.

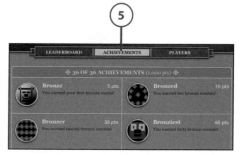

Can Your Friends Beat Your Scores? Issue Challenges

Proud of your high scores and achievements in Game Center and want to see if your friends can do better? Then you need to issue Challenges. These are messages that you can send to your friends to challenge them to beat your score or achievement in Game Center–compatible games. You need iOS 6 to issue Challenges. If you're running iOS 6, here's what you do:

1. Open Game Center and tap the game you want to challenge your friend in.

2. To challenge a friend to beat your high score, tap Leaderboard.

3. Tap your friend's name.

4. If your score is higher than your friend's, tap Send Challenge. If Send Challenge isn't active, your score is lower.

5. You see the person you're challenging and the score you want them to beat. Add a message ("Think you can beat me? Good luck!") and tap Send.

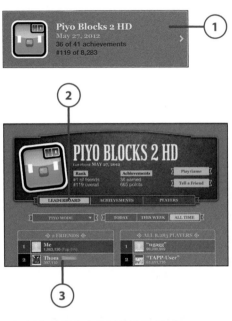

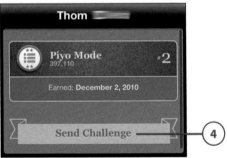

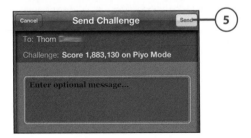

Issuing Achievement Challenges

You can also challenge your friends to top your achievements.

1. Open Game Center and tap the game you want to challenge your friend in.

2. Tap Achievements.

3. Find the achievement you want and tap it. If Challenge Friends is active, tap it. If it's not, your friends have achieved this goal and you haven't.

4. You see the person you're challenging and the score you want them to beat. Add a message ("No way you're getting this far!") and tap Send.

Challenging People to Games

For the games that let you play against someone via the Internet, you don't actually use Game Center directly to challenge someone else to a game. Instead, you do it from within the game you want to play. Although many games are similar in how they do this, the process varies from game to game. Here's how to challenge a friend in the popular game Fruit Ninja:

1. Find the multiplayer, online, or head-to-head option in the game and tap it.

2. To play a friend, tap Invite Friends.

3. Select the friend you want to play.

4. Tap Next.

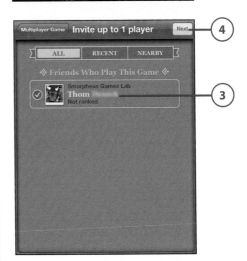

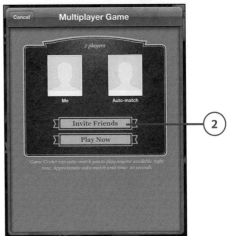

5. To invite your friend to play, either use Game Center's prewritten message or write your own.

6. Tap Send. The game lets you know when your friend has accepted your invitation and you start your match.

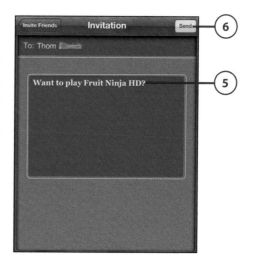

Hotseat Games

Another multiplayer option is called the hotseat game. It's called that because you and your friend play on the same iPad, passing it back and forth when you're on the hotseat, aka when it's your turn. To play a hotseat game, you don't use Game Center. Instead, just look for the head-to-head or versus option in the game you want to play with your friend and select that.

Be Safe: On Game Center

Using Game Center to play games against other people is relatively safe. That's because there's really no way for people to contact you through Game Center except to play games. It's only if they ask to do something other than play that you need to take precautions. Here are some rules of thumb:

- Never give your full name, address, phone number, or where you go to school to someone on Game Center.

- If someone on Game Center asks you to send them a picture of yourself, your family, or your friends, don't do it.

- If someone you don't know sends you a message through Game Center, tell a parent, teacher, or other adult you trust right away.

Check out the tips in "Be Safe: Texting, Chatting, Using Social Media, and Emailing" in Chapter 5, "Talk to Me: Texting, Chatting, and Email," for other good rules to follow.

Awesome Apps

Tens of thousands of games are available in the App Store. Whether you like racing or flying, fighting or adventure, puzzles or board games, or any other type of game, the App Store has it. With so many to choose from, you'll find lots of games you'll love. There's no way to list all the available games, of course, but here are some suggestions for games you might enjoy:

- **Angry Birds HD**—Perhaps the most famously addictive game on the iPad. The concept is simple: You put birds in a slingshot and shoot them at pigs hiding in buildings to try to knock them down. Sounds easy, but with complicated challenges and birds with different powers, it's a challenge you'll never want to stop playing. If you like this one, be sure to check out Angry Birds: Space as well! **Free or full version $0.99**

- **Cut the Rope HD**—This is another super popular, addictive game. In it, a box has been delivered to you that contains a monster named Om Nom. To take care of Om Nom, you have to feed him the only thing he eats: candy. In the game's 250 levels, you swipe across the screen to drop candy into Om Nom's mouth while also keeping it safe from other creatures that want to grab it. **Free lite version or $1.99**

- **Fruit Ninja HD**—This is one of my favorite games. In it, pieces of fruit are thrown into the air and you have to swipe across the screen to chop them into slices with your ninja sword. You earn extra points for combinations, special fruit, and multiple slices. You can play against the game, versus a friend on your iPad, or head-to-head using Game Center. Once you start chopping this fruit, you won't want to stop. **$2.99**

- **Minecraft – Pocket Edition**—Want to be the master of your own world? Minecraft lets you build and maintain whatever structures and places you can think of. You choose to just build and fly through the world you create, or you can play a version that requires you to collect resources to deal with hunger and health. For free, you get the first 18 levels, but you can't save your game. To get the other 18 levels and the ability to save, buy the paid version. **Free or $6.99**

- **Plants versus Zombies HD**—Anyone who knows anything about zombies is aware that they just keep shuffling toward you unless you stop them. In this hit game, a horde of zombies is approaching your house and you have to stop them from reaching it by flinging plants at them. Lucky for you, each different plant has different powers to repel the undead. Battle 26 kinds of zombies over 50 levels and find out if you have a green thumb when it comes to zombie combat. **$6.99**

- **Real Racing 2 HD**—Like fast cars and racing? Then you'll want to check out Real Racing 2. In it, you get to drive 30 different real-life sports cars through 15 real-life racing locations. You can race against the game or challenge up to 15 other players using Game Center. One of the coolest things is that you control your car by tilting your iPad—just like turning a steering wheel. **$6.99**

- **Ticket to Ride**—This is the iPad version of the popular and engrossing strategy board game about railroads. In it, you try to build a railroad network that links together various cities. The iPad version lets you play against the game, versus your friends on the same iPad, or use Game Center or other online tools to play against your friends on Macs, PCs, or other iOS devices. **$6.99**

- **Touch Pets Dogs 2 and Touch Pets Cats**—Do you love cats or dogs? Would you like a virtual pet to take care of and play with? Then these two games—one for dogs, the other for cats—are for you. In them, you adopt a puppy or kitten and then teach them tricks, play games with them, wash and dress them, and take them on missions. You can even have your pet play with your friends' virtual pets from their iPads.

  Free

Pet Bob by rubbing him with your finger

Learn tips for making your battery last longer.

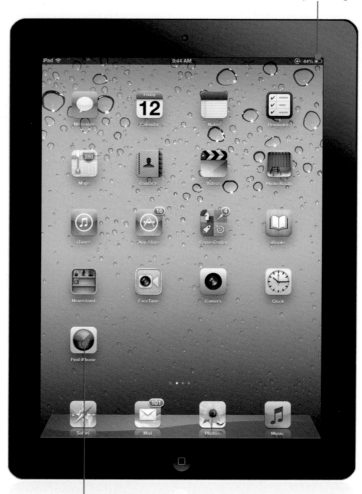

Discover how to get a lost or stolen iPad back with Find My iPad.

In this chapter, you find out what to do when something goes wrong with your iPad. Most of the time, the iPad works pretty smoothly, and you rarely have problems. But when problems do happen, you don't want to be stuck asking someone for help and then waiting for them to help you. After you read this chapter, you won't have to because this chapter covers:

→ Restarting a frozen iPad

→ Making your battery last longer

→ Finding a lost iPad

→ Saving your iPad if it gets wet

→ Backing up your iPad

→ Redownloading purchases from iCloud

Fixing Problems Yourself

Some problems that can happen to your iPad are too serious or too complicated to try to fix yourself. If your screen cracks or the speaker stops working, don't try taking the iPad apart; instead, ask your parents for help. (Chances are they'll need to contact Apple at an Apple Store, on the Web, or by phone.) But you don't want other problems to prevent you from doing things you want to do, such as playing a game or browsing the Web, or things you need to do, such as your homework. This chapter helps you figure out how to solve some of the most common iPad problems.

Restarting a Frozen iPad

Sometimes your iPad might not work the way you expect it to, or it has a problem you can't figure out. There are also some rare circumstances when your iPad just won't work at all; its screen has frozen, the buttons are locked, and nothing you touch or swipe works. When any of these things happen, restarting your iPad is a smart first step to try to fix it. A restart doesn't fix every problem, but you'll be surprised how many problems it does fix.

Restarting Your iPad

You can always try to turn the iPad on and off, as described in the section "Turning an iPad On and Off" of Chapter 1, "Please Touch: How the iPad Works." If your iPad is frozen and doesn't respond when you touch the screen or press the Home button, then hold down the power button until a power off slider appears. When it does, slide it to the right.

A wheel appears in the center of the screen until the iPad shuts down. When the iPad is off, hold down the power button until the white Apple logo appears on the screen. When it appears, release the button and your iPad should start up normally.

Hard Resetting Your iPad

If a basic restart doesn't work, it's possible your iPad has a more serious problem. In that case, you need to do what's called a hard reset:

1. Hold down both the button at the top-right and the Home button for 10 to 15 seconds. The red slider might appear, but don't touch it and don't let go of the buttons.

2. Keep holding until the iPad's screen goes black and turns off.

3. You can then turn it on like normal.

Make Your Battery Last Longer

Your iPad isn't much good if it doesn't work because its battery has run out. The iPad can run a pretty long time on a charged battery—it depends on what you're using it for, but you can expect to get 8 to 10 hours of use out of a full battery—but if you want to get every last minute out of it, here are some tips you should try.

You get to all of these options by first tapping the Settings app. When you're there, follow the instructions in each tip.

- **Use Auto-Brightness**—The iPad can automatically detect how much light is around it. When it does that, the screen can brighten or dim based on the light. By automatically having the screen dim when extra brightness isn't needed, you can save battery power. Tap Brightness & Wallpaper and then move the Auto-Brightness slider to On. (You can also move the Brightness slider manually; the lower the brightness, the more battery you save.)

- **Turn off data push**—Push is a setting that automatically moves your email from the Internet to your iPad without you having to check your email. It's basically a way to stay up to date as quickly as possible. That's handy, but the downside is that it takes up battery life. To turn it off and just let your email show up when you open the Mail app, tap Mail, Contacts, Calendar, tap Fetch New Data, and then move the Push slider to Off.

- **Fetch email less often**—I just mentioned that you can set your iPad to automatically check for new email. It's fun to get new email, but the more often you check for it, the more battery life you use. So, unless you need to get your email all the time, set your iPad not to check too often. Tap Mail, Contacts, Calendar, tap Fetch New Data, and then tap Every 30 Minutes, Hourly, or Manually (which gives you the biggest battery savings).

- **Turn off Bluetooth**—You'll probably only use Bluetooth for connecting wireless keyboards. If you're not connected to a keyboard, you can save battery life by turning Bluetooth off. Tap Bluetooth and move the slider to Off.

- **Turn off 4G**—Connecting to the Internet always uses more battery life because you have to send data back and forth. If you have a 4G iPad but don't need to connect to a 4G network right now (or are in a place where there's no 4G signal for your iPad to look for), turning off 4G saves battery life. To do this, tap General, Cellular Data, and move the slider to Off.

- **Turn off Wi-Fi**—If you're not connected to the Internet and don't need to be (like when you're on a bus or car trip), or if you're using 4G instead (assuming your iPad has 4G), turn off Wi-Fi. Tap Wi-Fi and then move the Wi-Fi slider to Off.

- **Turn off Location Services**—Location Services is an iPad feature that can figure out where you are geographically and give you data based on it. It's especially good when you want to find nearby stores and restaurants or you need to get directions. If you don't need to find local information, turn off Location Services until you do. Tap Privacy, tap Location Services, and move the Location Services slider to Off.

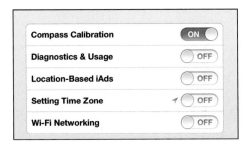

- **Turn off other Location Services**—Even if you leave your main Location Services on, there are some other, advanced settings that you can turn off to save some extra battery power. To do that, tap Privacy, tap Location Services, tap System Services, and move all the sliders on that screen to Off *except* Compass Calibration. Because it's the option that helps your iPad know where you are when using location-specific apps and tools, leave that one set to On.

- **Turn off Equalizer**—There's a setting in the Music app that automatically changes how your music sounds: It can add bass to rap music or the echo of a concert hall to a classical music performance. Doing that, though, takes up battery life. If you're not using that setting, turn it off. Tap Music, tap EQ, and then tap Off.

- **Lock the screen sooner**—Keeping the iPad's screen lit up can take up a lot of battery life. If you're not using your iPad, putting it to sleep sooner saves more battery. You can control how quickly the iPad goes to sleep when you're not using it. To do this, tap General, tap Auto-Lock, and choose 2 Minutes or 5 Minutes.

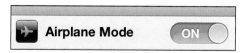

- **Use Airplane Mode**—One handy tip for saving battery life is called Airplane Mode. You can use this when you're not connected to 4G or Wi-Fi and don't expect to be anytime soon. Airplane Mode (named that because it's required for using your iPad on an airplane) turns off 4G, Wi-Fi, and a number of other features that can drain your battery. To use it, tap the Settings app and then move the Airplane Mode slider to On.

Finding a Lost iPad

We all try to take good care of our expensive possessions, including our iPads, but sometimes we lose them or, worse, they get stolen. It's very upsetting when this happens, but luckily a lost or stolen iPad isn't necessarily gone for good. If you turned on Find My iPad (check out "Lost and Found: Setting Up Find My iPad," in Chapter 2, "Getting Started: Set Up and Sync Your iPad," for more information) before your device was lost or stolen, you might be able to get it back.

Using Find My iPad

Find My iPad uses the Internet and the iPad's Location Awareness features to try to figure out where your iPad is. To locate your lost or stolen iPad, follow these steps:

1. Use any desktop, laptop, iPhone, or iPad that's connected to the Internet to go to www.icloud.com (there's also a free app from Apple for iPhone and iPad that you can get).

2. Enter your Apple ID and password.

3. Click the arrow to log in.

4. Click the Find My iPhone icon (don't worry, it works for iPads too).

5. Tap the Devices menu to see all your iOS devices. The website spends some time trying to locate your iPad on a map. When you've found your iPad, tell a parent or teacher and ask them to help you get it back. Never try to get your lost iPad back yourself; that can be dangerous.

6. When the website finds your iPad, you see it appear on the map as a green dot.

Using the Map

You can drag around and zoom in or out on the map to get more information about where your iPad is located. You can even go so far as to see the building it's in.

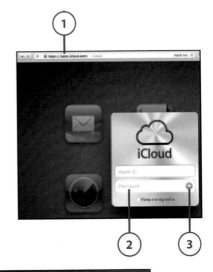

7. **Play Sound**—Choosing this causes the iPad to make a noise (good if it's lost under dirty clothes in your room and you want to find it).

8. **Lost Mode**—If you didn't already add a passcode to your iPad, you can do it now. This stops the person who has your iPad from using it or accessing your info. Click it and then set a four-digit code.

9. **Erase iPad**—To take a really drastic step, you can delete all the information on your iPad. This way, the person who has it can't read your email or look at your photos. Don't do this on your own because it can mean losing important information. If you think this is a good option, check with your parents (or your teachers) and see if they want to do this for you. If they decide to do it, they should click the Erase iPad button.

It's Not All Good

ICLOUD.COM REQUIREMENTS

The computer you want to use to find your lost or stolen iPad has to meet certain requirements. For a Mac, it has to be running OS X 10.7.2 or higher. For a PC, it has to be running Windows Vista or 7, with iCloud Control Panel 1.1 installed (a free download from Apple). If you're not sure what you have, ask your parents. If the computer you're using doesn't meet those requirements, icloud.com doesn't let you log in. In that case, you can download the free Find My iPhone app from the App Store onto another iPhone, iPad, or iPod touch and use it to find your iPad. When you do that, you need to sign in to the app using *your* Apple ID, not the Apple ID of the person who owns the device you're using. The app works the same way as the website.

It's Not All Good

WHEN FIND MY IPAD DOESN'T WORK

Find My iPad is a pretty cool technology, and it's a big help in locating a lost or stolen iPad, but there are some situations where it doesn't work, such as the following:

- **If you don't have Find My iPad turned on**—If you want to use Find My iPad, you have to turn it on before your iPad gets lost. After the iPad is gone, it's too late to turn on Find My iPad.

- **If the iPad isn't connected to the Internet**—Because Find My iPad relies on the Internet to locate your iPad, if the iPad isn't online, you can't find it. You can see where it was the last time it was connected to the Web, but you can't see where it is now.

- **If the iPad is turned off**—Just like with the Internet connection, if your iPad is turned off, you can use Find My iPad to see where your iPad was the last time it was on, but not where it is now.

What to Do If Your iPad Gets Wet

If there's any rule you have to follow about taking care of your iPad, it's this: Don't get it wet. A drop of water on the iPad's screen or back is okay if you wipe it off, but dropping the iPad in the bath because you were reading in the tub spells trouble. Knocking over a glass of juice or soda onto it can be worse because those drinks can do even more damage than water. Either way, getting your iPad wet is a bad idea because electronics aren't designed to get wet, and when they do, they can be damaged or stop working altogether—which could be the end of your iPad!

Or maybe not. If your iPad gets really wet, try these tips to dry it out. They won't save every iPad—sometimes too much water gets in and the iPad is ruined—but they will save some:

- **Don't turn it on**—This is super important. If your iPad gets soaked, don't turn it on. That could cause the electronics to short-circuit. If your iPad was on, though, hold down the power button until it shuts down. (This isn't the same as pressing the button to put it to sleep. Hold the button until the iPad's screen shuts off completely.)

- **Shake out the water or let it drain**—Get as much of the water out as possible. A good way to do that is to turn the iPad so that the dock connector is facing down and let the water drain out. Also try shaking the iPad to get water out.

- **Try rice**—Even after the water has drained, some water will still be stuck in the nooks and crannies inside your iPad. Believe it or not, the way to get it out involves rice. Get some dry, uncooked rice and a big plastic bag. Put a scoop or two of rice into the bag and then put your iPad in the bag, too. Keep it there for one to two days. Believe it or not, the rice sucks the moisture out of the iPad and absorbs it! This trick has saved many iPads.

After you've tried these tips and your iPad appears dry, you can turn it on. It might work perfectly or it might not work at all. Maybe the most frustrating outcome, though, is if it sort of works and sort of doesn't. For example, maybe your iPad seems to work, but the speaker doesn't make noise. Or everything works but the screen is streaky. In these cases, try the rice again. If that still doesn't work, your iPad might be broken for good. You should tell your parents and find out what they want to do.

Backing Up Your iPad

The iPad is very reliable, but sometimes accidents happen and the things you have stored on it can get erased or lost. When you have music, photos, email, and school papers stored on your iPad, you don't want to take any chances of losing important items.

To prevent that, you have to make copies of everything on your iPad. This is called *backing up your data*. There are two main ways to do this: backing up using iCloud and backing up by syncing with a desktop or laptop computer.

Maybe the easiest way to back up your iPad is by using the iCloud account you created when you set up the iPad (check out Chapter 2 for more info). iCloud is Apple's web-based service for storing your data. It automatically copies data there and lets you download it later if you need it.

Backup Using iCloud

If you chose to back up to iCloud during the setup process, there's nothing to change: You're already backing up to iCloud. If you didn't do that, though, you have to turn this feature on. To do that, make sure you have an iCloud account (it's the same as your Apple ID), you're signed in to it, you're connected to the Internet, and you have opened the Settings app. Then follow these steps:

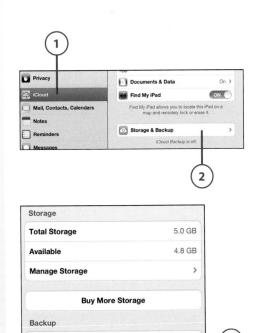

1. Tap iCloud from the Settings options.

2. Tap Storage & Backup.

3. Move the iCloud Backup slider to On.

How Much Storage Do You Get?

iCloud gives you 5GB of storage for free. If you need more, you can buy it for $20 to $100 per year.

4. Tap OK in the pop-up window to agree to iCloud backup. Your iPad spends a moment turning on the backup feature and then you're all set. From now on, backups to iCloud happen automatically whenever you're connected to the Web.

5. After you've turned iCloud backup on, you have to make sure all the stuff you want saved is getting backed up. Return to the iCloud screen in the Settings app.

6. On the iCloud screen, you see all the kinds of apps and data that iCloud can back up. For each one that you want to store, move the slider to On. When you're done, you can just press the Home button and go do something else. Your changes are automatically saved.

It's Not All Good

BACKING UP MUSIC

iCloud is great for backing up lots of kinds of data from your iPad, but one thing it doesn't do is back up music. All the music you buy from the iTunes Store is stored in your iCloud account (more on that in the next section), but any music you get from another source—such as a CD or Amazon's music store—isn't stored there.

For that, you either need to back up your music from your computer or use Apple's iTunes Match service, which uploads all your music to Apple's servers and stores it there in case you need it later. iTunes Match costs $25 per year, so ask your parents to research whether your computer is compatible with it and if they want to get it.

Backup by Syncing

The other way to back up your iPad is to use your computer: Every time you sync your iPad to a computer, you're creating a backup. That's because the iPad transfers all its data to your computer for use there or in case of emergency. Pretty easy, huh?

If you don't back up to iCloud, just make sure to sync your iPad to your computer regularly (try every day or two) and you'll have backups when you need them.

The good thing about this option is that it also backs up your music onto your computer, so you don't have to worry about iTunes Match. It's a good idea to back up the data on your computer too, just in case.

Restoring Your Data from Backup

Let's say something bad happens and you lose some or all of the information on your iPad. If you've been backing up regularly, then it's okay—you just need to restore your data from the backup. It's important to know that when you restore your iPad, you can't pick and choose what you want to restore. Instead, you have to erase everything on your iPad and replace it with the backup. That's usually okay, because you want to get back lost data anyway, but it's important to know because you might lose new data you added since the last backup.

Restoring from iCloud

To restore your iPad from an iCloud backup, make sure you're connected to the Internet (there's no way to reach iCloud otherwise) and tap the Settings app to open it. After you've done that, follow these steps:

1. Tap General.

2. Scroll to the bottom of the screen. Tap Reset.

3. Tap Erase All Content and Settings. Be sure you mean it, though—this erases everything from your iPad.

4. Tap Erase in the pop-up window. A second window pops up, making sure you really want to do this. If you do, tap Erase again.

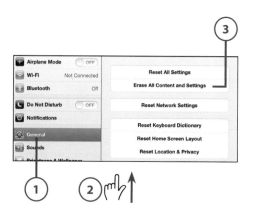

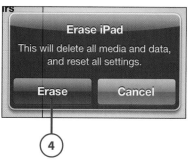

Redoing Setup

When your iPad restarts, you go through the same set up process you did when the iPad was new. Check out Chapter 2 if you want a refresher on that.

5. After you've redone the initial setup, you have a choice of what backup you want to restore your data from. Tap Restore from iCloud Backup.

6. Sign in to your iCloud account. When asked about agreeing to the Terms of Service, tap the Agree button in the pop-up window.

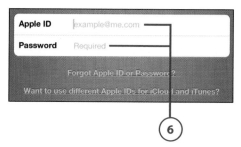

7. You now have a choice of what iCloud backup you want to use. Tap the one you prefer (probably the most recent one, but not always) and then tap Restore. The backup begins to download to your iPad. How long this takes depends on how much data and how many apps you have to download.

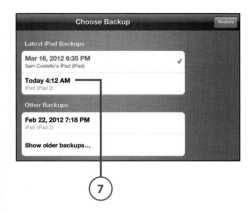

Restoring from iTunes

Just like you can back up your data using your computer, you can also use those backups on your computer to restore information to your iPad. To restore your iPad using a backup from your computer, follow these steps:

1. Connect your iPad to the computer you sync it with. It syncs again. When that's done, click Restore in the iTunes window. When you do this, some windows pop up asking if you're sure you want to do this. Click the buttons that let you continue.

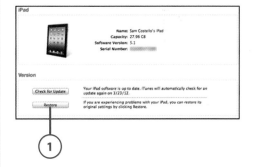

2. A box appears on the screen giving you two options: to set the iPad up like new or to restore from a backup. Click the Restore From button.

3. Select the backup you want to use (usually the most recent one) from the drop-down.

4. Click Continue to proceed. Your iPad restarts and all the things you've stored on it are erased. After a minute or so, the white Apple logo appears on the iPad's screen. You then have to repeat the initial setup process from Chapter 2 of updating your sync settings to make sure to sync all the music, apps, and other data you want on your iPad.

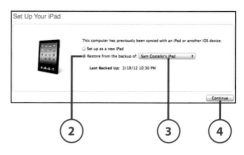

It's Not All Good

GETTING YOUR MUSIC BACK

You already know that backing up to iCloud doesn't back up your music. You might be surprised, though, that when you restore from backup on your computer, your music isn't automatically added to your iPad, either. That doesn't mean it's lost, though—it just means that you have to sync again.

When you restore from backup, it's like you're starting over from scratch with your iPad. When you do that, you have to change some of your settings again, including your music sync settings. Just follow the steps on syncing music from Chapter 2's section on syncing with iTunes and your music will be back on your iPad in no time.

Redownloading from iCloud

Although iCloud doesn't back up all of your music or other data, it does offer a neat feature: It stores and lets you redownload almost anything you've bought from the iTunes or App Stores. This way, if you accidentally delete or lose any music, apps, books, or TV shows you've gotten from iTunes or the App Store, you can easily get them back again—for free!

How to Redownload Purchases

To redownload your iTunes purchases from iCloud, make sure your iPad is connected to the Internet, open the iTunes Store app from your iPad's home screen, and then follow these steps:

1. Tap Purchased from the list of icons along the bottom of the screen. This is the section that shows everything you've bought from iTunes.

2. In the Purchased section, you have three choices of what to see: TV Shows, Music, and Movies. Not all options show up, just those that you've bought things in. Tap the option you want.

3. You can choose to see either everything you've bought from iTunes or just the purchased items not on your iPad. I'd choose the second option because that's what you're looking to download.

4. In TV shows, there's a list of the shows you've purchased. The same is true for Movies. In Music, you see a list of all the artists you've bought songs or albums by.

5. For TV shows, tap the show you want to redownload an episode from and then tap the season.

6. When you've found the TV episode, movie, song, or album you want to download, tap the iCloud button next to it. You might be asked to enter your Apple ID again. After you've done that, the video or music downloads to your iPad and you'll be able to enjoy it in no time.

>>>*Go Further*

REDOWNLOADING APPS

Redownloading apps works in a very similar way, except with one major change: To do it, you have to use the App Store app.

To redownload apps, tap the App Store app to launch it and then tap the Purchased menu. There, you see all the apps not installed on your iPad. Find the one you want and tap the iCloud button. The app redownloads.

Keep your iPad safe and secure
by using a passcode and the
other tips in this chapter.

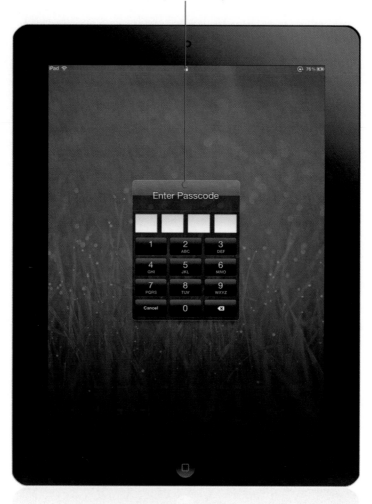

In this chapter, you find out how to take good care of your iPad—and what's on it—to keep it working as long as possible. Taking care of your iPad means:

→ Keeping your iPad safe
→ Protecting your data
→ Protecting your privacy
→ Keeping your iPad clean

18

Taking Care of Your iPad

Think about everything your iPad can do: browse the Web, play games, help you learn, show movies. It's a pretty amazing device. Getting something so cool and so powerful isn't cheap. If your parents bought your iPad, they worked hard to earn the money they used. If you bought it yourself, then you know how hard it was to work and save enough money. Show that you appreciate your parents' hard work or your own by working hard to take care of your iPad and make it last a long time.

Keeping Your iPad Safe

Because iPads are so cool—and so expensive—a lot of people want them. You're lucky; you have one. Not everyone is as lucky as you. Most people who don't have iPads can accept that, but some people may not and they may try to take yours without asking.

Having your iPad stolen would be upsetting for both you and your parents—and, depending on a lot of things, you or your parents might not be able to buy another one. Therefore, you have to take good care of your iPad at all times.

To keep it from getting lost or stolen, follow these tips:

- **Always keep your eye on it**—Always know where your iPad is. If you're using it in public, don't leave it alone while you do something else. Before you leave somewhere you've been using it—whether that's school, a friend's house, or in public—double-check to make sure you have it with you so you don't accidentally leave it behind.

- **Store it in a safe place**—Make sure to keep your iPad someplace safe. Your backpack or book bag can be a good place. Carrying it under your arm down the street probably isn't.

- **Don't lend it to strangers**—Because iPads are so cool, strangers may ask to look at or borrow yours. Don't let them. Only let people you know and trust—your friends, teachers, or family—use your iPad. And make sure to get your iPad back from them before you go somewhere else.

- **Be careful about using it in public**—Most people are nice and won't want to take your iPad, but some people aren't so nice. Because of that, be careful about using your iPad in public. Using it on a bus or subway might not be a great idea. Using it in a restaurant or library is probably okay.

If your iPad does get lost or stolen, be sure to tell your parents or teachers right away and ask them to help you. Together, you can use Find My iPad, which I cover in Chapter 17, "Fixing Problems Yourself," to try to locate it.

Protecting Your Data

Besides keeping your iPad safe, you also want to keep what's on it safe. The content of your iPad—your email, songs, friends' addresses, and photos—is called *data*. When it comes to your data, you definitely want to keep it safe and make sure that people you don't know or like can't get to or see your personal data.

A good way to keep your data safe is to set a passcode lock. A passcode lock is a password you put on your iPad. Anyone who wants to use your iPad needs to know the passcode to unlock it. If they don't know the passcode, they can't use the iPad.

Setting a Passcode Lock

To set a passcode lock on your iPad, start by tapping the Settings app and then follow these steps:

1. Tap General from the Settings app.

2. Tap Passcode Lock.

3. Tap Turn Passcode On.

4. Type a four-digit passcode. Make sure this is an easy number for you to remember. (If you forget it, you'll be locked out of your iPad, too!) Type it again to confirm, and your passcode is set.

Testing Your Passcode

To see how your passcode works, lock your iPad and then try to press the on/off button to wake it up. After you slide to unlock, you have to enter the passcode to unlock the iPad.

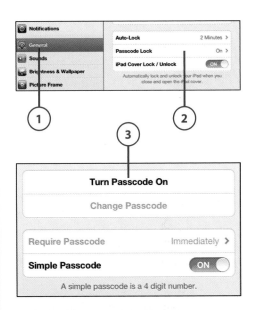

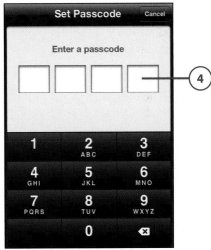

Passcode Options

After you've set a passcode, you have a number of options you can use with it:

1. **Change Passcode**—Tap this and enter your passcode if you want to create a new one.

2. **Require Passcode**—This lets you choose when your iPad asks for the passcode. It immediately asks for the passcode when you unlock the iPad, but you can also choose certain amounts of time after the unlock, if you want.

3. **Simple Passcode**—Want a more secure passcode than just four numbers? Move this slider to Off, enter your current passcode, and then type any password you want. (If you want some tips on creating a good password, read "Go Further: Good Passwords," in Chapter 2, "Getting Started: Set Up and Sync Your iPad.") Just make sure you remember this one, too!

4. **Siri**—You can use Siri, your voice-activated digital assistant, even when your iPad is locked and secured with a passcode. This means that you can use it without unlocking your iPad—which also means that anyone who gets your iPad can use Siri to send emails or messages or place FaceTime calls. If you don't want that, move this slider to Off.

5. **Picture Frame**—If this is On, your iPad can display your photos even when it's locked. Move the slider

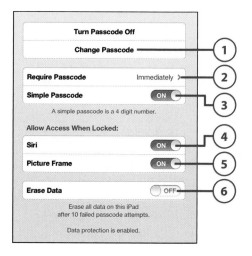

to Off to prevent strangers from looking at your photos even if they can't see any of your other data.

6. **Erase Data**—If you want to really stop someone who's trying to get unauthorized access to your iPad, use this setting. When it's turned on, all the data is erased from your iPad when someone enters the wrong passcode ten times. This is why it pays to remember your passcode: You don't want to erase all your data just because you forgot your code, do you?

> ## >>>Go Further
>
> ## WHAT IF YOU FORGET YOUR PASSCODE?
>
> If you do forget your passcode, you're not permanently locked out of your iPad. To get around your passcode and set a new one, you need to restore your iPad from backup (as described in Chapter 17). To do this, you first erase your iPad—and the passcode you forgot—and then put a new copy of your data back onto your iPad. After you've done that, your iPad will be back to new. And this time, use a passcode you can remember!

Protecting Your Privacy

Other people's prying eyes aren't the only way someone might see your data when you don't want them to. Many apps, especially those that work with your address book or calendar, can see your data—and maybe even copy it to their computers. Some people don't care about this, but others take it very seriously. Luckily, if you have iOS 6, your iPad has a built-in way to control what apps can use your personal data.

Ask your parents for help with this one. They'll have a good idea about what information is OK to share with some apps and what isn't.

Changing Your Privacy Settings

When you're running iOS 6 on your iPad, you can choose what apps can access your personal data.

1. Tap the Settings app on your home screen.

2. Tap Privacy.

3. You see a list of the kinds of personal information apps might want to use, including your location, contacts, and calendars. To begin customizing those settings, tap Location Services.

4. Location Services are the iPad's GPS-style features that figure out where you are geographically and give you information based on that. On this screen, there's a list of all the apps that use Location Services. Move the sliders to On for the apps that you want to know your location, and switch the ones you don't to Off. Keep in mind, though, that turning off Location Services in some apps could disable some features (like a restaurant-finder app that wants to tell you where to eat within three blocks of your current location; without Location Services, it can't).

5. Tap each of the other items—Contacts, Calendar, and so on—to see which apps want access to that data. Move the sliders to On or Off depending on your preference (again, remember that your choice might affect how the app works).

6. When you're done, press the home button; your choices are saved automatically.

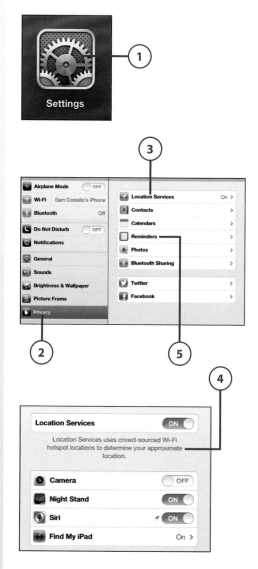

As I've repeated many times throughout this book, when it comes to things that happen online or what information, if any, you should share with apps or websites, it's always smart to talk to your parents about what to do. They'll have good ideas about how to be safe and secure when you use your iPad.

Caring for Your iPad

The outside of the iPad is pretty tough, but the electronics that make it work on the inside are very delicate. That means you can damage your iPad quite badly if you're not careful. Here are some important tips to keep in mind to make sure you take good care of your iPad.

Keep It Away from Water and Food

Food and water are the enemies of electronic devices such as the iPad. If they get inside the iPad, they can ruin it. So, even though it might be tempting to use your iPad at the table while you eat, or to read on it in bed while also drinking a glass of water, you shouldn't. If you're eating or drinking, put your iPad somewhere else where a spill can't hurt it.

If you do end up getting your iPad wet, don't panic. A little water on the front or back probably isn't a huge deal. Just wipe it off with a soft towel or cloth. If your iPad gets *really* wet, though, check out the tips for what to do that I cover in Chapter 17.

Don't Drop It

This might seem obvious, but another way to take care of your iPad is to make sure you don't drop it. The iPad is tough, but not so tough that it can survive a lot of drops. This is especially true of the screen. The iPad's screen is made of glass, like a window, and it can break like a window, too. Keep a tight grip on your iPad and pay attention when you're holding or carrying it so you don't accidentally drop it. Most iPads can survive small drops, but big ones, or lots of them, can ruin your iPad.

Cases and Screen Protectors

One good way to save your iPad from the occasional drop or the scratches that come from a lot of use is to protect it with a case, a screen protector, or a Smart Cover.

- **Cases** are like a holder you can slip your iPad into that cushion it from drops and protect it from scratches while still letting you use it. I recommend that pretty much everyone get a case for their iPad. When you get your iPad, ask your parents about getting a case for safekeeping. **Cases cost $30–$90.**

- **Screen protectors** are clear, thin plastic films that stick to your screen. When you put a screen protector on your iPad, you won't be able to see it, but it will save your screen from getting scratched (though, if you drop it without a case, a screen protector can't stop the screen from cracking or breaking). Screen protectors can be pretty tough to install, so ask your parents to help you. **Screen protectors cost $5–$20.**

- **Smart Covers** are a little like cases and a little like screen protectors. They're colorful and are used to cover an iPad's screen. What's neat about them, though, is that they're magnetic—they just snap onto the iPad—and the iPad knows when a Smart Cover is on. If a Smart Cover is over the screen, the iPad goes to sleep. Open the Smart Cover, and the iPad wakes right up. Pretty cool. **Smart Covers cost $39–$69.**

What to Use—and Not Use—for Cleaning

Even if you take good care of your iPad, don't get food or water on it, and use a case, the screen is still going to get dirty. That's because you're always touching the screen, and you have dirt and oil on your skin all the time.

To clean that gunk off your iPad's screen, though, you can't use just anything. You want to make sure you don't accidentally damage the screen when you clean it.

To be safe when cleaning your iPad's screen, you have two options. First, you can buy a kit for cleaning an iPad screen. These generally include some cleaning spray or foam and a soft cloth for wiping the screen. They usually cost between $10 and $15.

Your second option is to clean it yourself. In this case, you don't need to buy anything. You just need a soft, lint-free cloth or towel and a little water. First, turn off the iPad and then follow these steps:

1. Lightly wet the cloth under a faucet—emphasis on *lightly*. This really should be just *a bit* of water.

2. Wipe the iPad's screen with the cloth a few times until it looks clean.

3. Never use window cleaner, soap, paper towels, or other cleaning products because they can scratch or damage the screen.

Index

Symbols

A

Q–R

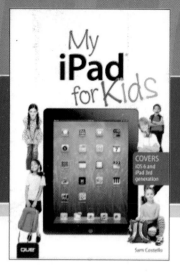